Blueprints

Land Law

Blueprints

Your plan for learning

Land Law

Elliot Schatzberger

PEARSON

Harlow, England • London • New York • Boston • San Francisco • Toronto • Sydney • Auckland • Singapore • Hong Kong
Tokyo • Seoul • Taipei • New Delhi • Cape Town • São Paulo • Mexico City • Madrid • Amsterdam • Munich • Paris • Milan

PEARSON EDUCATION LIMITED
Edinburgh Gate
Harlow CM20 2JE
United Kingdom
Tel: +44 (0) 1279 623623
Web: www.pearson.com/uk

First published 2014 (print and electronic)

ISBN: 978-1-4479-0494-6 (print)
      978-1-4479-0495-3 (PDF)
      978-1-292-01514-9 (eText)

British Library Cataloguing-in-Publication Data
A catalogue record for the print edition is available from the British Library

Library of Congress Cataloging-in-Publication Data
A catalog record for the print edition is available from the Library of Congress

10 9 8 7 6 5 4 3 2 1
18 17 16 15 14

Print edition typeset in 10/12pt Helvetica Neue LT Pro by 35
Printed in Great Britain by Henry Ling Ltd., at the Dorset Press, Dorchester, Dorset

NOTE THAT ANY PAGE CROSS REFERENCES REFER TO THE PRINT EDITION

Brief contents

Contents

Tables of cases and statutes

CASES

STATUTES

Acknowledgements

We are grateful to the following for permission to reproduce copyright material:

Figures

Figure 1.2 from Land Registry, Crown copyright; Figure 5.1 from Land Registry, Crown copyright (ref: LR/HO) 10/12.

Text

Extract on pages 80 and 81 from Schedule 3 LRA 2002, http://www.landregistry.gov.uk/professional/law-and-practice/act-and-rules, Land Registry, Crown copyright.

In some instances we have been unable to trace the owners of copyright material, and we would appreciate any information that would enable us to do so.

How to use this guide

Blueprints was created for students searching for a smarter introductory guide to their legal studies

This guide will serve as a primer for deeper study of the law – enabling you to get the most out of your lectures and studies by giving you a way in to the subject which is more substantial than a revision guide, but more succinct than your course textbook. The series is designed to give you an overview of the law, so you can see the structure of the subject and understand how the topics you will study throughout your course fit together in the big picture. It will help you keep your bearings as you move through your course study.

Blueprints recognises that students want to succeed in their course modules

This requires more than a basic grasp of key legislation; you will need knowledge of the historical and social context of the law, recognition of the key debates, an ability to think critically and to draw connections among topics.

Blueprints addresses the various aspects of legal study, using assorted text features and visual tools

Each Blueprints guide begins with an **Introduction**, outlining the parameters of the subject and the challenges you might face in your studies. This includes a **map** of the subject highlighting the major areas of study.

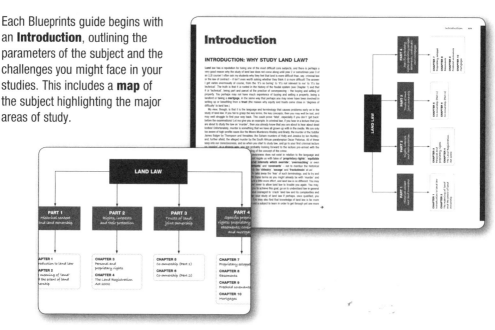

Each **Part** of the guide also begins
with an Introduction and a map of
the main topics you need to grasp
and how they fit together.

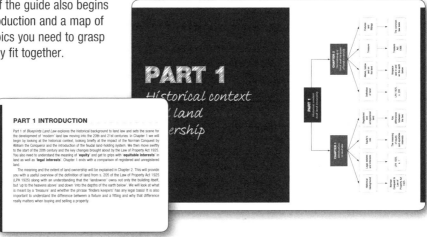

Each guide includes advice on the
specific **study skills** you will need
to do well in the subject.

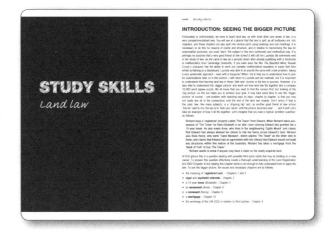

Each chapter starts with a
Blueprint of the topic area to
provide a visual overview of the
fundamental buildings blocks of
each topic, and the academic
questions and the various outside
influences that converge in the
study of law.

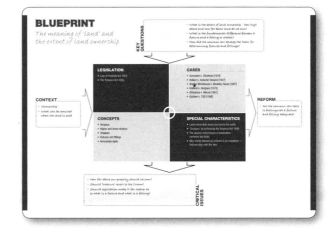

A number of text features have been included in each chapter to help you better understand the law and push you further in your appreciation of the subtleties and debates:

Setting the scene illustrates why it is important to study each topic.

Setting the scene

The ownership of land has always been a highly contentious issue – not least due to the fact that land has always been a valuable commodity. It has also been, and will probably always be a 'political hot potato'. On the 'far left' of the political spectrum, at the top of Karl Marx's agenda in his 1848 Communist Manifesto was the view that society should work towards the 'abolition of property/ownership of land', arguing that 'modern bourgeois society . . . has sprouted from the ruins of feudal society'. However, giving a more 'capitalist' viewpoint, the economist Milton Friedman argued that private land ownership has the ability to 'make a positive contribution to freedom – or at least an enhancement of choice . . .'. (see below). This argument was echoed by journalists such as Heath who, shortly after the death of Margaret Thatcher, stated that 'one of Lady Thatcher's greatest legacies was to increase home ownership, allowing families to buy council homes at a discount. Her

Cornerstone highlights the fundamental building blocks of the law.

CORNERSTONE

Alienability

Whether a right is purely personal or is proprietary is vital in relation to one of the fundamental principles underpinning land law – **alienability**. The concept of alienability means that the owner of a property should be able to sell without any hidden rights getting in the way of that sale. The best way for you to start to understand this topic is to look at *why* the difference matters.

Application shows how the law applies in the real world.

APPLICATION

Emilia Jones and Finn Matthews buy a property together in 1897. Both names are recorded on the title deeds (the land is *unregistered*). In 1910, Max wishes to buy the property. The contract for sale names Emilia Matthews and Finn Matthews as the legal owners. Max would not be able to rely on the names on the contract as being the true legal owners as the current title deeds show the same forenames but different surnames. Max would need to see a copy of the marriage certificate (assuming a marriage has taken place between Emilia and Finn between 1897 and 1910). In an alternative scenario, if the contract for sale only states the name of Emilia Jones as the seller, Max would need to find out what had happened to Finn – maybe the two have separated, or maybe Finn has died. If the latter is true, Max would need proof of death and need to take a look at the probate documents which would show what has happened to Finn's

Intersection shows you connections and relationships with other areas of the law.

INTERSECTION

A full discussion of the issue of overriding interests in *Rosset* can be found in Chapter 4. Actual occupation would now come under LRA 2002, Schedule 3, paragraph 2 – but the common law 'rule' for needing to have a pre-existing proprietary interest before being able to claim actual occupation was in place at the time of *Rosset*.

Reflection helps you think critically about the law, introducing you to the various complexities that give rise to debate and controversy.

'The Plane Crash Rule?'

Perhaps even more strangely, there is a quaint English law doctrine known as the *commorientes* rule, which states that if joint tenants die simultaneously and the order in which they died cannot therefore be ascertained, the general rule is that the property vests automatically in the estate of the *youngest* of the joint tenants, as 'the deaths are presumed to have occurred in order of age so that the younger is presumed to have survived the elder' (LPA 1925, s. 184).

REFLECTION

Context fills in some of the historical and cultural background knowledge that will help you understand and appreciate the legal issues of today.

> **CONTEXT**
>
> There are many social and economic reasons why the law on adverse possession exists. First, it is arguably more desirable for a property not to stand empty and abandoned for many years – it could start to fall apart and damage may be done to other property or to people passing by. Secondly, if whole neighbourhoods decided to move to the Cayman Islands, then not a single property in that locality would be 'saleable' and as such the housing market would start to stagnate. Social reasoning also suggests that it is better for the homeless to be housed in abandoned properties than to be left on the street.

Take note offers advice that can save you time and trouble in your studies.

> ember of the club to play golf on the club's course. The right was rely personal. The first characteristic in *Ellenborough* is therefore that there needs to be a 'dominant tenement' – land which is pable of taking the benefit of the easement, and a 'servient nement' – land which grants the easement and as such carries e burden of that easement. These two pieces of land must be entifiable at the time of the grant as in the case of *London and enheim Estates* v. *Ladbroke Retail Parks* [1993] where no easement was present due to there being no dominant land at the time e easement was granted.
>
> **Take note**
> The same is not true of a profit à prendre, which is also a proprietary right to take something from another person's land. This is also covered by section 1(2)(a) of the LPA 1925. This right does exist without a dominant

Key points lists the main things to know about each topic.

> ## KEY POINTS
>
> - A covenant is an agreement between two freeholders. Essentially this is contractual in nature and is binding only on the original covenantor and covenantee.
> - If the 'rules' are satisfied, then a covenant is capable of being a proprietary right which may bind third parties outside the statutory exceptions of section 56 of the LPA 1925 and the Contract (Rights of Third Parties) Act 1999.

Core cases and statutes summarises the major case law and legislation in the topic.

> ## CORE CASES AND STATUTES
>
> | Case | About | Importance |
> | --- | --- | --- |
> | *Tulk* v. *Moxhay* (1848) 2 Ph 774 | Land in the centre of Leicester Square. | This is the first case which established that only a negative covenant is capable of running with the land and binding a third party. |
> | *Smith & Snipes Hall Farm* v. *River Douglas* [1949] 2 KB 500 | Sets down the four main conditions for the benefit running at common law. | This case suggests that the benefit will nearly always run with the land at common law – especially with the statutory provision |

Further reading directs you to select primary and secondary sources as a springboard to further studies.

> ## FURTHER READING
>
> Bowcott, O. 'Supreme court rules on property rights for unmarried couples', *The Guardian*, Wednesday 9 November 2011 http://www.guardian.co.uk/law/2011/nov/09/court-rules-property-rights-unmarried
> This gives an excellent overview of the judgment in *Jones* v. *Kernott* – explains why the Supreme Court awarded 90 per cent to
>
> http://www.landregistry.gov.uk/public/guides/public-guide-18
> This useful practice guide sets down the rules and relevant practice forms available for declaring a trust of land.
>
> Law Commission Report *Cohabitation: The Financial Consequences of Relationship Breakdown* (No 307, 31 July 2007) www.parliament.uk/briefing-papers/

A **glossary** provides helpful definitions of key terms.

> **Adverse possession** Occupation of land taken to the exclusion of the original owner. The procedure to claim has been made more difficult under the LRA 2002.
>
> **Alienability** The ability to transfer property from one party to another.
>
> **Beneficial interest** The rights of a beneficiary in relation to property held under a trust. It is a particular type of equitable interest.
>
> *Caveat emptor* Buyer beware – especially important when buying a property.
>
> **E-conveyancing** The method of electronic conveyancing for which the LRA 2002 paved the way. The aim is that all property will be transferred electronically with completion, stamp duty payment and registration of title all happening simultaneously.
>
> **Easement** A proprietary right enjoyed by (the owner of) one piece of land (the dominant tenement) to use proximate land (the servient tenement).
>
> **Equitable interest** A right recognised by

What is a Blueprint?

Blueprints provide a unique plan for studying the law, giving you a visual overview of the fundamental building blocks of each topic, and the academic questions and the various outside influences that converge in the study of law.

At the centre are the 'black-letter' elements, the fundamental building blocks that make up what the law says and how it works.

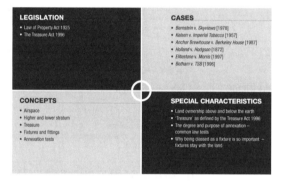

As a law student you will need to learn what questions or problems the law attempts to address, and what sort of issues arise from the way it does this that require critical reflection.

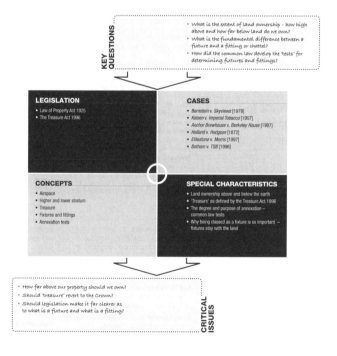

To gain a more complete understanding of the role of law in society you will need to know what influencing factors have shaped the law in the past, and how the law may develop in the near future.

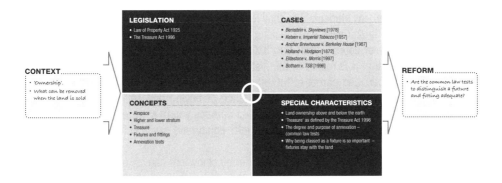

You can use the Blueprint for each topic as a framework for building your knowledge in the subject.

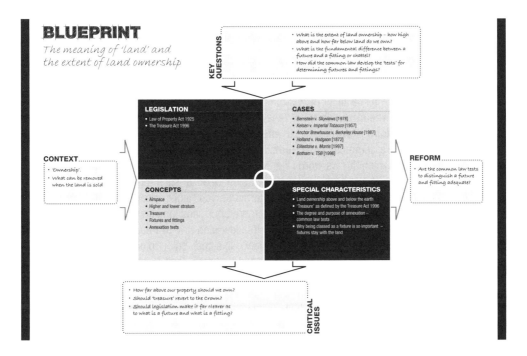

Introduction

INTRODUCTION: WHY STUDY LAND LAW?

Land law has a reputation for being one of the most difficult core subjects, and there is perhaps a very good reason why the study of land law does not come along until year 2 or sometimes year 3 of an LLB course! I often ask my students why they feel that land is more difficult than, say, criminal law or the law of contract – it isn't even worth asking whether they think it *is* more difficult! The answer I get varies enormously of course, from the 'it's so boring' to 'it's not relevant to me' to 'it's too technical'. The truth is that it *is* rooted in the history of the feudal system (see Chapter 1) and that it *is* 'technical', being part and parcel of the practice of conveyancing – the buying and selling of property. You perhaps may not have much experience of buying and selling a property, being a landlord or taking a **mortgage**, in the same way that perhaps you may never have been involved in setting up or benefiting from a **trust** (the reason why equity and trusts come close in 'degrees of difficulty' to land law.)

My view, though, is that it is the language and terminology that causes problems early on in the study of land law. If you fail to grasp the key terms, the key concepts, then you may well be lost, and may well struggle to find your way back. This could prove 'fatal', especially if you don't 'get back' before the examinations! Let me give you an example. In criminal law, if you hear in a lecture that you are about to study the law on 'murder', then you already know that you are about to hear about dead bodies! Unfortunately, murder is something that we have all grown up with in the media. We are only too aware of high-profile cases like the Moors Murderers Hindley and Brady; the murder of the toddler James Bulger by Thompson and Venables; the Soham murders of Holly and Jessica by Ian Huntley; and, further afield, the alleged murder by the South African paralympian Oscar Pistorius. All of these seep into our consciousness, and so when you start to study law, and go to your first criminal lecture on 'murder', in a strange way, you are probably looking forward to the lecture pre-armed with the confidence of at least a basic understanding of the concept of the crime.

I would argue that the same level of awareness does not exist in relation to the language and terminology of land law. The media does not regale us with tales of '**proprietary rights**'; '**equitable interests**'; '**registered land**'; '**unregistered interests which override**'; '**overreaching**' or even perhaps the slightly more common '**easements**' and '**covenants**' – not to mention the historical background to land law which throws words like '**chivalry**', '**socage**' and '**frankelmoin**' at us!

My task, in the writing of this book, is to take away the 'fear' of such terminology, and to try and make you as familiar and comfortable with these terms as you might already be with 'murder' and 'theft'. Everything worth understanding takes a little more effort, and land law is no different. You may have a desire only to pass the module, and never to allow land law to trouble you again. You may, though, and I hope that this book will help you to achieve this goal, go on to understand law in general far more comprehensively, because you have managed to 'crack' land law and its complexities and nuances. You may of course go on to use your study of land law if perhaps, once qualified, you become a *bona fide* land law practitioner. You may also find that knowledge of land law is far more useful in a practical way, much more than just a subject to learn in order to get through yet one more core law module.

→

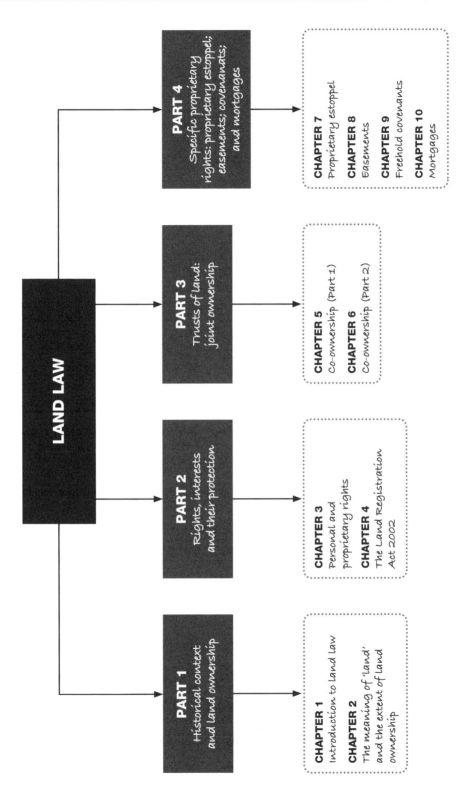

LAND LAW

PART 1
Historical context
and land ownership

CHAPTER 1
Introduction to land law

CHAPTER 2
The meaning of 'land'
and the extent of land
ownership

PART 2
Rights, interests
and their protection

CHAPTER 3
Personal and
proprietary rights

CHAPTER 4
The Land Registration
Act 2002

PART 3
Trusts of land:
joint ownership

CHAPTER 5
Co-ownership (Part 1)

CHAPTER 6
Co-ownership (Part 2)

PART 4
Specific proprietary
rights: proprietary estoppel;
easements; covenants;
and mortgages

CHAPTER 7
Proprietary estoppel

CHAPTER 8
Easements

CHAPTER 9
Freehold covenants

CHAPTER 10
Mortgages

Before we move on, let me give you a few practical examples, other than the more obvious 'study to pass' reason, as to why the study of land law has enormous relevance:

- A dispute with a neighbour over a boundary – this involves **easements** (Chapter 8) and possibly **adverse possession** (Chapter 4).
- Taking out a loan from a bank to buy a property – more obviously, this involves the law on **mortgages** (Chapter 10).
- An agreement that your neighbour will not turn their property into a music venue or bar – the law on **covenants** deals with this (Chapter 9).
- You buy a property with your partner, but are unsure of who owns what percentage of the property – this is covered by the law of **co-ownership** (Chapters 5 and 6).

So, perhaps we are far more aware of such land law issues than we may have believed, it is simply the terminology and the 'rules' that need to be understood. The purpose of this book is to help you understand not only why it is necessary to study land law, but also to teach you how to study and how to apply what is, in fact, a very living breathing subject.

STUDY SKILLS

Land law

INTRODUCTION: SEEING THE BIGGER PICTURE

Fortunately or unfortunately, we have to teach land law, as with most other core areas of law, in a very compartmentalised way. You will see at a glance that this text is split, as all textbooks are, into chapters, and those chapters are also split into various parts using headings and sub-headings. It is necessary to do this for reasons of clarity and structure, and in relation to memorising the law for examination purposes, you must 'learn' the subject in this very systematic and methodical way. It is perhaps no surprise that a very good friend at law school (I will call her Lucinda) did extremely well in her study of law, as she came to law as a second career after already qualifying with a Doctorate in mathematics from Cambridge University. If you have seen the film *The Beautiful Mind*, Russell Crowe's character has the ability to work out complex mathematical equations in super-fast time whilst scribbling on a blackboard. Lucinda was able to do exactly the same with a law problem, taking a very systematic approach – even with a hangover! When I try to help you to understand how to plan for examinations later on in this section, I will return to Lucinda and her methods, but it is important to understand that learning land law in these 'bite-size' chunks is the key to success. However, it is also vital to understand the '*bigger picture*' and work out how land law fits together like a complex 10,000 word jigsaw puzzle. We all know that you need to find the corners first, but looking at the 'big picture' on the box helps you to achieve your goal. It may take some time to see the 'bigger picture' of course – one problem with teaching topic by topic, chapter by chapter, is that you may not really see all of the connections until the end of the land law module. Don't worry if that is the case: law, like many subjects, is a 'dripping tap' and, as another good friend at law school 'Darren' said to me, the key is to 'hold your nerve' until the picture becomes clear . . . and it will! Let's take an example of how it all fits together. Let's imagine that you have a typical 'problem question' as follows:

> Richard buys a 'registered' property called 'The Tower' from Edward. When Richard takes possession of 'The Tower' he finds Elizabeth in an attic room claiming Edward had granted her a 10-year lease. He also meets Anne, who lives in the neighbouring 'Castle Mount' and claims that Edward had always allowed her (Anne) to ride her horse across Edward's land. Richard also finds Henry, who owns 'Tudor Mansion', which adjoins 'The Tower' on the other side to Anne, and claims that Edward had an agreement with him (Henry) that Edward would not build any structures within five metres of the boundary. Richard has taken a mortgage from the 'Bank of York' to buy 'The Tower'.
>
> Richard wants to know if anyone may have a claim on his newly acquired land.

At first glance this is a question dealing with possible third party rights that may be binding on a new owner. To answer this question effectively needs a thorough understanding of the Land Registration Act 2002 (Chapter 4) but reading this chapter alone is not enough to fully understand how to apply the law. To see the bigger picture, the issues and necessary chapters are as follows:

- the meaning of '**registered land**' – Chapters 1 and 4
- **legal** and **equitable interests** – Chapter 2
- a 10-year **lease** (Elizabeth) – Chapter 3
- an **easement** (Anne) – Chapter 8
- a **covenant** (Henry) – Chapter 9
- a **mortgage** – Chapter 10
- the workings of the LRA 2002 in relation to third parties – Chapter 4.

To answer this question in an examination would need an in-depth understanding of each issue (and chapter) but would also need you to be able to 'put it all together' to give a coherent and structured piece of advice to poor Richard! Again, the aim of this book is to help you to be able to do exactly that.

Land law in action

Before the case of *Stack* v. *Dowden* [2007] appeared before the House of Lords, presided over by Baroness Hale, it had long been established that if you lived as an unmarried couple with your partner, where one partner was named as the sole legal owner, the *unnamed* partner could only lay claim to a percentage of the property if they had contributed to the purchase price at the time of purchase (a resulting trust) or contributed to purchase price or mortgage payments after the purchase (a constructive trust). This of course, in situations where the male partner was named as the sole legal owner, left unmarried women, in particular, in a very precarious position. In the case of *Lloyds Bank* v. *Rosset* in 1991 (note *199*1 not *18*91), Lord Bridge decided that, even though married, Mrs Rosset had absolutely no percentage of the ownership of a property held solely in her husband's name. The fact that she had been overseeing renovations and project managing the builders was no indication of ownership – she was only doing, according to Lord Bridge, 'what any good wife should do'!

When the case of *Stack* v. *Dowden*, an unmarried couple, came before the Lords, it just so happened that Baroness Hale was in the driving seat. She decided that the *Rosset* approach was no longer appropriate in the 21st century. She decided that a couple's joint ownership should be based not just on a purely mathematical computation of early contributions to purchase and mortgage payments. She made it very clear that the law must 'move on' and that a 'holistic approach' should be taken which takes into account the entire 'course of dealing' within a relationship. It was only fair to calculate percentage ownership in terms of the entire input into the relationship – any and all contributions financial or otherwise could be used to compute the 'quantification' of the partner's share. *A first rate example of 'land law in action' in the 21st century*. The impact of this ruling was felt in *Jones* v. *Kernott* [2011] where Miss Jones was awarded a 90 per cent share of the property to her ex-partner Kernott's 10 per cent. This was based on her 'holistic' contribution even though there seemed to be an agreement in existence from the early part of their relationship which stated a 50/50 share of ownership. Mr Kernott's 'abandonment' of Miss Jones, leaving her alone for many years to pay for the mortgage on the property and take care of the maintenance, allowed the share to 'ambulate' or move over the years, resulting in a finding of 90/10. I explain all of this in far more detail in Chapter 5, but it serves as an excellent example of how land law lives, breathes and develops.

Look out for recent cases at the Court of Appeal or the Supreme Court, and keep an eye out for land law related 'stories', especially in the business press. Commercial property disputes, squatting and matrimonial breakdowns sell newspapers nearly as much as a murder!

SPECIFIC STUDY SKILLS

When studying law, it is essential to be able to apply a number of skills and techniques which you may have already picked up on your way to the study of land law. Some of these skills have hopefully been developed since the early part of your studies in law, probably from when you began studying the English Legal System and the development and workings of the common law. You will hopefully have already developed certain skills in applying case law; using statutes; referring to academic sources; and, more generally, answering problem and essay questions. Here are just a few more tips on how to apply these skills effectively, specifically in a 'land law' context:

Study skill: essay writing

There are certain questions which lend themselves more obviously to an essay answer rather than a problem question. Essentially, your preparation should not really be any different whether the question is an essay or a problem. You still need to learn and apply case law and statute, but the key difference with an essay is that you are not required to *apply* the law to a given scenario. Rather you are expected to explain the law and perhaps, depending on the question, to critique the law in that particular area. You should still explain cases and statutory provisions but also add some judicial comment and even academic critique where relevant. Let's take the example of co-ownership once again. Here is a typical essay question:

> The law on co-ownership is confused and in need of reform, especially in relation to unmarried couples. Discuss.

You would hopefully recognise that the essay is asking you to 'discuss' the law, meaning that there is a need to be a little critical in your approach rather than merely descriptive. The essay should of course have an introduction, main body and conclusion, like any other. In the introduction you should set the scene and lay down the objectives of the essay you are about to write. I suggest that you do not *start* with a 'conclusion' (a pet hate of mine). Conclusions should only be found in one place – at the *end* of the essay! Once you have set the objectives – maybe here saying that you are about to analyse the historical development of the law on co-ownership, by explaining the thread of case law running from *Pettitt* and *Gissing* through to *Rosset* and then on to the 'holistic' approach in *Stack* and *Jones* (Chapter 5) – you move on to the main body, which will of course explain these cases in some detail. It is always a good idea in an essay to refer where possible to the judges where they have made an impact: Denning in *Eves* v. *Eves* in 1975, Bridge in *Rosset*, and of course Hale in *Stack* and *Jones*. A really sound essay, with critical analysis, will explain why Hale was advocating a holistic approach in *Stack* – berating Parliament for failing to legislate for unmarried couples in this area of law. It should also go into some detail on Lord Neuberger's dissenting voice in *Stack*, explaining his reasoning clearly. The essay should also build to a discussion of case law post-*Stack* and *Jones*, looking to what the law is saying on this right now. If possible, your essay should contain a few academic references, including authors such as Martin Dixon who has written extensively in *The Conveyancer* journal on this and many other topics. The conclusion should sum up your points, but also end with a strong clear statement which either agrees or disagrees that the law needs reform.

Study skill: problem questions

The key difference here is that you need to apply the law to the facts of your scenario. It is not so important in answering a problem question to give critique, or even academic opinion. Only the law is really necessary. Think of it as dealing with a client in practice. If a client comes to you for advice, asking whether he has a strong claim, he doesn't want to hear '. . . ah yes, Professor Dixon on page 47 says . . .' The client wants to know the *law* itself – their legal position. Hence answering a problem question needs you to carry out a legal dissection of your scenario. Harvard Law School developed a method for analysing and planning an answer to a problem question – and this method is widely used across the globe. It is commonly referred to as the IRAC method of case study/problem analysis. Not pretending to be wiser than Harvard Law School of course, I nevertheless like to teach this as the **P**IRAC method as I believe Harvard ignored the obvious start point! So what is the PIRAC method of case analysis – let's use it to analyse the problem question I posed earlier:

Richard buys a 'registered' property called 'The Tower' from Edward. When Richard takes possession of 'The Tower' he finds Elizabeth in an attic room claiming Edward had granted her a 10-year lease. He also meets Anne, who lives in the neighbouring 'Castle Mount' and claims that Edward had always allowed her (Anne) to ride her horse across Edward's land. Richard also finds Henry, who owns 'Tudor Mansion', which adjoins 'The Tower' on the other side to Anne, and claims that Edward had an agreement with him that Edward would not build any structures within five metres of the boundary. Richard has taken a mortgage from the 'Bank of York' to buy 'The Tower'.

Richard wants to know if anyone may have a claim on his newly acquired land.

PIRAC:

P – start by looking at who the ***parties*** are and who you are asked to advise – here the parties are all of those highlighted earlier, and you are asked to advise Richard, the new proprietor of 'The Tower'.
I – what are the ***issues***? The issues here are that Richard has bought the land but there are pre-existing rights that may be binding on him: the lease; the overriding interest of 'actual occupation'; the easement; the covenant and the mortgage.
R – this stands for the ***rule of law*** – in other words, what law are you going to rely on and apply to the scenario? The start point here, as always where relevant, is statute – here the Law of Property Act 1925 for definitions of leases, easements and mortgages, and the LRA 2002 to see how these rights, along with covenants, may be binding. Then case law should be used to argue your position.
A – this is for ***application*** – the most vital part of any problem question. You need to take the law on leases from the relevant sections of the LPA 1925 and use the LRA 2002 sections (ss. 27–29 and Sch. 3, para. 1) to apply the law to Elizabeth's lease. You also need some basic 'lease' case law (such as *Street* v. *Mountford*) to back up your points. Elizabeth may also be in 'actual occupation' so Schedule 3, paragraph 2 and relevant cases such as *Chhokar* will also help here. Anne's easement may need application of the case law on easements (*Re Ellenborough Park*) and Schedule 3, paragraph 3 to the LRA 2002. Henry's covenant will need to be analysed through case law – and an explanation of covenants needing a 'notice' under LRA 2002, ss. 32–35 will be necessary. Finally, mortgage law will be needed – relevant case law and application of LPA 1925, ss. 101–105 (detail on all of these points can be found in the chapters highlighted above).
C – finally you will need to draw ***conclusions*** as to whether Richard is bound by any or all of the pre-existing interests. Never sit on the fence; always try to come to a solid conclusion. Remember that land law is civil law not criminal, so you only need to be sure '*on the balance of probabilities*' in order to advise your client (meaning 51% to 49%); you never need to be sure '*beyond a reasonable doubt*'.

I should stress that this is a way of planning a problem question answer, not necessarily the style in which your answer should be written. You may also need to apply PIRAC a number of times within one problem question if there are numerous issues or parties. We will deal with style – the use of the law – next.

Study skill: how to apply cases, statutes and academic opinion

Whether you are answering an essay or a problem question in an examination or a coursework, or even if you are trying to advise a client in practice, the key to your success is in being able to apply the law to your scenario. I always tell my students that you can't arrive in court and argue to the judge that the court should favour your client simply because it would be 'fair', or that your client is a 'good person'. Whether you are arguing academically or professionally you will be expected to refer to your 'source of law' and give your '*authority*'. This means that you must *use* the law to argue your point. Let me give you an example from the world of English Literature. If you studied this subject at school or college you may well have studied a play such as Shakespeare's *Romeo and Juliet*. You may be faced with an essay question asking you to discuss Juliet's dilemma as to the fact that Romeo is part of the enemy Montague clan. You would of course want to refer to *the* famous speech by Juliet, found at the start of the 'balcony scene' which starts 'Romeo Romeo, wherefore art thou Romeo'. Contrary to the popular misconception, this is not Juliet asking where Romeo is – she is asking why he is *called* Romeo – why he is a Montague. In order to make this point in an essay, though, you would need to reference the text of the play: 'according to Act 2, Scene 2 . . .' This would be your 'authority' and would score the points in your essay. This principle is exactly the same when referring to or applying law. It is necessary always to refer to either the name of a case, the provisions of a statute, or European law where appropriate (though the latter is not really a part of the study of land law). So how do you go about this?

The first thing to remember, especially in a problem question, is that you *apply* the point of law to the facts of your scenario rather than give a full explanation of the facts of the case itself. You are aiming to use the *ratio* of the case to help prove your point. It may be appropriate to set out what I call the 'trigger facts' – by that I mean the briefest of facts of the case that help you to apply the law to your scenario. In an essay, however, you may have more scope to explain the facts of the case itself, as, of course, there is no need for application to a given scenario. In an essay, you may also want to refer to academic opinion, though, as I suggested above, this is not strictly necessary in a problem question. The best way to explain what I mean here is to give you an example.

Let's take the situation of Elizabeth again. You may remember that Richard has bought 'The Tower' and has now found Elizabeth in an attic room. Leaving the lease to one side, you would need to advise Richard that Elizabeth may have another proprietary right (if the lease in itself is not binding as it may not be on the register and is not an overriding interest – see Chapters 3 and 4), that being the right of a person in '*actual occupation*'. You would first refer to the LRA 2002, Sch. 3, para. 2 (Sch. 3 rather than Sch. 1 as this is land which is already registered land). You would explain that Sch. 3, para. 2 sets down that a person in actual occupation may have a binding 'interest which overrides' if Richard either knows Elizabeth is there, or '*on a reasonably careful inspection of the land it is reasonably obvious*' that she is in occupation. However, though statute is always the start point when applying the law, where relevant, the next stage is to use case law to 'put the flesh on the bones' of the statute. You would need to apply a number of cases here, all of which carry a relevant ratio. First, Elizabeth must have a proprietary right to begin with, as in *National Provincial* v. *Ainsworth*. Don't forget to apply the ratio: she *does* have such a right – the lease. Secondly, she must be there at the time of the transfer to Richard – as in *Abbey National* v. *Cann* where Mrs Cann's furniture was there before transfer but she was not. Thirdly, even if she is away at the time of the transfer, if she can show evidence of an intention to return and there is also evidence of her physical presence, then she is still in actual occupation. *Chhokar* v. *Chhokar* can be applied here, where Mr Chhokar sold the house while his wife was away in hospital giving birth. Intention to return was clear as there was enough evidence of her presence: Mr Chhokar had only hidden some of her belongings, not all. Hence, to conclude, Elizabeth may have an 'overriding interest' which may bind Richard (note that it would be the terms of her lease which then bind). All of this is explained in far more detail in Chapter 4 – but that is how you would apply the law. You will see that I applied the ratios and, where it helps, gave brief facts of the cases to strengthen the application of the law to the scenario. Of course, if your scenario has slightly different facts to the actual case, then you would need to 'distinguish' the case from your scenario to argue a different outcome. For example, if Elizabeth's belongings were completely hidden, this can be distinguished from *Chhokar*, and the conclusion may be that she is not in discoverable actual occupation at all. As I suggested above, if this was an essay question on overriding interests, you may well also include any academic opinion or judicial comment – especially dissenting judgments (see Hale/Neuberger in Chapter 5) that you have read.

Study skill: how to prepare for an examination

There have been many books written on how to prepare for examinations, but I thought I would give a little advice on how to prepare specifically for an examination in law. As I explained at the beginning of this section, it is necessary when writing any answer to a legal question to support your arguments with relevant law. This means that it is necessary to learn and memorise many cases to help achieve this goal. Your aim is to apply relevant case law as I have demonstrated above, but how do you go about remembering many cases and their points of law? Different students memorise in different ways of course. You may memorise by writing out the cases many times over. You may take a more 'audible' approach and repeat cases to yourself many times or you may simply read them over and over. My fellow student at law school, 'Lucinda', memorised by writing cases and their points of law on sticky notes and placed them over all available wall space at her home. Another friend, let's call her Marion, made up sentences starting with the first letter of each case name in the order in which the cases were to be applied. For example, if Marion was trying to remember the line of cases for co-ownership (Chapter 5), *Pettitt, Gissing, Eves, Rosset, Stack* and *Jones* for example, she would try to remember 'purple geese eat radishes sprouts and jelly' – the more ridiculous the sentence, the easier to remember! Of course, there is more than one way to skin a cat, but the key point here is to have a method, any method, to aid your memory. You may decide to formulate a table of cases with the name, the point of law and the brief trigger fact, then use the table to help you memorise. I have given you such a table at the end of each chapter to get you started. You will also find useful websites in the Further Reading section at the end of each chapter. As I said, there are many methods out there to help you learn how to memorise, but I can't stress enough how important it is to find and use a method which works for you.

I hope, having read this section carefully, that some of the 'fear' of studying land law may have been removed. Land law is certainly not just a 'historical' subject rooted in the feudal Middle Ages! It is, given the economic climate, perhaps now more than ever a living, breathing subject, and one that I hope you will study, digest, understand, and even enjoy!

PART 1

Historical context and land ownership

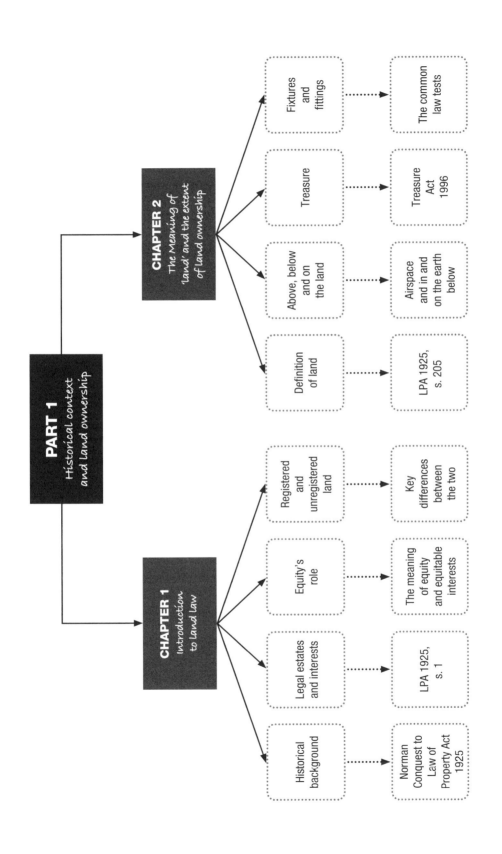

PART 1
Historical context and land ownership

CHAPTER 1
Introduction to land law

- Historical background
  ⋯▶ Norman Conquest to Law of Property Act 1925
- Legal estates and interests
  ⋯▶ LPA 1925, s. 1
- Equity's role
  ⋯▶ The meaning of equity and equitable interests
- Registered and unregistered land
  ⋯▶ Key differences between the two

CHAPTER 2
The meaning of 'land' and the extent of land ownership

- Definition of land
  ⋯▶ LPA 1925, s. 205
- Above, below and on the land
  ⋯▶ Airspace and in and on the earth below
- Treasure
  ⋯▶ Treasure Act 1996
- Fixtures and fittings
  ⋯▶ The common law tests

PART 1 INTRODUCTION

Part 1 of *Blueprints Land Law* explores the historical background to land law and sets the scene for the development of 'modern' land law moving into the 20th and 21st centuries. In Chapter 1 we will begin by looking at the historical context, looking briefly at the impact of the Norman Conquest by William the Conqueror and the introduction of the feudal land-holding system. We then move swiftly to the start of the 20th century and the key changes brought about by the Law of Property Act 1925. You also need to understand the meaning of '**equity**' and get to grips with '**equitable interests**' in land as well as '**legal interests**'. Chapter 1 ends with a comparison of registered and unregistered land.

The meaning and the extent of land ownership will be explained in Chapter 2. This will provide you with a useful overview of the definition of land from s. 205 of the Law of Property Act 1925 (LPA 1925) along with an understanding that the 'landowner' owns not only the building itself, but 'up to the heavens above' and down 'into the depths of the earth below'. We will look at what is meant by a 'treasure' and whether the phrase 'finders keepers' has any legal basis! It is also important to understand the difference between a fixture and a fitting and why that difference really matters when buying and selling a property.

CHAPTER 1

Introduction to land law

BLUEPRINT

Introduction to land law

LEGISLATION

- Law of Property Act 1925
- Land Registration Act 1925/2002

CONTEXT

- All land is 'owned' by the Crown
- All land is only 'held' by freeholders or leaseholders
- 96% of land in England and Wales is registered land

CONCEPTS

- Legal and equitable rights
- Personal and proprietary rights
- The feudal system of land ownership
- Registered and unegistered land
- Equity's darling

- Should equitable ownership be recognised at all?
- Should ALL land be subject to compulsory registration with NO hidden interests?

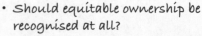

- What is the fundamental difference between a legal and an equitable interest in land?
- How did the 1925 legislation simplify land law?
- What are the key differences between registered and unregistered land?

CASES

- *Walsingham's Case* [1573]
- *Midland Bank* v. *Green* [1981]

SPECIAL CHARACTERISTICS

- The legal proprietary rights at s1(1) and s1(2) LPA 1925
- Equitable proprietary rights at s1(3) LPA 1925
- The protection of proprietary rights against third parties

REFORM

- Is the feudal system totally dead?
- Is the register a true reflection of the reality?

CRITICAL
ISSUES

Setting the scene

Oliver Cromwell described land law in England as a 'tortuous and ungodly jumble' and, from its origins in 1066 until the start of the 20th century, Cromwell's assessment was probably not far off the mark! Megarry and Wade suggest that English land law 'has tended to have an unenviable reputation for complexity'. Echoing Cromwell, they suggest that 'this reputation was thoroughly deserved' but that, since 1925, due to 'simplifying' legislation, 'this is no longer the case'. (See Further Reading below.) There are, of course, many excellent textbooks which give a profoundly scholarly explanation of the history of land law. I have set down some of these texts in the Further Reading section below. The purpose of *this* book will be to explain the workings of 'modern' English land law. However, it is always useful to set this in context. As such, a basic understanding of the historical background helps to set the scene. Just as a house will be in danger of subsidence without a solid foundation, the understanding of English land law can be undermined without some awareness of its roots.

BRIEF HISTORICAL BACKGROUND – THE NORMAN CONQUEST TO THE LAW OF PROPERTY ACT 1925

History tells us that William the Conqueror landed in England in September 1066, and defeated the last Anglo-Saxon King, Harold, at the Battle of Hastings in October 1066. Prior to William being crowned King in Westminster Abbey on Christmas Day 1066, the previous Anglo-Saxon system of 'landholding' was far from 'easy to grasp and . . . expressed in a bewildering variety of formulae' according to Pollock and Maitland (see Further Reading). William I replaced the entire system and imposed the *feudal system* where all land was *held* rather than owned – by way of **tenure** (from the Latin *tenere* 'to hold'). The idea behind this tenure is that land was 'granted' in return for various services – hence absolute ownership did not and could not exist. The owner of the land was of course, and theoretically still is, the Crown. There were a number of categories of tenure. These included:

- Knight service – agreement by the tenant to supply knights for the monarch's battles

- Frankalmoin – agreement to provide spiritual services

- Socage – agreement to provide agricultural services.

The process of land 'redistribution' didn't really begin in earnest until the 12th century, after the Domesday Book (completed in 1086) had compiled a detailed list of land ownership before and after the Conquest. This allowed the monarch to re-allocate land to a select band of Norman nobles in what Cooper refers to as the 'Norman land-grab' (see below). The families were known as 'tenants in chief' but were also able to grant 'sub-tenancies' (to use the modern term), known as the process of *sub-infeudation*. The land could not be sold or bequeathed – the tenant was said to enjoy *seisin* or *possession* of the land – a concept that is vitally important to understand even in the context of 'modern' land law. It was this 'right of possession' that could be protected, and not a right of ownership *per se*.

As time moved on, the feudal system of *tenure* began to change. The statute of *Quia Emptores* in 1290 replaced *subinfeudation* with *substitution* where a new tenant could replace an existing one. By the 13th century *knight service* tenants paid money (*scutage*) rather than provide armed men. *Socage* and *Frankalmoin* were also on the decline, and land started to become a 'commodity' which could be transferred a little more easily. The Statute of Wills in 1540 allowed most land to be left in a will. By this time, a system of complex rights in and over land had started to be the norm, including the rights of 'commoners' to take profits from common land. These included:

- *pasture*: the right to keep cattle, horses, sheep or other animals on the common land
- *piscary*: the right to fish
- *turbary*: the right to take turf
- *pannage*: the right to feed pigs
- *estovers*: the right to take wood.

By the 17th century, especially after the Cromwellian '*interregnum*' where royal estates were seized, land started to have a substantial commercial value. In 1660, the Tenures Abolition Act disposed of most forms of remaining tenures, and the Inclosure Acts of 1750–1850 allowed large plots of common land to be enclosed and put into the hands of private owners. By the 19th century land law had become extremely complex, with many large English estates held under '*strict settlement*' – a legal mechanism, the primary purpose of which was to allow land to be kept within family (usually aristocratic) ownership. However, as the need to transfer land as a valuable commodity increased, reform started to take place, with the Settled Land Act 1882 allowing for such 'strict settlements' to be sold. (See Chapter 6 – Trusts of Land and Appointment of Trustees Act 1996 finally 'outlawed' any new strict settlements from being created.)

As the 20th century approached, land law was no longer a slave to its ancient feudal roots. Due to the needs of 'modern society', law reforms were put in place changing the way land was 'owned' and the way that ownership was recorded. Through the Law of Property Act 1925, the Land Charges Act 1925 and the Land Registration Act 1925, the foundations of modern land law were laid.

LEGAL ESTATES AND INTERESTS IN LAND – SECTION 1 OF THE LAW OF PROPERTY ACT 1925

CORNERSTONE

Legal Ownership of Land

Prior to 1925, there were a number of ways in which a person could take legal 'ownership' of land. Of course, as stated above, this 'ownership' was really only a way of 'holding' the land – but with *almost* all of the rights of an absolute owner. The legal owner could sell the property, lease it to a tenant or sub-tenant, take a mortgage secured on the property, build and extend (within planning control laws) and even destroy the property if they so desired. It is also vital to understand that it is said that a 'legal right' in or over the land has the capability to '*bind the world*' – it may be binding on a third party due to its very nature as a 'legal right'. This is not the case with an *equitable* right (see below). It must also be said that the right needs to be *proprietary* rather than *personal* for it to be binding on third parties (like successors in title or banks taking possession). This distinction will be dealt with in detail in Chapter 3.

Due to the fact that the Crown was (and is) the real owner, the 'ownership' or 'proprietary right' is that of an '*estate in land*' or an '*interest in or over land*' and prior to 1925 there were a number of these estates and interests in land capable of being 'legal' **estates**. After the Law of Property Act 1925, these were greatly reduced, and the key starting point post-1925 is the Law of Property Act 1925, s. 1 which sets down proprietary rights capable of being legal (emphasis added):

1   Legal estates and equitable interests

(1)   The only estates in land which are capable of subsisting or of being conveyed or created at law are –
  (a)   *An estate in fee simple absolute in possession*;
  (b)   *A term of years absolute.*

(2)   The only interests or charges in or over land which are capable of subsisting or of being conveyed or created at law are –
  (a)   *An easement*, right, or privilege in or over land for an interest equivalent to an estate in fee simple absolute in possession or a term of years absolute;
  (b)   *A rentcharge* in possession issuing out of or charged on land being either perpetual or for a term of years absolute;
  (c)   A charge by way of *legal mortgage*;
  (d)   [. . .] and any other similar charge on land which is not created by an instrument;
  (e)   *Rights of entry* exercisable over or in respect of a legal term of years absolute, or annexed, for any purpose, to a legal rentcharge.

(3)   *All other estates, interests, and charges in or over land take effect as equitable interests.*

As explained above, the owner of the land holds an 'estate' or an interest in that land. As far back as *Walsingham's Case* (1573) it was clear that 'the land itself is one thing, and the estate in land is another thing, for an estate in the land is a time in the land, or land for a time, and there are diversities of estates, which are no more than diversities of time'. The idea of holding the land for an *almost* indefinite time is borne out by the feudal doctrine of *escheat* which states that a 'freeholder' may 'own' their land until there are no longer any heirs or descendants who can take the property. At that point the Crown is said to take title to the property by '*escheat*'. This part of our feudal heritage, at least in theory, remains to the present day, with the Administration of Estates Act 1925, s. 46(1)(vi) allowing for property of an intestate deceased to 'return' to the Crown *bona vacantia* where no one else is able to take the estate. Generally now, *escheat* only occurs where there is an estate subject to bankruptcy proceedings under the Insolvency Act 1986.

Legal estates prior to 1925

Prior to 1925 there were a number of ways in which to hold legal **title** (see Figure 1.1). These were:

1. *Fee simple*: this was tantamount to absolute ownership and could be sold or left in a will. This remains as a legal estate today as '*freehold ownership*' (see below).
2. *Life estate*: this was an estate in land that, as it suggests, lasted only as long as the life of the 'owner' of the land. Once they died, the property returned to the person or state of the grantor. This 'estate' can still exist – but only as a trust of land *in equity* (see below).

3. *Fee tail*: in 1285, the statute *De Donis Conditionabilis* allowed for a fee tail estate to be recognised as a legal estate in land. This term 'tail' derived from the French word *taille*, which suggests a limitation on inheritance of such an estate. Only direct male descendants (fee tail male) or female descendants (fee tail female) could take the land – clearly the aim being to keep the property within the family. From 1925, however, these estates were also only recognised as equitable and since the Trusts of Land and Appointment of Trustees Act 1996 no new fee tails can be created – they will simply be seen as a trust of land.

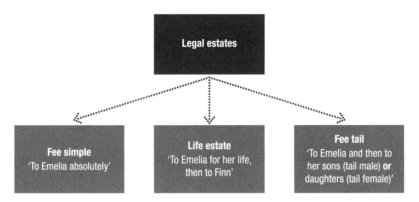

Figure 1.1 Legal estates prior to 1925

Legal estates after 1925

As illustrated above, section 1(1) of the Law of Property Act 1925 has greatly simplified 'legal owner-ship'. It reduced the number of estates capable of being 'legal estates' to just two:

1. **The fee simple absolute in possession** (s. 1(1)(a)): this is more commonly known, especially in conveyancing terms, as *the freehold estate*, which equates to absolute ownership (with some limitations – see Chapter 2).
2. **The term of years absolute** (s. 1(1)(b)): this is known as the *leasehold estate* and is based on a certain or fixed time period for ownership 'carved out' of the freehold and granted by the freeholder – at the end of that time period the property '*reverts*' to the freehold owner.

The fee simple absolute in possession

Fee simple: This illustrates that the *grant* of the land is *inheritable* and as such is the closest to full ownership that is possible. Other than third party rights in and over the land, and such other restrictions found in planning laws and general laws of negligence and nuisance, the 'fee simple' suggests an almost unrestricted use of the land. In *Walsingham's Case* (1573) it was stated that 'he

> **Take note**
>
> In relation to legal owners of a property, due mainly to the desire to ease conveyancing practice, the Law of Property Act 1925, s. 34(2) states that there can be a maximum of four legal owners of a single piece of land.

who has a fee simple in land has a time in the land without end or the land for a time without end'. As such the 'owner' is said to hold the land freely – and therefore is the *freeholder* of that land.

Absolute: The word 'absolute' signifies that there should be no limitations placed on 'fee simple' ownership. Traditionally a fee simple could be 'conditional' or 'determinable':

APPLICATION

The conditional or determinable fee simple

Conditional:

'To Zyg on the condition that he becomes a stockbroker'

The grantor has the choice of whether to enforce a condition or not – and the condition may be void for being contrary to public policy. It is possible even today to have a legal estate based on a conditional fee simple (though rare) under section 7(1) of the Law of Property Act 1925.

Determinable:

'To Zyg until he becomes a stockbroker'

Even though the 'event' may be the same as the event which forms the basis for a condition, if worded as ending the fee simple on the occurrence of such an event, it will be seen as a determinable fee simple and will only be an equitable estate in land, not legal. The right *will* end at the time Zyg becomes a stockbroker.

In possession: This simply means that the 'owner' must take immediate physical possession of the property, or be in 'receipt of rents and profits' – for example, as a landlord with a tenant in possession. The tenant will also have a legal estate – a '*leasehold*' estate.

The term of years absolute

This is defined at section 205(1)(xxvii) of the LPA 1925 as an estate in land for a fixed, certain or ascertainable time period. It states that 'years' can also mean a time period of less than a year. If the property is purchased leasehold, then the freeholder holds the property '*on reversion*': that is the freeholder or freeholder's estate will 'take back' the title of the property at the end of the time period. It is also possible, of course, for the 'owner' to 'lease' the property by creating a landlord–tenant relationship or for a leasehold tenant already 'renting' under a 'lease' to create a 'sub-lease' to a 'sub-tenant' for a period of time shorter than the original lease (see Chapter 3).

There is also a *third* form of ownership known as **commonhold**, which was introduced by the Commonhold and Leasehold Reform Act 2002. However, this is really a subsection of freehold ownership, the idea being that the commonhold interest is 'carved out' of an existing freehold estate, usually by a property developer of a new development, with the idea of creating individual 'commonhold' units that are owned by each unit holder, where the common areas are owned collectively by the '*commonhold*

Take note

It is useful to understand here that in land law terminology 'leasehold ownership' can mean either that the leaseholder has purchased a property leasehold from the freeholder (for example, on a 99-year lease) or they may be simply 'renting' from the freeholder with a tenancy agreement (see Chapter 3).

association'. The unit holders will be the registered owners of their individual units, whereas the common areas will be registered in the name of the 'association' collectively. The concept was born to solve old common law problems of the accountability of 'common parts' such as waste bin areas and staircases. Traditionally cases such as *Liverpool City Council* v. *Irwin* [1977] needed to rely on contractual implied terms to solve any disputes as to liability for these common areas. The 2002 Act sought to create a statutory regime which allows a *commonhold association*, like a business organisation, to hold property registered in its name.

> **REFLECTION**
>
> Commonhold has been described as 'an unknown quantity' which is still surrounded by 'nervousness' due to this 'new legal arrangement along the lines of an American condominium' needing full cooperation by a majority of the members of the 'association' who then share the full costs of repairs and maintenance (see Further Reading below). Selling commonhold units has been described by Smytherman as 'like trying to sell seats on the first test flight of a new prototype airliner, with . . . the pilot being a student [on] his first solo flight' (see below).

Legal interests after 1925

As explained above, section 1(2) of the Law of Property Act 1925 sets down five categories of interests that are *capable* of being legal interests. It is important to understand that they are not *automatically* legal interests, however. Generally, if not created in accordance with the relevant formalities (usually by deed – see Chapter 3) then they may be equitable interests rather than legal (see below).

INTERSECTION . . . .

A full discussion of the creation and protection of the two key interests in land capable of being legal can be found in their own substantive chapters: easements can be found in Chapter 8; mortgages can be found in Chapter 10. It is not necessary to deal with the substantive law on easements or mortgages here.

Easements: LPA 1925, section 1(2)(a)

This provision states that an 'easement, right or privilege' which is 'equivalent to an estate in fee simple absolute in possession [freehold] or a term of years absolute [leasehold]' can be a legal interest. This means that it must be for ever (like a freehold interest) or for a fixed, certain or ascertainable time period (like a leasehold). However, for an easement to be 'legal' it must also be created by deed following the formalities at section 52(1) of the LPA 1925.

Mortgages: LPA 1925, section 1(2)(c)

Once again, if the relevant formalities are satisfied (see Chapter 10) and the mortgage is a 'legal charge' created by deed, then the mortgage is also a key interest in land that is capable of being (and nearly always will be) a legal interest.

> **Take note**
>
> The right of entry of a landlord is dealt with thoroughly in the specific study of landlord and tenant law but is outside the remit of this book.

Rights of entry: LPA 1925, section 1(2)(e)

This is the right of re-entry onto the land in default of a rent charge (see below – of historical interest only) or the right of a landlord to re-enter a property where a tenant is in breach of a tenancy covenant such as a repair obligation or non-payment or rent.

Rent charges: LPA 1925, section 1(2)(b); Miscellaneous charges: LPA 1925, section 1(2)(d)

The 'rent charge' was traditionally a payment of money for the use of (usually agricultural) land rather than a 'normal' rent. However, since the introduction of the Rent Charges Act 1977, no new rent charges could be created – and, as such, this 'interest' is of historical interest only. This is also true of the 'miscellaneous charges' at section 1(2)(d) of the LPA 1925.

It is important to understand that all of the estates and rights listed at section 1 of the LPA 1925 are *capable* of being legal proprietary interests – that is, legal interests in or over the land itself.

INTERSECTION

A detailed explanation of the difference between purely personal rights (such as that of a 'licence' which gives permission for you to be on someone else's land and prevents you from being a trespasser) and proprietary rights (rights in or over the land itself) is given at Chapter 3. It is VITAL to understand that only proprietary rights, legal *or* equitable, are capable of binding a third party.

THE MEANING OF EQUITY AND EQUITY'S ROLE IN LAND LAW; EQUITABLE INTERESTS

LPA 1925, section 1(3) – All other proprietary interests: *equitable only*

Section 1(3) of the LPA 1925 states that all other rights, not listed at section 1, are proprietary rights that can *only ever be equitable* rather than legal. These will generally be dealt with in substantive chapters on each interest, but it is useful to list them here:

- beneficiaries' interests under a trust of land
- restrictive covenants
- proprietary estoppel rights
- estate contracts.

As stated above, though, it is also perfectly possible to have an equitable easement, lease or mortgage, especially where the formalities at section 52 of the LPA 1925 (creation by deed) have not been satisfied. If the interest is not created by deed, then provided it satisfies the formalities requirements at section 53(1)(a) of the LPA 1925 (in writing and signed) or the alternative requirements at section 2 of the Law of Property (Miscellaneous Provisions) Act 1989 (see Chapter 3 for details) then the proprietary interest will be *equitable* and may still be binding on a third party. It is vital therefore to understand exactly what 'equity' means and to understand the role equity plays within land law.

Equity – a brief history

For a thorough understanding of the 'birth' and development of equity within English law, there are many textbooks available on Equity and Trusts (including the Blueprints textbook on the subject). However, to understand land law fully, as suggested above, it is vital to have a working knowledge of how equity 'fits in' to the overall operation of land law.

In 1066, when the common law was introduced to England by William the Conqueror, if a claim was to be brought (a writ) then it was brought before the King's Court. This process allowed for limited remedies, such as the equivalent of damages – but if there was no writ, there was no real remedy. The Provisions of Oxford 1258 restricted any writs being brought without permission of the King. However, as the workload increased, and a realisation that the common law was proving rather rigid and inflexible, some 'writs' were handed over to the Lord Chancellor who was said to act as the 'keeper of the King's Conscience'. The Lord Chancellor eventually set up the Courts of Chancery and dealt with petitions based on the merits of each particular case and decided on principles of fairness and justice – hence equity. It is also said that 'equity acts in personam' to enable a personal claim to be brought against a defendant rather than just a common law action *in rem* focusing on the 'thing' – the property itself.

Apart from allowing more diverse claims to come before the Chancery Court, equity also allowed for different remedies such as specific performance and injunctions.

INTERSECTION

In Chapter 9, the equitable proprietary right of a 'restrictive covenant' is discussed in detail. Although the common law remedy of damages is available (see below) should your neighbour breach a covenant, money is not really the general aim. For example, if the agreement was to prevent your neighbour using their land as commercial property, a money remedy will not really suffice. As covenants are equitable, equity allows the equitable remedy of injunction – to stop the land being used for a purpose outside the covenant. However, the Senior Courts Act 1981 at section 50 also expressly allows for common law remedies such as damages to be awarded in place of an equitable remedy. (See Chapter 9 – *Jaggard* v. *Sawyer* [1995], where damages were awarded for a breach of covenant.)

As time went on, the King's Court (common law) and the Chancellor's Court of Equity worked independently. A claimant would need to decide whether the common law or equity would provide the better solution. The common law gave certainty, but equity gave flexibility. In the *Earl of Oxford's Case* (1616) the conflict came to a head with the ruling that where there was a clash between the common law and equity, 'equity should prevail'.

As equity developed further, the Lord Chancellor gave his judgment based not on precedent, but based on the Chancellor's own, often moral, opinion. In the 17th century, the respected jurist John Selden proclaimed that the outcome of a case heard in the Chancery Courts of equity was totally unpredictable as 'equity varies with the length of the Chancellor's foot'. As a response, Lord Nottingham, the Lord Chancellor at the time, introduced a more 'rule-based' system to attempt to create a little more certainty. Through the Judicature Acts 1873–75 the courts of common law and the courts of equity finally merged, with claimants being able to plead common law cases but heard with equitable principles being applied if relevant. In *Pugh* v. *Heath* (1882) it was stated that a court 'is now not a Court of Law or a Court of Equity, it is a Court of complete jurisdiction' although section 25 of the Judicature

Act 1873 stated quite clearly that where there was a conflict between common law and equity, equity will prevail. This is also now found in the Senior Courts Act 1981, section 49(1).

Equity's role in land law

As stated earlier, the common law only recognises legal title – any other rights are not recognised. The role of equity, therefore, is to 'step in' to recognise the equitable rights of owners and/or third parties. As such, those proprietary rights not listed at section 1 of the LPA 1925 or proprietary rights that have not been created in satisfaction of the formalities remain as equitable rights – and it is only due to the existence of equity that these rights are recognised and can be enforced. These rights include **beneficial interests** under a trust of land; restrictive covenants; estate contracts; and estoppel rights. They also include equitable leases, easements and mortgages if formalities have not been met.

INTERSECTION

Each of these key equitable rights will be discussed in detail in the following chapters:

Equitable leases: Chapter 3

Estate contracts: Chapter 4

Beneficiaries' interests under a trust of land: Chapters 5 and 6

Proprietary estoppel rights: Chapter 7

Equitable easements: Chapter 8

Restrictive covenants: Chapter 9

Equitable mortgages: Chapter 10

The 'enforceability' of equitable rights in land law

As explained above, in relation to enforcing a right, the traditional difference between common law and equity was the remedy available. However, this has now merged under section 50 of the Senior Courts Act 1981. Traditionally the other major difference between a common law right and an equitable right was that common law rights were 'attached to the land not the owner' and as such would 'run with the land' binding successors in title whereas a person claiming an equitable right in the land, prior to 1925 especially, could be defeated by '*equity's darling*' or the '*bona fide purchaser for value without notice*'. Put simply, this meant that if you were claiming an equitable right, your 'opponent' could challenge that right by arguing that they had bought the land in good faith (*bona fide*) for some *value* (though not necessarily market value as consideration needs to be sufficient but not necessarily economically adequate – a general principle of the contract law rules of consideration) and without any knowledge of your right being in existence (*without notice*). This was seen as an 'absolute, unqualified, unanswerable defence' against a person claiming an equitable right (James LJ in *Pilcher* v. *Rawlins* (1872)). However, this 'doctrine of notice' as it was called, only really applied to *unregistered land* – as with the advent of *registered land* with the introduction of the Land Registration Act 1925, the 'doctrine of notice' was effectively replaced with the presumption of knowledge of a pre-existing interest if it appears on the property register (see Chapter 4) or the presumption of an interest which overrides the register (see also Chapter 4). Section 198 of the LPA 1925 states that the entry of an interest on the property register is 'deemed actual notice' of that interest. Hence 'equity's darling' and the doctrine of notice has 'no application in registered land' (Mummery LJ in *Barclays Bank* v. *Boulter* [1998]) and, as unregistered land is virtually consigned to history, 'equity's darling' and 'notice' only remain as a *principle* in registered land – the mirror principle (see Chapter 4), which suggests that all interests on the property register should reflect the reality of ownership.

> ### Take note
>
> As unregistered land is largely now historical, with around 96 per cent of all land in England and Wales being registered, this textbook will refer fleetingly to unregistered land – the detail of unregistered or 'traditional' conveyancing is unnecessary. As such, this text will focus almost entirely on land law in a 'registered land' context. However – some basic background can be found below.

BRIEF INTRODUCTION TO THE CONCEPT OF REGISTERED AND UNREGISTERED LAND

Prior to 1925, most of the land in England and Wales was 'unregistered' – it was only with the introduction of a major system of land registration under the Land Registration Act 1925 that land began to be 'registered'. It is vital to understand that this Act has been repealed and replaced with the Land Registration Act 2002. (See Chapter 4 for a detailed discussion and explanation of the LRA 2002 and how it operates.) The general idea is that with *registered land* there is ONE document known in conveyancing terms as the Official Copy of the Register (see Figure 1.2) – and this is the document which will be the subject of a 'search' by your conveyancer or solicitor (or, of course, yourself) when purchasing a property. The 'mirror principle' referred to above suggests that this one document is a true reflection of all pre-existing rights and interests that are attached to the land you are purchasing. The only 'crack in the mirror' as Professor Martin Dixon puts it (see below) are the 'interests which override' the register but may still be binding on a new purchaser or a bank taking possession (see Chapter 4).

Land Registry

Official copy of register of title

| Title number CS705289 | Edition date 19.11.2008 |

— This official copy shows the entries in the register of title on 15 January 2009 at 11:50:13.
— This date must be quoted as the "search from date" in any official search application based on this copy.
— The date at the beginning of an entry is the date on which the entry was made in the register.
— Issued on 15 January 2009
— Under s.67 of the Land Registration Act 2002, this copy is admissible in evidence to the same extent as the original.
— For information about the register of title see Land Registry website www.landregistry.gov.uk or Land Registry Public Guide *1 – A guide to the information we keep and how you can obtain it.*
— This title is dealt with by Land Registry Croydon office.

A: Property register
The register describes the registered estate comprised in the title.

CORNSHIRE : DEVONBRIDGE

1. (19.12.1989) The Freehold land shown edged with red on the plan of the above Title filed at the Registry and being 13 Augustine Way, Kerwick, (PL14 3JP).

2. (19.12.1989) The land has the benefit of a right of way on foot only over the passageway tinted brown on the filed plan.

3. (19.12.1989) The land has the benefit of the rights granted by but is subject to the rights reserved by the Transfer dated 5 December 1989 referred to in the Charges Register.

4. (19.12.1989) The land has the benefit of a right of drainage through the pipe shown by a blue broken line on the filed plan so far as such pipe lies outside the land in this title.

5. (14.09.2006) The land edged and numbered in green on the title plan has been removed from this title and registered under the title number or numbers shown in green on the said plan.

B: Proprietorship register
This register specifies the class of title and identifies the owner. It contains any entries that affect the right of disposal.

Title absolute

Figure 1.2 The Official Copy of the Register
Source: from Land Registry, Crown copyright

Title Number CS705289

1. (19.11.2008) PROPRIETOR: PAUL JOHN DAWKINS and ANGELA MARY DAWKINS both of 13 Augustine Way, Kerwick, Maradon, Cornshire PL14 3JP.

2. (19.11.2008) The price stated to have been paid on 12 November 2008 was £325,500.

3. (19.11.2008) No disposition by a sole proprietor of the registered state (except a trust corporation) under which capital money arises is to be registered unless authorised by an order of the court.

4. (19.11.2008) RESTRICTION: No disposition of the registered estate by the proprietor of the registered estate is to be registered without a written consent signed by the proprietor for the time being of the charge dated 12 November 2008 in favour of Weyford Building Society referred to in the charges register or their conveyancer.

C: Charges register

This register contains any charges and other matters that affect the registered estate.

1. (19.12.1989) A Conveyance of the land tinted yellow on the filed plan and other land dated 19 May 1924 made between (1) Allan Ansell (Vendor) and (2) Frances Amelia Moss (Purchaser) contains covenants details of which are set out in the schedule of restrictive covenants hereto.

2. (19.12.1989) A Conveyance of the land tinted pink of the filed plan and other land dated 16 August 1926 made between (1) Edward Philip Green (Vendor) and (2) Peter John Brown and Hannah Sarah Brown contains covenants details of which are set out in the schedule of restrictive covenants hereto.

3. (19.12.1989) A Transfer of the land in this title dated 5 December 1989 made between (1) Freeman Builders Limited and (2) James Michael Pritchard and Molly Carol Pritchard contains restrictive covenants.

    NOTE: Copy filed

4. (19.12.1989) The land is subject to rights of way on foot only over the passageway tinted blue on the filed plan.

5. (19.11.2008) REGISTERED CHARGE dated 12 November 2008.

6. (19.11.2008) PROPRIETOR: WEYFORD BUILDING SOCIETY of Society House, The Avenue, Weyford, Cornshire CN12 4BD.

Schedule of restrictive covenants

1. The following are details of the covenants contained in the Conveyance dated 19 May 1924 referred to in the Charges Register: -

    "And the Purchaser for himself his heirs, executors, administrators, and assigns hereby covenants with the Vendor its heirs and assigns that he will perform and observe the stipulations set out in the first schedule hereto so far as they relate to the hereditaments hereby assured.

                    THE FIRST SCHEDULE

Figure 1.2 (*continued*)

Title Number CS705289

    a) The Purchaser shall within 3 months from the date of his purchase erect (if not already erected) and afterwards maintain in good condition a good and sufficient open pale or other approved fence or hedge on the sides of the plot marked 'T' on the plan within the boundary.

    b) No external alterations whatsoever shall be made to the premises without the written consent of the Vendor.

    c) The premises shall not be used for the purpose of a public house or hostel or any purpose connected with the sale of intoxicating liquor."

NOTE: The 'T' marks referred to above do not affect the land in this title.

2.   The following are details of the covenants contained in the Conveyance dated 16 August 1926 referred to in the Charges Register: -

"And the purchaser for themselves their heirs and executors administrators and assigns hereby covenants

that they would not erect or carry on upon any part said pieces of land delineated on said plan and coloured Green and Pink respectively any Manufactory whatsoever or upon any part of said pieces of land delineated on said plan any Mill Hospital Lunatic Asylum Steam Engine Barracks Beer Shop Gasworks Limeworks Pottery Brickworks or carry or permit or suffer to be carried on any noisome noisy dangerous or offensive trade business or occupation whatsoever.

And would not at any time thereafter uncope or dig for any stone sand or clay or use any stone Quarry Sand Pit or Clay pit for the purpose of selling Stone Sand or Clay in or upon any part of said land and premises or use said land and premises or any part thereof as a cemetery or Burial Ground nor bore for water or sink any well on any part of said land and premises which should require any power beyond manual labour to pump or force up the water or sell any water from off said land and premises.

NOTE: The land coloured pink on the filed plan forms part of the land coloured green and coloured pink referred to in the first paragraph above.

End of register

Figure 1.2 (*continued*)

The problem with *unregistered land*, however, is that a new purchaser did not have the 'luxury' of perusing one single document. The purchaser would have to search through a number of 'title deeds' going back at least 15 years to satisfy the requirement that they had what was referred to as a 'good root of title' (Law of Property Act 1969, s. 23). They would also need to check the Land Charges Register in which, under the Land Charges Act 1972, they would be able to see the entry of certain equitable interests such as covenants; easements; mortgages; estate contracts; and matrimonial rights of occupation. These were (are) known as Land Charges and if registered were deemed to give 'actual notice' (LPA 1925, s. 198 – see above). If the rights were not entered they could still bind under the 'doctrine of notice' (see above) but certain equitable rights could also be overreached – where the proprietary right (usually a beneficiary under a trust) could be replaced with a monetary payment (see *Kingsnorth Finance* v. *Tizard* [1986]). Overreaching still plays a major role in *registered land* and this will be discussed later (see Chapter 4). Hence, with unregistered land, an entry not on the Land Charges Register, especially of an equitable interest, would generally not be binding against a third party as it would be defeated by 'equity's darling':

APPLICATION

Midland Bank v. *Green* [1981]

Farmer Green owned a farm estate (unregistered land) worth approximately £40,000. He agreed with his son Geoffrey that Geoffrey could take an 'option to purchase' the farm at any time within the next 10 years. This agreement – an equitable proprietary right in the form of an estate contract – was backed up by consideration with Geoffrey paying a nominal amount for the agreement in order to make it legally binding. Six years into the 10-year period Geoffrey introduced his wife-to-be to his father who disapproved of his choice of partner. To avoid the farm falling into the hands of his son and his wife, Farmer Green transferred the farm to his own wife Evelyne for the sum of £500. The question for the court was whether the estate contract should be enforced as a pre-exisiting equitable interest or did Evelyne defeat the claim by being 'equity's darling'.

At first instance, Oliver J found that she was the 'bona fide purchaser of a legal estate, for value, without notice' and as Geoffrey had failed to register the estate contract as a Class C(iv) Land Charge it was invalid under section 13(2) of the LCA 1925. In the Court of Appeal, however, Lord Denning MR found in favour of Geoffrey – arguing that she had not given 'money or money's worth' for the purchase – £500 being a 'gross underpayment'. The House of Lords reminded Lord Denning that 'consideration need not be economically adequate' and restored the findings of Oliver J. The House made it very clear that if a person has an interest that needs to be entered on the register to bind a third party – especially an equitable interest – then it will be void if not entered on the register. The farmer's wife was indeed the *bona fide* purchaser for 'money or money's worth', and due to the lack of an entry on the register, was indeed also 'without notice'.

As stated above, though, the remainder of this book will focus on registered land, though the principles behind the 'traditional' system of conveyancing, and even those of the feudal system, still play their part in the study and operation of 'modern land law'.

As such, a proprietary right in or over the land, whether legal or equitable, is a valuable commodity, not least because it may have the effect of binding a third party. Although traditionally unravelling these proprietary rights from the 'ungodly jumble' may well have been 'tortuous', according to Megarry (see below), thanks to the 1925 legislation, 'the structure of modern land law' helps to 'ease the burden on purchasers without defeating the interests of others unfairly'.

REFLECTION

KEY POINTS

- 'Modern' land law has its roots in the feudal system of 'tenures' introduced by William the Conqueror after the Battle of Hastings. The Crown owned all land but gave land to 'hold' in return for various services to the monarch.

- The feudal system was eventually replaced by a system of land ownership which included various 'legal estates' in land such as the fee simple, the life estate and the fee tail.

- The number of legal estates in land and interests over land were greatly reduced and simplified by the LPA 1925. The two remaining estates capable of being 'legal' are the 'freehold' and 'leasehold' estates and the key interests are the easement, the mortgage and the right of re-entry by a landlord. These rights and estates are capable of being 'legal' if they satisfy formality requirements – such as being created by deed.

- All other proprietary interests or rights (LPA 1925, s. 1(3)) are only ever equitable. These include the covenant; the beneficiaries' interests under a trust of land; the proprietary estoppel interest; and the estate contract. If formalities are not satisfied, then there can also be an equitable lease, mortgage and easement.

- The role of equity within land law is to allow for different remedies such as specific performance and injunctions but also serves to recognise rights that are not recognised by the common law – especially the rights of beneficiaries under a trust.

- Courts of Equity sprang up alongside the King's courts from the time of William I – to allow more flexibility – and at the time of the Judicature Acts 1873–1875 the two courts merged, with equity prevailing where there was a conflict with the common law.

- Traditionally an equitable claim could be defeated by 'equity's darling' but this was based on the 'doctrine of notice' which is largely historical since the introduction of registered land. Legal rights are attached to the land and are said to 'run with the land' to bind all future third parties.

- Registered land is now the system used for conveyancing in England and Wales – around 96 per cent of all land is registered. This allows a purchaser to search one document containing all pre-existing proprietary rights – except those which override the register – the Official Copy of the Register. If a purchaser buys unregistered land they must search back through numerous documents to find a 'good root of title' going back at least 15 years. They must also check the Land Charges Register for any equitable land charges.

- This textbook will focus on registered land only – though the principles behind unregistered conveyancing are still relevant.

CORE CASES AND STATUTES

Case	About	Importance
Walsingham's Case (1573)	Historical overview of land ownership.	The ownership is 'in the land' for a period of time – *not* the full ownership of the land itself – which is held by the Crown.
Midland Bank v. *Green* [1981] AC 513	Wife pays her husband farmer £500 for a farm worth £40,000 in 'breach' of an equitable estate contract held by their son.	If an interest is not entered on the register (and not an overriding interest) then the interest will be void against third parties as that third party has no 'notice' of the interest. Traditionally, in unregistered land, an unprotected right will be defeated by 'equity's darling'.

Statute	About	Importance
LPA 1925, s. 1(1)	Sets down at s. 1(1) the two remaining legal estates in land.	Freehold and leasehold.
LPA 1925, s. 1(2)	Section 1(2) gives the interests capable of being legal.	Easements, mortgages and rights of re-entry.
LPA 1925, s. 1(3)	Section 1(3) sets down that all other proprietary rights are only ever equitable.	These include covenants, proprietary estoppel rights, beneficiary interests under a trust, estate contracts. All of the rights at s. 1(1) and (2) will only be equitable if the formalities for creation (deed) are not satisfied.

FURTHER READING

Clark, R. 'Leasehold has us tied in chains', *The Telegraph*, Jan. 2006: www.telegraph.co.uk/property
A critical account of leasehold ownership.

Cooper, A. 'Extraordinary privilege: the trial of Penenden Heath and the Domesday inquest', *The English Historical Review*, 1 November 2001
More historical context – useful for background understanding.

Megarry's Manual of the Law of Real Property (8th edn, Sweet & Maxwell, 2002)
As above – a practical and detailed approach to the subject of land law.

Megarry & Wade, *The Law of Real Property* (7th edn, Thomson, 2008) (ed. Martin Dixon)
The 'bible' when it comes to a detailed 'practitioner' account of land law.

Pollock, Sir Fredrick and Maitland, F.W. *The history of English law before the time of Edward I* **(2nd edn, 1898)**
As above – this gives great historical detail of the medieval system of land holding.

Scrutton, Sir Thomas Edward, *Land in fetters; or, The history and policy of the laws restraining the alienation and settlement of land in England*
(1885) http://books.google.co.uk/ books?id=0wQ9AAAAIAAJ
Gives the history of land law – especially the feudal system of land holding.

Smytherman, B. 'What's the future for Commonhold', *The Property Network,* **14 March 2010: www.network.propertyweek.com**
Critique of the 'commonhold' innovation created by the Commonhold and Leasehold Reform Act.

CHAPTER 2

The meaning of 'land' and the extent of land ownership

BLUEPRINT

The meaning of 'land' and the extent of land ownership

KEY QUESTIONS

LEGISLATION

- Law of Property Act 1925
- The Treasure Act 1996

CONTEXT

- 'Ownership'.
- What can be removed when the land is sold

CONCEPTS

- Airspace
- Higher and lower stratum
- Treasure
- Fixtures and fittings
- Annexation tests

- How far above our property should we own?
- Should 'treasure' revert to the Crown?
- Should legislation make it far clearer as to what is a fixture and what is a fitting?

- What is the extent of land ownership – how high above and how far below land do we own?
- What is the fundamental difference between a fixture and a fitting or chattel?
- How did the common law develop the 'tests' for determining fixtures and fittings?

CASES

- *Bernstein* v. *Skyviews* [1978]
- *Kelsen* v. *Imperial Tobacco* [1957]
- *Anchor Brewhouse* v. *Berkeley House* [1987]
- *Holland* v. *Hodgson* [1872]
- *Elitestone* v. *Morris* [1997]
- *Botham* v. *TSB* [1996]

REFORM

- Are the common law tests to distinguish a fixture and fitting adequate?

SPECIAL CHARACTERISTICS

- Land ownership above and below the earth
- 'Treasure' as defined by the Treasure Act 1996
- The degree and purpose of annexation – common law tests
- Why being classed as a fixture is so important – fixtures stay with the land

CRITICAL ISSUES

Setting the scene

The ownership of land has always been a highly contentious issue – not least due to the fact that land has always been a valuable commodity. It has also been, and will probably always be a 'political hot potato'. On the 'far left' of the political spectrum, at the top of Karl Marx's agenda in his 1848 Communist Manifesto was the view that society should work towards the 'abolition of property/ownership of land', arguing that 'modern bourgeois society . . . has sprouted from the ruins of feudal society'. However, giving a more 'capitalist' viewpoint, the economist Milton Friedman argued that private land ownership has the ability to 'make a positive contribution to freedom – or at least an enhancement of choice . . .'. (see below). This argument was echoed by journalists such as Heath who, shortly after the death of Margaret Thatcher, stated that 'one of Lady Thatcher's greatest legacies was to increase home ownership, allowing families to buy council homes at a discount. Her right to buy policy . . . in the 1980s and 1990s . . . played a central role in changing the aspiration and culture of the UK public, as well as enabling many more people to own assets' (see below).

It is important however, at least historically, to remember, as stated in the Preamble to the Land Registration Act 2002, that 'the concepts of leasehold and freehold derive from medieval forms of tenure *and are not ownership*' at all (see Chapter 1). As explained in Chapter 1, land 'ownership' takes the form of 'holding' the land either in '**fee simple absolute**' or for a '**term of years**', but in lay-man's terms, to understand the extent of your *ownership* is vital. Knowing exactly what is 'owned' is essential in giving a complete picture of all rights in and over your land and all obligations to others, especially third parties such as neighbours, lenders or new purchasers. A lack of knowledge or under-standing of what is 'owned' can lead to difficulties, disputes and, of course, expensive litigation. To set the scene further, the 'land ownership' argument at the start of Chekov's short play *The Proposal* highlights, in simple terms, how land ownership disputes can cause chaos and confusion:

Lomov: . . . The Lomovs and the Chubukovs have always had the most friendly, and I might almost say the most affectionate, regard for each other. And, as you know, my land is a near neighbour of yours. You will remember that my Oxen Meadows touch your Birchwoods.

Natalya Stepanovna: Excuse my interrupting you. You say, 'my Oxen Meadows . . .'. But are they yours?

Lomov: Yes, mine.

Natalya Stepanovna: What are you talking about? Oxen Meadows are ours, not yours! How long have they been yours?

Lomov: How long? As long as I can remember . . . you can see from the documents, honoured Natalya Stepanovna. Oxen Meadows, it's true, were once the subject of dispute, but now everybody knows that they are mine. There's nothing to argue about. You see, my aunt's grandmother gave the free use of these Meadows in perpetuity to the peasants of your father's grandfather, in return for which they were to make bricks for her. The peasants belonging to your father's grandfather had the free use of the Meadows for forty years, and had got into the habit of regarding them as their own . . .'

As such, gaining a thorough understanding as to exactly what is meant by 'land' and 'property' as well as an understanding as to what the extent of that ownership is – the *size and shape* of your land; how *far above* the land is yours; how *far below* the land is owned by you; what *objects in or on* the land form part of your ownership; and which objects are *fixtures* and which are *fittings* are all key questions which need answering. This chapter will attempt to do exactly that.

DEFINITION OF LAND – LAW OF PROPERTY ACT 1925, SECTION 205

First, it is important to realise that 'land' does not just mean the 'land' itself. Of course, it is true to say that 'plots' of land can be purchased as bare plots of land, undeveloped and without any structures or buildings 'sat' on that plot. For the purposes of land law though, land means far more than that. There is a Latin maxim or phrase that states *superficies solo cedit*, which translated literally means 'the surface yields to the ground' or, put more straightforwardly, everything built on the land belongs to the owner of that piece of land. This becomes all the more important when selling the property as *all of the land* including anything 'fixed' to the land will automatically become part of the sale. This was clarified in section 62(1) of the LPA 1925 which states that 'any conveyance of land shall be deemed to include . . . all buildings, erections, fixtures . . .' attached to the land unless otherwise stated in the sale contract (s. 62(4)). Land is defined, though in rather complex terms, at section 205(1)(ix) of the LPA 1925 (see Figure 2.1):

CORNERSTONE

LPA 1925, section 205(1)(ix)

. . . land of any tenure, mines and minerals, whether or not held apart from the surface, buildings or part of buildings (whether the division is horizontal, vertical or made in any other way) and other corporeal hereditaments; also a manor, an advowson, and a rent and other incorporeal hereditaments, and an easement, right, privilege or benefit in, over or derived from land.

The Interpretation Act 1978, at Schedule 1 further clarifies that 'land' includes 'buildings and other structures, land covered with water, and any estate, interest, easement, servitude or right in or over land'.

It is vital to understand that section 205 refers to both *corporeal* and *incorporeal* hereditaments. The former includes what may be described as 'tangibles' in or on the land – the earth, clay or rock, and also buildings, hedges, fences, trees and plants. Blackstone in his *Commentaries* (see Chapter 1) described such rights as 'substantial and permanent objects' which can be seen or touched. Again, as explained in Chapter 1, land law is also concerned with 'intangible' rights that may affect the landowner and his successors in title. These 'incorporeal' rights include the 'proprietary rights' illustrated in Chapter 1 – for example, the easement (such as a right of way); the covenant (a restrictive promise between neighbouring landowners); and the rights of a beneficiary under a trust. With reference once again to Blackstone, these rights cannot be 'touched' – they 'exist only in contemplation' but nevertheless can be binding on third parties as such a right can be said to be 'attached' to the land itself and 'run with the land' to bind new buyers or lenders taking back possession.

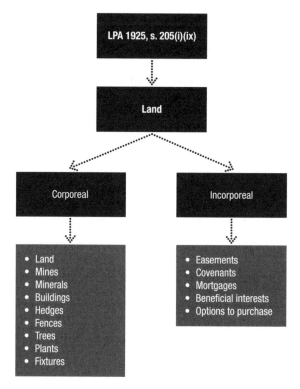

Figure 2.1 This definition of land s. 205 LPA 1925

Rights above, below and on the surface of the land

Airspace – above the land

As stated above, it is important to understand that the 'owner' of the property does not just own the building itself, or even the plot of land upon which the property stands. There is a Latin maxim or phrase which states *Cuius est solum eius est usque ad coelum et ad inferos*, which roughly translated means that the owner of a piece of land also owns 'up to the heavens above' and 'down to the depths of the earth below'. In relation to the 'airspace' above a property or a piece of land, it was suggested by Griffiths J in *Bernstein of Leigh (Baron)* v. *Skyviews & General Ltd* [1978] that the maxim is a 'colourful phrase' and the extent of ownership of airspace is simply 'up to a reasonable height'. The 'airspace' is generally said to be split between the 'lower stratum' and the 'higher stratum' to allow for the 'rules' of such ownership to be practicable. In terms of the 'higher stratum' it was confirmed in *Bernstein* and also at section 76 of the Civil Aviation Act 1982 that there is no ownership at such a height where it is reasonable to expect aircraft to fly (see Figure 2.2).

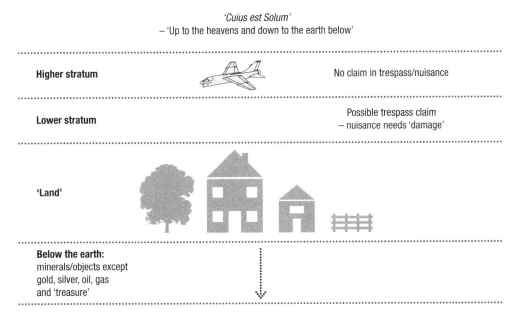

'Cuius est Solum'
– 'Up to the heavens and down to the earth below'

Higher stratum — No claim in trespass/nuisance

Lower stratum — Possible trespass claim
– nuisance needs 'damage'

'Land'

Below the earth:
minerals/objects except
gold, silver, oil, gas
and 'treasure'

Figure 2.2 The extent of land ownership

APPLICATION

Section 76 of the Civil Aviation Act 1982 states that 'the lower stratum is unlikely to extend beyond an altitude of much more than 500 or 1,000 feet above roof level, this being roughly the minimum permissible distance for normal overflying by any aircraft' (Rules of the Air Regulations 2007, Sch. 1, s. 3(5)).

This clearly suggests that there can generally be no claim in the 'higher stratum' for the two possible actions in tort law for nuisance or for trespass.

For cases relating to the 'lower stratum' it was stated in *Bernstein* that a landowner *can* claim ownership of airspace to such a height 'as is necessary for the ordinary use and enjoyment of his land and the structures upon it'. As stated above, this claim will almost exclusively be for trespass rather than nuisance. Traditionally, however, the courts were slow to accept a claim for such 'trespass'. In *Pickering* v. *Rudd* (1815) a balloon flying over a property was not seen as actionable trespass. In *Lemmon* v. *Webb* [1894] encroaching tree branches were effectively judged a nuisance rather than trespass. As the twentieth century developed, though, the courts became more flexible in their approach. In *Gifford* v. *Dent* [1926] a sign projecting from a wall almost five feet over property was seen as trespass. In *Kelsen* v. *Imperial Tobacco Ltd* [1957] McNair J stated the judicial preference for a trespass claim rather than a claim in nuisance:

APPLICATION

'That leads me to the next and in some ways most interesting point of the case, namely, whether an invasion of an airspace by a sign of this nature does give rise to an action in trespass or whether the rights, if any, of the owner of the airspace are not limited to complaining of nuisance; for if his rights are so limited it is clear on the facts of this case that no nuisance was created since the presence of this sign in the position where it was on this wall caused no inconvenience and no interference with the plaintiff's use of his airspace . . .'

Take note

In tort law, there are two possible claims relating to the 'invasion' of your property. One is to make a claim in nuisance claiming that a third party is 'causing a substantial and unreasonable interference' with your 'use or enjoyment' of your land. However, this is tricky in two main ways. Firstly, there must be 'interference' – and this may be problematic as the 'invasion' of your airspace may not really interfere with your use of the land. Secondly, the nuisance must cause some tangible 'damage' to the property. As such, the more straightforward claim is one of trespass, which is 'actionable per se' meaning that there is no need to establish damage of any kind. The case law, therefore, on the 'invasion' of airspace (lower stratum) tends to be based on claims for trespass rather than nuisance.

There have often been problems with 'jibs' (arms) of cranes overhanging property. In the case of *Woollerton and Wilson Ltd* v. *Richard Costain Ltd* [1970] a crane jib was overhanging the roof of property by some 50 feet. Trespass was established, though an injunction was delayed by 12 months to allow the defendant time to finish the building work and no damages were awarded. In the more recent case of *Anchor Brewhouse Developments Ltd* v. *Berkley House (Docklands Developments) Ltd* [1987] another swinging crane was seen as trespass, with Scott J suggesting that especially where the trespass is ongoing and continuing, an injunction should ordinarily be granted. The delayed injunction in the *Woollerton* case came under fire by Sir Thomas Bingham in the restrictive covenant case of *Jaggard* v. *Sawyer* [1995] (see Chapter 9). He stated that 'the fact that a plaintiff has suffered only nominal damage cannot in common sense be a reason for confining his remedy to an injunction if the court is then, by suspending the injunction, to deny him any remedy at all.' In *Laiqat* v. *Majid* [2005] an extractor fan at a height of around six metres above ground level protruding across into the claimant's property was also an interference with airspace and therefore an actionable trespass, even though the actual protrusion, though six metres high, was only around 750 mm into the claimant's garden!

Below the surface

As stated earlier, the Latin maxim *cuius est solum* also extends ownership beneath the surface of the land. Generally speaking anything found *below the surface* is owned by the landowner even if they are unaware that the object is there (*Elwes* v. *Brigg Gas Company* (1886)). This is also the case where the object is found by a third party, unless the original owner of the object is known. In *Waverley Borough Council* v. *Fletcher* [1995] Fletcher discovered a medieval brooch below the surface of the council-owned parkland. Though the first instance judge found in favour of the 'finder', the Court of Appeal reversed the decision, stating that in cases where the object is found below the surface, and where the original owner is unknown, the landowner has a better claim for title than the finder – 'finders keepers' did not hold sway with the Court of Appeal where the object was *in* and not *on* the land! Lord Justice Auld stated that 'Such objects were to be treated as an integral part of the realty'. This is due to the fact that the 'strata' under the surface of the land is 'owned' by the landowner. In *Bocardo SA* v. *Star Energy UK Onshore Ltd* [2011] the Supreme Court held that a landowner was able to succeed in a trespass action against an oil company that had placed pipelines up to 3,000 feet below the land's surface.

In relation to *minerals* themselves found under the surface the general rule is that ownership is with the landowner, though there are of course substantial exceptions to this such as coal, natural gas and oil that are 'state-owned' and are governed by statute, and would require a licence to extract. A licence would also be needed to extract *water* running through the land in a 'defined channel' such as a stream or river, other than water that may be used for the landowners' personal or general agricultural use. The owner may also fish in water running through such a 'defined channel'. The *Case of Mines* (1586) sets down that gold and silver are owned by the Crown (see 'Treasure' below). As stated above, trees, plants, flowers and hedges, due to the fact that they are rooted within the ground, are also owned by the landowner.

On the surface

There is a subtle but important difference, however, in relation to items found *on* the land. Generally, as explained by Lord Justice Auld in the *Waverley* case, where an object is found unattached to the land, then if it is not possible to ascertain the true owner, the 'finders keepers' presumption applies, provided the finder has been invited onto the land and is not a trespasser. The only exception to this is where the landowner can establish that they intended at all times to exercise control over the land, property and all objects found on the land. In such a case, the 'finders keepers' presumption can be rebutted in favour of the landowner. In *Bridges* v. *Hawkesworth* (1851) a customer found some money in an envelope which had been dropped in a public area of a shop. The customer handed them over to the owner of the shop, but the true owner did not come forward to claim the money. Patterson J subsequently awarded the money to the customer as the envelope was in a public area and not under the express control of the shopkeeper. This was followed in *Parker* v. *British Airways Board* [1982] where a passenger was judged to be able to keep a gold bracelet found on the floor of a public lounge at Heathrow Airport.

In relation to wild animals found on the land, the general rule is that where the species are not protected, the owner has a 'qualified right' to catch and kill the animal as in *Blade* v. *Higgs* (1865) and once caught and killed the animal becomes the personal property of the owner.

Treasure

There are specific statutory provisions if 'treasure' is found *in or on* the land under the Treasure Act 1996. If 'treasure' is found on the land, section 4 states that the treasure will generally belong to the Crown, and the finder is bound to report the find to the *local coroner* within 14 days of finding it (s. 8). It is a criminal offence not to do so. However, section 10 allows a compensatory payment up to the full value to be paid to the finder and/or the owner or occupier of the land.

....APPLICATION

Treasure Act 1996

Section 1 of the Treasure Act 1996 defines 'treasure' as being any object *at least 300 years old* when found, which:

- is not a coin, but has metallic content of which at least 10 per cent by weight is precious metal (means gold or silver) (s. 1(1)(a)(i)).
- is one of at least two coins in the same find having a metal content of at least 10 per cent precious metal (s. 1(1)(a)(ii)).
- is one of at least ten coins in the same find, all of which must be at least 300 years old (s. 1(1)(a)(iii)).

Objects of material other than precious metal, and which are found as part of the same find, are also treasure (see (s. 1(1)(d)).

FIXTURES AND FITTINGS

When a property is sold, a contract for that sale is drawn up by the conveyancer or solicitor dealing with the property and that contract is signed by both parties and upon 'exchange of contracts' the terms within the contract become legally binding. In order to ease conveyancing, and also in order to avoid some of the harsher rules of general contract law, the Law Society developed the 'Standard Conditions of Sale' (now the 5th Edition) (see Figure 2.3) and this document is expressly incorporated into every sale of a property. The document contains a large number of clauses which deal with such matters as insurance and risk; completion dates; and remedies for breach. At the end of the document is a section known as 'Special Conditions' and generally, at special condition 3a and 3b, it states that the sale of the property *includes* all listed *contents* which the seller has agreed to sell to the buyer, but *excludes* all listed *fixtures*. This pre-assumes that if fixtures are *not* listed as to be excluded from the sale, then they will form part of the land itself and will remain with the property.

CONTRACT

Incorporating the Standard Conditions of Sale (Fifth Edition)

For conveyancer's use only

Buyer's conveyancer: ______________________

Seller's conveyancer: ______________________

Law Society Formula: [A / B / C / Personal exchange]

The information above does not form part of the Contract

Date :

Seller :

Buyer :

Property (freehold/leasehold) :

Title number/root of title :

Specified incumbrances :

Title guarantee (full/limited) :

Completion date :

Contract rate :

Purchase price :

Deposit :

Contents price (if separate) :

Balance :

The seller will sell and the buyer will buy the property for the purchase price.

WARNING	**Signed**
This is a formal document, designed to create legal rights and legal obligations. Take advice before using it.	Seller/Buyer

SCS1_2/1

Figure 2.3 Standard Conditions of Sale – 5th Edition

STANDARD CONDITIONS OF SALE (FIFTH EDITION)
(NATIONAL CONDITIONS OF SALE 25TH EDITION, LAW SOCIETY'S CONDITIONS OF SALE 2011)

1. GENERAL

1.1 Definitions

1.1.1 In these conditions:
- (a) 'accrued interest' means:
  - (i) if money has been placed on deposit or in a building society share account, the interest actually earned
  - (ii) otherwise, the interest which might reasonably have been earned by depositing the money at interest on seven days' notice of withdrawal with a clearing bank less, in either case, any proper charges for handling the money
- (b) 'clearing bank' means a bank which is a shareholder in CHAPS Clearing Co. Limited
- (c) 'completion date' has the meaning given in condition 6.1.1
- (d) 'contents price' means any separate amount payable for contents included in the contract
- (e) 'contract rate' means the Law Society's interest rate from time to time in force
- (f) 'conveyancer' means a solicitor, barrister, duly certified notary public, licensed conveyancer or recognised body under sections 9 or 23 of the Administration of Justice Act 1985
- (g) 'lease' includes sub-lease, tenancy and agreement for a lease or sub-lease
- (h) 'mortgage' means a mortgage or charge securing the repayment of money
- (i) 'notice to complete' means a notice requiring completion of the contract in accordance with condition 6.8
- (j) 'public requirement' means any notice, order or proposal given or made (whether before or after the date of the contract) by a body acting on statutory authority
- (k) 'requisition' includes objection
- (l) 'transfer' includes conveyance and assignment
- (m) 'working day' means any day from Monday to Friday (inclusive) which is not Christmas Day, Good Friday or a statutory Bank Holiday.

1.1.2 In these conditions the terms 'absolute title' and 'official copies' have the special meanings given to them by the Land Registration Act 2002.

1.1.3 A party is ready, able and willing to complete:
- (a) if he could be, but for the default of the other party, and
- (b) in the case of the seller, even though the property remains subject to a mortgage, if the amount to be paid on completion enables the property to be transferred freed of all mortgages (except any to which the sale is expressly subject).

1.1.4 These conditions apply except as varied or excluded by the contract.

1.2 Joint parties

If there is more than one seller or more than one buyer, the obligations which they undertake can be enforced against them all jointly or against each individually.

1.3 Notices and documents

1.3.1 A notice required or authorised by the contract must be in writing.

1.3.2 Giving a notice or delivering a document to a party's conveyancer has the same effect as giving or delivering it to that party.

1.3.3 Where delivery of the original document is not essential, a notice or document is validly given or sent if it is sent:
- (a) by fax, or
- (b) by e-mail to an e-mail address for the intended recipient given in the contract

1.3.4 Subject to conditions 1.3.5 to 1.3.7, a notice is given and a document is delivered when it is received.

1.3.5
- (a) A notice or document sent through a document exchange is received when it is available for collection.
- (b) A notice or document which is received after 4.00pm on a working day, or on a day which is not a working day, is to be treated as having been received on the next working day.
- (c) An automated response to a notice or document sent by e-mail that the intended recipient is out of the office is to be treated as proof that the notice or document was not received.

1.3.6 Condition 1.3.7 applies unless there is proof:
- (a) that a notice or document has not been received, or
- (b) of when it was received.

1.3.7 A notice or document sent by the following means is treated as having been received as follows:

(a) by first-class post:	before 4.00pm on the second working day after posting
(b) by second-class post:	before 4.00pm on the third working day after posting
(c) through a document exchange:	before 4.00pm on the first working day after the day on which it would normally be available for collection by the addressee
(d) by fax:	one hour after despatch
(e) by e-mail:	before 4.00pm on the first working day after despatch.

1.4 VAT

1.4.1 The purchase price and the contents price are inclusive of any value added tax.

1.4.2 All other sums made payable by the contract are exclusive of any value added tax and where a supply is made which is chargeable to value added tax, the recipient of the supply is to pay the supplier (in addition to any other amounts payable under the contract) a sum equal to the value added tax chargeable on that supply.

1.5 Assignment and sub-sales

1.5.1 The buyer is not entitled to transfer the benefit of the contract.

1.5.2 The seller cannot be required to transfer the property in parts or to any person other than the buyer.

1.6 Third party rights

Unless otherwise expressly stated nothing in this contract will create rights pursuant to the Contracts (Rights of Third Parties) Act 1999 in favour of anyone other than the parties to the contract.

2. FORMATION

2.1 Date

2.1.1 If the parties intend to make a contract by exchanging duplicate copies by post or through a document exchange, the contract is made when the last copy is posted or deposited at the document exchange.

2.1.2 If the parties' conveyancers agree to treat exchange as taking place before duplicate copies are actually exchanged, the contract is made as so agreed.

2.2 Deposit

2.2.1 The buyer is to pay or send a deposit of 10 per cent of the purchase price no later than the date of the contract.

2.2.2 If a cheque tendered in payment of all or part of the deposit is dishonoured when first presented, the seller may, within seven working days of being notified that the cheque has been dishonoured, give notice to the buyer that the contract is discharged by the buyer's breach.

2.2.3 Conditions 2.2.4 to 2.2.6 do not apply on a sale by auction.

2.2.4 The deposit is to be paid:
- (a) by electronic means from an account held in the name of a conveyancer at a clearing bank to an account in the name of the seller's conveyancer or (in a case where condition 2.2.5 applies) a conveyancer nominated by him and maintained at a clearing bank or
- (b) to the seller's conveyancer or (in a case where condition 2.2.5 applies) a conveyancer nominated by him by cheque drawn on a solicitor's or licensed conveyancer's client account

2.2.5 If before completion date the seller agrees to buy another property in England and Wales for his residence, he may use all or any part of the deposit as a deposit in that transaction to be held on terms to the same effect as this condition and condition 2.2.6.

2.2.6 Any deposit or part of a deposit not being used in accordance with condition 2.2.5 is to be held by the seller's conveyancer as stakeholder on terms that on completion it is paid to the seller with accrued interest.

2.3 Auctions

2.3.1 On a sale by auction the following conditions apply to the property and, if it is sold in lots, to each lot.

2.3.2 The sale is subject to a reserve price.

2.3.3 The seller, or a person on his behalf, may bid up to the reserve price.

2.3.4 The auctioneer may refuse any bid.

2.3.5 If there is a dispute about a bid, the auctioneer may resolve the dispute or restart the auction at the last undisputed bid.

2.3.6 The deposit is to be paid to the auctioneer as agent for the seller.

3. MATTERS AFFECTING THE PROPERTY

3.1 Freedom from incumbrances

3.1.1 The seller is selling the property free from incumbrances, other than those mentioned In condition 3.1.2.

3.1.2 The incumbrances subject to which the property is sold are:
- (a) those specified in the contract
- (b) those discoverable by inspection of the property before the date of the contract.
- (c) those the seller does not and could not reasonably know about
- (d) those, other than mortgages, which the buyer knows about
- (e) entries made before the date of the contract in any public register except those maintained by the Land Registry or its Land Charges Department or by Companies House
- (f) public requirements.

3.1.3 After the contract is made, the seller is to give the buyer written details without delay of any new public requirement and of anything in writing which he learns about concerning a matter covered by condition 3.1.2.

3.1.4 The buyer is to bear the cost of complying with any outstanding public requirement and is to indemnify the seller against any liability resulting from a public requirement.

3.2 Physical state

3.2.1 The buyer accepts the property in the physical state it is in at the date of the contract unless the seller is building or converting it.

3.2.2 A leasehold property is sold subject to any subsisting breach of a condition or tenant's obligation relating to the physical state of the property which renders the lease liable to forfeiture.

3.2.3 A sub-lease is granted subject to any subsisting breach of a condition or tenant's obligation relating to the physical state of the property which renders the seller's own lease liable to forfeiture.

3.3 Leases affecting the property

3.3.1 The following provisions apply if any part of the property is sold subject to a lease.

3.3.2
- (a) The seller having provided the buyer with full details of each lease or copies of the documents embodying the lease terms, the buyer is treated as entering into the contract knowing and fully accepting those terms.
- (b) The seller is to inform the buyer without delay if the lease ends or if the seller learns of any application by the tenant in connection with the lease; the seller is then to act as the buyer reasonably directs, and the buyer is to indemnify him against all consequent loss and expense.
- (c) Except with the buyer's consent, the seller is not to agree to any proposal to change the lease terms nor to take any step to end the lease.
- (d) The seller is to inform the buyer without delay of any change to the lease terms which may be proposed or agreed.
- (e) The buyer is to indemnify the seller against all claims arising from the lease after actual completion; this includes claims which are unenforceable against a buyer for want of registration.
- (f) The seller takes no responsibility for what rent is lawfully recoverable, nor for whether or how any legislation affects the lease.
- (g) If the let land is not wholly within the property, the seller may apportion the rent.

4. TITLE AND TRANSFER

4.1 Proof of title

4.1.1 Without cost to the buyer, the seller is to provide the buyer with proof of the title to the property and of his ability to transfer it, or to procure its transfer.

4.1.2 Where the property has a registered title the proof is to include official copies of the items referred to in rules 134(1)(a) and (b) and 135(1)(a) of the Land Registration Rules 2003, so far as they are not to be discharged or overridden at or before completion.

4.1.3 Where the property has an unregistered title, the proof is to include:
- (a) an abstract of title or an epitome of title with photocopies of the documents, and
- (b) production of every document or an abstract, epitome or copy of it with an original marking by a conveyancer either against the original or an examined abstract or an examined copy.

4.2 Requisitions

4.2.1 The buyer may not raise requisitions:
- (a) on any title shown by the seller before the contract was made
- (b) in relation to the matters covered by condition 3.1.2.

4.2.2 Notwithstanding condition 4.2.1, the buyer may, within six working days of a matter coming to his attention after the contract was made, raise written requisitions on that matter. In that event, steps 3 and 4 in condition 4.3.1 apply.

4.2.3 On the expiry of the relevant time limit under condition 4.2.2 or condition 4.3.1, the buyer loses his right to raise requisitions or to make observations.

4.3 Timetable

4.3.1 Subject to condition 4.2 and to the extent that the seller did not take the steps described in condition 4.1.1 before the contract was made, the following are the steps for deducing and investigating the title to the property to be taken within the following time limits:

Step	Time Limit
1. The seller is to comply with condition 4.1.1	Immediately after making the contract
2. The buyer may raise written requisitions	Six working days after either the date of the contract or the date of delivery of the seller's evidence of title on which the requisitions are raised, whichever is the later
3. The seller is to reply in writing to any requisitions raised	Four working days after receiving the requisitions
4. The buyer may make written observations on the seller's replies	Three working days after receiving the replies

The time limit on the buyer's right to raise requisitions applies even where the seller supplies incomplete evidence of his title, but the buyer may, within six working days from delivery of any further evidence, raise further requisitions resulting from that evidence.

4.3.2 The parties are to take the following steps to prepare and agree the transfer of the property within the following time limits:

Step	Time Limit
A. The buyer is to send the seller a draft transfer	At least twelve working days before completion date
B. The seller is to approve or revise that draft and either return it or retain it for use as the actual transfer	Four working days after delivery of the draft transfer
C. If the draft is returned the buyer is to send an engrossment to the seller	At least five working days before completion date

4.3.3 Periods of time under conditions 4.3.1 and 4.3.2 may run concurrently.

4.3.4 If the period between the date of the contract and completion date is less than 15 working days, the time limits in conditions 4.2.2, 4.3.1 and 4.3.2 are to be reduced by the same proportion as that period bears to the period of 15 working days. Fractions of a working day are to be rounded down except that the time limit to perform any step is not to be less than one working day.

4.4 Defining the property

The seller need not:
- (a) prove the exact boundaries of the property
- (b) prove who owns fences, ditches, hedges or walls
- (c) separately identify parts of the property with different titles further than he may be able to do from information in his possession.

4.5 Rents and rentcharges

The fact that a rent or rentcharge, whether payable or receivable by the owner of the property, has been, or will on completion be, informally apportioned is not to be regarded as a defect in title.

4.6 Transfer

4.6.1 The buyer does not prejudice his right to raise requisitions, or to require replies to any raised, by taking any steps in relation to preparing or agreeing the transfer.

4.6.2 Subject to condition 4.6.3, the seller is to transfer the property with full title guarantee.

SCS1_2/2

Figure 2.3 *(continued)*

4.6.3 The transfer is to have effect as if the disposition is expressly made subject to all matters covered by condition 3.1.2 and, if the property is leasehold, is to contain a statement that the covenants set out in section 4 of the Law of Property (Miscellaneous Provisions) Act 1994 will not extend to any breach of the tenant's covenants in the lease relating to the physical state of the property.

4.6.4 If after completion the seller will remain bound by any obligation affecting the property which was disclosed to the buyer before the contract was made, but the law does not imply any covenant by the buyer to indemnify the seller against liability for future breaches of it:

(a) the buyer is to covenant in the transfer to indemnify the seller against liability for any future breach of the obligation and to perform it from then on, and

(b) if required by the seller, the buyer is to execute and deliver to the seller on completion a duplicate transfer prepared by the buyer.

4.6.5 The seller is to arrange at his expense that, in relation to every document of title which the buyer does not receive on completion, the buyer is to have the benefit of:

(a) a written acknowledgement of his right to its production, and

(b) a written undertaking for its safe custody (except while it is held by a mortgagee or by someone in a fiduciary capacity).

4.7 **Membership of company**

Where the seller is, or is required to be, a member of a company that has an interest in the property or has management responsibilities for the property or the surrounding areas, the seller is, without cost to the buyer, to provide such documents on completion as will enable the buyer to become a member of that company.

5. RISK, INSURANCE AND OCCUPATION PENDING COMPLETION

5.1.1 The property is at the risk of the buyer from the date of the contract

5.1.2 The seller is under no obligation to the buyer to insure the property unless:

(a) the contract provides that a policy effected by or for the seller and insuring the property or any part of it against liability for loss or damage is to continue in force, or

(b) the property or any part of it is let on terms under which the seller (whether as landlord or as tenant) is obliged to insure against loss or damage.

5.1.3 If the seller is obliged to insure the property under condition 5.1.2, the seller is to:

(a) do everything necessary to maintain the policy

(b) permit the buyer to inspect the policy or evidence of its terms

(c) if before completion the property suffers loss or damage:

(i) pay to the buyer on completion the amount of the policy monies which the seller has received, so far as not applied in repairing or reinstating the property, and

(ii) if no final payment has then been received, assign to the buyer, at the buyer's expense, all rights to claim under the policy in such form as the buyer reasonably requires and pending execution of the assignment hold any policy monies received in trust for the buyer

(d) cancel the policy on completion.

5.1.4 Where the property is leasehold and the property, or any building containing it, is insured by a reversioner or other third party, the seller is to use reasonable efforts to ensure that the insurance is maintained until completion and if, before completion, the property or building suffers loss or damage the seller is to assign to the buyer on completion, at the buyer's expense, such rights as the seller may have in the policy monies, in such form as the buyer reasonably requires.

5.1.5 If payment under a policy effected by or for the buyer is reduced, because the property is covered against loss or damage by an insurance policy effected by or on behalf of the seller, then, unless the seller is obliged to insure the property under condition 5.1.2, the purchase price is to be abated by the amount of that reduction.

5.1.6 Section 47 of the Law of Property Act 1925 does not apply.

5.2 **Occupation by buyer**

5.2.1 If the buyer is not already lawfully in the property, and the seller agrees to let him into occupation, the buyer occupies on the following terms.

5.2.2 The buyer is a licensee and not a tenant. The terms of the licence are that the buyer:

(a) cannot transfer it

(b) may permit members of his household to occupy the property

(c) is to pay or indemnify the seller against all outgoings and other expenses in respect of the property

(d) is to pay the seller a fee calculated at the contract rate on a sum equal to the purchase price (less any deposit paid) for the period of the licence

(e) is entitled to any rents and profits from any part of the property which he does not occupy

(f) is to keep the property in as good a state of repair as it was in when he went into occupation (except for fair wear and tear) and is not to alter it

(g) if the property is leasehold, is not to do anything which puts the seller in breach of his obligations in the lease, and

(h) is to quit the property when the licence ends.

5.2.3 The buyer is not in occupation for the purposes of this condition if he merely exercises rights of access given solely to do work agreed by the seller.

5.2.4 The buyer's licence ends on the earliest of: completion date, rescission of the contract or when five working days' notice given by one party to the other takes effect.

5.2.5 If the buyer is in occupation of the property after his licence has come to an end and the contract is subsequently completed he is to pay the seller compensation for his continued occupation calculated at the same rate as the fee mentioned in condition 5.2.2(d).

5.2.6 The buyer's right to raise requisitions is unaffected.

6. COMPLETION

6.1 **Date**

6.1.1 Completion date is twenty working days after the date of the contract but time is not of the essence of the contract unless a notice to complete has been served.

6.1.2 If the money due on completion is received after 2.00pm, completion is to be treated, for the purposes only of conditions 6.3 and 7.2, as taking place on the next working day as a result of the buyer's default.

6.1.3 Condition 6.1.2 does not apply and the seller is treated as in default if:

(a) the sale is with vacant possession of the property or any part of it, and

(b) the buyer is ready, able and willing to complete but does not pay the money due on completion until after 2.00pm because the seller has not vacated the property or that part by that time.

6.2 **Arrangements and place**

6.2.1 The buyer's conveyancer and the seller's conveyancer are to co-operate in agreeing arrangements for completing the contract.

6.2.2 Completion is to take place in England and Wales, either at the seller's conveyancer's office or at some other place which the seller reasonably specifies.

6.3 **Apportionments**

6.3.1 On evidence of proper payment being made, income and outgoings of the property are to be apportioned between the parties so far as the change of ownership on completion will affect entitlement to receive or liability to pay them.

6.3.2 If the whole property is sold with vacant possession or the seller exercises his option in condition 7.2.4, apportionment is to be made with effect from the date of actual completion; otherwise, it is to be made from completion date.

6.3.3 In apportioning any sum, it is to be assumed that the seller owns the property until the end of the day from which apportionment is made and that the sum accrues from day to day at the rate at which it is payable on that day.

6.3.4 For the purpose of apportioning income and outgoings, it is to be assumed that they accrue at an equal daily rate throughout the year.

6.3.5 When a sum to be apportioned is not known or easily ascertainable at completion, a provisional apportionment is to be made according to the best estimate available. As soon as the amount is known, a final apportionment is to be made and notified to the other party. Any resulting balance is to be paid no more than ten working days later, and if not then paid the balance is to bear interest at the contract rate from then until payment.

6.3.6 Compensation payable under condition 5.2.5 is not to be apportioned.

6.4 **Amount payable**

The amount payable by the buyer on completion is the purchase price and the contents price (less any deposit already paid to the seller or his agent) adjusted to take account of:

(a) apportionments made under condition 6.3

(b) any compensation to be paid or allowed under condition 7.2

(c) any sum payable under condition 5.1.3.

6.5 **Title deeds**

6.5.1 As soon as the buyer has complied with all his obligations under this contract on completion the seller must hand over the documents of title.

6.5.2 Condition 6.5.1 does not apply to any documents of title relating to land being retained by the seller after completion.

6.6 **Rent receipts**

The buyer is to assume that whoever gave any receipt for a payment of rent or service charge which the seller produces was the person or the agent of the person then entitled to that rent or service charge.

6.7 **Means of payment**

The buyer is to pay the money due on completion by a direct transfer of cleared funds from an account held in the name of a conveyancer at a clearing bank and, if appropriate, an unconditional release of a deposit held by a stakeholder.

6.8 **Notice to complete**

6.8.1 At any time after the time applicable under condition 6.1.2 on completion date, a party who is ready, able and willing to complete may give the other a notice to complete.

6.8.2 The parties are to complete the contract within ten working days of giving a notice to complete, excluding the day on which the notice is given. For this purpose, time is of the essence of the contract.

6.8.3 On receipt of a notice to complete:

(a) if the buyer paid no deposit, he is forthwith to pay a deposit of 10 per cent

(b) if the buyer paid a deposit of less than 10 per cent, he is forthwith to pay a further deposit equal to the balance of that 10 per cent.

7. REMEDIES

7.1 **Errors and omissions**

7.1.1 If any plan or statement in the contract, or in the negotiations leading to it, is or was misleading or inaccurate due to an error or omission by the seller, the remedies available to the buyer are as follows.

(a) When there is a material difference between the description or value of the property, or of any of the contents included in the contract, as represented and as it is, the buyer is entitled to damages.

(b) An error or omission only entitles the buyer to rescind the contract:

(i) where it results from fraud or recklessness, or

(ii) where he would be obliged, to his prejudice, to accept property differing substantially (in quantity, quality or tenure) from what the error or omission had led him to expect.

7.1.2 If either party rescinds the contract:

(a) unless the rescission is a result of the buyer's breach of contract the deposit is to be repaid to the buyer with accrued interest

(b) the buyer is to return any documents he received from the seller and is to cancel any registration of the contract.

7.2 **Late completion**

7.2.1 If there is default by either or both of the parties in performing their obligations under the contract and completion is delayed, the party whose total period of default is the greater is to pay compensation to the other party.

7.2.2 Compensation is calculated at the contract rate on an amount equal to the purchase price, less (where the buyer is the paying party) any deposit paid, for the period by which the paying party's default exceeds that of the receiving party, or, if shorter, the period between completion date and actual completion.

7.2.3 Any claim for loss resulting from delayed completion is to be reduced by any compensation paid under this contract.

7.2.4 Where the buyer holds the property as tenant of the seller and completion is delayed, the seller may give notice to the buyer, before the date of actual completion, that he intends to take the net income from the property until completion. If he does so, he cannot claim compensation under condition 7.2.1 as well.

7.3 **After completion**

Completion does not cancel liability to perform any outstanding obligation under this contract.

7.4 **Buyer's failure to comply with notice to complete**

7.4.1 If the buyer fails to complete in accordance with a notice to complete, the following terms apply.

7.4.2 The seller may rescind the contract, and if he does so:

(a) he may:

(i) forfeit and keep any deposit and accrued interest

(ii) resell the property and any contents included in the contract

(iii) claim damages

(b) the buyer is to return any documents he received from the seller and is to cancel any registration of the contract.

7.4.3 The seller retains his other rights and remedies.

7.5 **Seller's failure to comply with notice to complete**

7.5.1 If the seller fails to complete in accordance with a notice to complete, the following terms apply.

7.5.2 The buyer may rescind the contract, and if he does so:

(a) the deposit is to be repaid to the buyer with accrued interest

(b) the buyer is to return any documents he received from the seller and is, at the seller's expense, to cancel any registration of the contract.

7.5.3 The buyer retains his other rights and remedies.

8. LEASEHOLD PROPERTY

8.1 **Existing leases**

8.1.1 The following provisions apply to a sale of leasehold land.

8.1.2 The seller having provided the buyer with copies of the documents embodying the lease terms, the buyer is treated as entering into the contract knowing and fully accepting those terms.

8.2 **New leases**

8.2.1 The following provisions apply to a contract to grant a new lease.

8.2.2 The conditions apply so that:
'seller' means the proposed landlord
'buyer' means the proposed tenant
'purchase price' means the premium to be paid on the grant of a lease.

8.2.3 The lease is to be in the form of the draft attached to the contract.

8.2.4 If the term of the new lease will exceed seven years, the seller is to deduce a title which will enable the buyer to register the lease at the Land Registry with an absolute title.

8.2.5 The seller is to engross the lease and a counterpart of it and is to send the counterpart to the buyer at least five working days before completion date.

8.2.6 The buyer is to execute the counterpart and deliver it to the seller on completion.

8.3 **Consent**

8.3.1 (a) The following provisions apply if a consent to let, assign or sub-let is required to complete the contract

(b) In this condition 'consent' means consent in the form which satisfies the requirement to obtain it.

8.3.2 (a) The seller is to apply for the consent at his expense, and to use all reasonable efforts to obtain it

(b) The buyer is to provide all information and references reasonably required.

8.3.3 Unless he is in breach of his obligation under condition 8.3.2, either party may rescind the contract by notice to the other party if three working days before completion date (or before a later date on which the parties have agreed to complete the contract):

(a) the consent has not been given, or

(b) the consent has been given subject to a condition to which a party reasonably objects. In that case, neither party is to be treated as in breach of contract and condition 7.1.2 applies.

9. CONTENTS

9.1 The following provisions apply to any contents which are included in the contract, whether or not a separate price is to be paid for them.

9.2 The contract takes effect as a contract for sale of goods.

9.3 The buyer takes the contents in the physical state they are in at the date of the contract.

9.4 Ownership of the contents passes to the buyer on actual completion.

SCS1_2/3

Figure 2.3 *(continued)*

SPECIAL CONDITIONS

1 (a) This contract incorporates the Standard Conditions of Sale (Fifth Edition).

(b) The terms used in this contract have the same meaning when used in the Conditions.

2 Subject to the terms of this contract and to the Standard Conditions of Sale, the seller is to transfer the property with either full title guarantee or limited title guarantee, as specified on the front page.

3 (a) The sale includes those contents which are indicated on the attached list as included in the sale and the buyer is to pay the contents price for them.

(b) The sale excludes those fixtures which are at the property and are indicated on the attached list as excluded from the sale

4 The property is sold with vacant possession.

(or)

4 The property is sold subject to the following leases or tenancies:

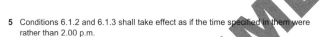

5 Conditions 6.1.2 and 6.1.3 shall take effect as if the time specified in them were   rather than 2.00 p.m.

6 **Representations**

Neither party can rely on any representation made by the other, unless made in writing by the other or his conveyancer, but this does not exclude liability for fraud or recklessness.

7 **Occupier's consent**

Each occupier identified below agrees with the seller and the buyer, in consideration of their entering into this contract, that the occupier concurs in the sale of the property on the terms of this contract, undertakes to vacate the property on or before the completion date and releases the property and any included fixtures and contents from any right or interest that the occupier may have.

Note: this condition does not apply to occupiers under leases or tenancies subject to which the property is sold.

Name(s) and signature(s) of the occupier(s) (if any):

Name

Signature

Notices may be sent to:

Seller's conveyancer's name:

    E-mail address:*

Buyer's conveyancer's name:

    E-mail address:*

*Adding an e-mail address authorises service by e-mail see condition 1.3.3(b)

Figure 2.3 *(continued)*

The reason for this 'rule' is that all *fixtures* are said to be part of the land, or 'annexed' to the land, and as such, unless otherwise stated in the special conditions of sale, will automatically transfer to the new owner. This reflects another Latin maxim *Quicquid plantatur solo, solo cedit* meaning that 'whatever is attached to the soil becomes part of it'. As suggested above, whether something is a fitting (or to use the traditional word '**chattel**') or a fixture becomes vitally important when the property is sold, as only 'fixtures' which are attached to the land (unless expressly excluded – s. 62(4)) are implied automatically to form part of the sale. It is worth taking a look at section 62(1) of the LPA 1925 in full.

As such, the key question is whether something is 'annexed' to the land and is therefore a fixture, or is simply a 'chattel' or 'fitting' that can be removed by the seller or sold to the buyer outside the cost of the property.

In certain scenarios, it may seem relatively obvious as to whether something is 'fixed' to the land. In *Chelsea Yacht and Boat Co Ltd* v. *Pope* [2000] a houseboat attached only by removable cables and pipes was said not to be 'attached' to the land. Similarly, in *Mew* v. *Tristmire Ltd* [2011] houseboats free-standing on wooden planks were once again said not to be 'attached' to the land. However, the question often arose as to whether purely 'physical' attachment alone would give rise to the item being classified as a fixture. Over the last 150 years, the courts have developed three main tests to determine whether an item is a 'chattel' (moveable *fitting*) or a fixture. These tests are known as:

1. the degree of annexation test;
2. the purpose of annexation test; and
3. the 'part and parcel' test.

The degree of annexation test

Originally, the test applied by the courts was simply to judge how firmly an object was attached to the land, and how much damage would be caused by its removal. The more securely the object was 'fixed' and the more damage likely to be caused by its removal, the more it was likely to be a 'fixture'. The seminal case setting down the guidance for this test was *Holland* v. *Hodgson* (1872), which concerned spinning looms bolted to the mill floor. Blackburn J stated that: 'There is no doubt that the general maxim of the law is, that what is annexed to the land becomes part of the land . . . When the article in question is no further attached to the land, than by its own weight it is generally to be considered a mere chattel.' Blackburn J pointed towards cases such as *Buckland* v. *Butterfield* (1820) where a veranda cemented onto a brick foundation was seen as a fixture. This test was used in *Montague* v. *Long* [1972] where a timber footbridge was fixed to the land by way of posts being driven six feet into the river bed secured in concrete. In *Deen* v. *Andrews* [1986] a free-standing greenhouse, though 'hefty' was only 'fixed' through its own weight and was therefore a chattel (fitting) not a fixture.

> ## Take note
>
> 62 General words implied in conveyances.
> (1) A conveyance of land shall be deemed to include and shall by virtue of this Act operate to convey, with the land, all buildings, erections, *fixtures*, commons, hedges, ditches, fences, ways, waters, water-courses, liberties, privileges, easements, rights, and advantages whatsoever, appertaining or reputed to appertain to the land, or any part thereof, or, at the time of conveyance, demised, occupied, or enjoyed with, or reputed or known as part or parcel of or appurtenant to the land or any part thereof.

The purpose of annexation test

In *Holland*, Blackburn expressed doubts that the 'degree of annexation' test was sufficient. He stated that on occasion it can be 'very difficult, if not impossible, to say with precision what constitutes an annexation . . . It . . . must depend on the circumstances of each case, and mainly on two circumstances . . . the degree of annexation and the object of the annexation.' Blackburn J gave the example of a dry stone wall, explaining that: 'blocks of stone placed one on the top of another without any mortar or cement . . . would become part of the land, though the same stones, if deposited in a builder's yard . . . would remain chattels.' He went on to suggest that in certain situations there is clear intention that the object should be a more permanent part of the land, the purpose of the object being to enhance that land, pointing to the case of *D'Eyncourt* v. *Gregory* (1866) where stone statues forming part of an ornamental garden, though not fixed to the ground, were held to be fixtures by way analysing the *purpose of the annexation*. This was followed in *Hamp* v. *Bygrave* [1982] in relation to stone ornaments in a landscaped garden.

In a number of cases, however, it was held that neither was there a sufficient degree of annexation nor was the purpose of the annexation to enhance the land itself. In *Hill* v. *Bullock* [1897] a display of stuffed birds, even though fixed to the wall, was held to be a 'fitting' or chattel. Similarly, tapestries fixed to the wall in *Leigh* v. *Taylor* [1902] were also classed as fittings. In *Berkley* v. *Poulett* [1977] the question arose as to paintings fixed to a wall, a marble statue sat on a plinth and a sundial resting on a pedestal. Scarman LJ, although referring to both the degree and purpose tests, preferred the annexation test, finding them all 'chattels' stating that: 'it remains significant to discover the extent of physical disturbance of the building or the land involved in the removal of the object. If an object cannot be removed without serious damage . . . the case for its having become a fixture is a strong one.' However, Scarman LJ did point out that 'today so great are the technical skills of affixing and removing objects to land or buildings' that objects which are firmly fixed can be removed carefully and without damage. It is perhaps due to the problems posed by both tests that the 'third way' was 'created' – an overall analysis of the object as 'part and parcel' of the land itself.

The 'part and parcel' test

In the case of *Elitestone Ltd* v. *Morris* [1997] the issue related to bungalows resting on their own weight. Lord Lloyd suggested that a third 'test' could be applied to ascertain whether an object was 'fixed' to the land – that being whether it had become 'part and parcel' of the land itself. The bungalows would have to be completely demolished to be removed and as such could be said to be 'part and parcel' of the land – a fixture.

As such a freehold landowner should not remove fixtures unless these are specified in the contract of sale 'special conditions' (see above). In *Taylor* v. *Hamer* [2002] the departing landowner removed flagstones from a landscaped garden which were there when the buyer inspected the property:

·· APPLICATION

Taylor v. *Hamer* [2002]

Sedley LJ:

> A house and grounds are put on the market. A prospective buyer looks them over and decides to buy. Before contracts are exchanged the vendor removes valuable fixtures without telling the purchaser. The purchaser exchanges and completes in the reasonable belief that the property he is buying is the property he was shown. Common sense and common decency both suggest that, if there is no good reason to do otherwise, the law ought to give the purchaser what he was led to think he was getting . . .

The situation is different, however, when it is a leaseholder or tenant leaving a property. In *Holland* Blackburn J referred to *Climie* v. *Wood* [1869] stating that a tenant may remove 'tenant fixtures' which are part of the '*tenant's trade'* or '*ornamental and domestic'* fixtures, but these must generally (with the exception of agricultural tenancies) be removed before the end of the tenancy. There is, of course, an obligation on the tenant to carry out any necessary repairs due to any damage caused on removal (*Mancetter Developments Ltd* v. *Garmanson Ltd* [1986])

It is worth reading the case of *Botham* v. *TSB Bank Plc* [1996] – see below. The judgment of Roch LJ in the Court of Appeal makes fascinating reading on this subject – the difference between a fixture and a fitting and the tests that are to be applied. The Court of Appeal needed to assess 109 separate items and decide whether the trial judge was correct in finding that 108 of them were fixtures! This would have allowed the possessing bank – the TSB – to sell all 108 items along with the property itself. This of course was the reason why Charles Botham appealed the finding of the trial judge. Roch LJ and his fellow judges reversed the findings of the trial judge, finding that a number of the objects were in fact fittings. This entire judgment is worth reading as it gives a detailed overview and application of how the common law tests are applied.

REFLECTION

KEY POINTS

- The definition of 'land' can be found at section 205 of the LPA 1925 and includes not just the land itself but objects 'fixed' to the land. It also includes 'incorporeal' rights such as easements or covenants.
- The extent of land ownership also includes 'up to the heavens above and down into the earth below' – meaning that a landowner owns 'airspace' into the 'lower stratum', that is up to a 'reasonable height' to enable a claim in trespass to be brought.
- The owner also owns things found in the earth below the property, with some exceptions such as oil, gas, or minerals. These generally belong to the state. This is also true of 'treasure' found in or on the land – though compensation may be payable under the Treasure Act 1996.
- Objects found *in* the ground generally belong to the landowner irrespective of who the finder might be, though things found *on* the land may be judged to be the property of the finder where the landowner has not expressed a sufficient level of control over the land (with the exception of 'treasure').
- At section 62(1) of the LPA 1925, the owner must leave all 'fixtures' with the property when selling that property – unless they are listed specifically as for removal (s. 62(4)). All 'fittings' or chattels can be removed by the landowner or sold separately to the buyer, though not as a way of defrauding on Stamp Duty.
- There are three common law tests for determining a fixture: the degree of annexation based on how firmly an object is fixed; the purpose of annexation based on the overall reason for the object being on the land; and the 'part and parcel' test which suggests that if an object has become an integral part of the landscape it may be seen as a fixture.
- Landowners may not remove fixtures (unless expressly stated in the conveyance) though tenants may remove tenant's 'trade' or 'ornamental or domestic' fixtures before the end of the tenancy and without causing or leaving damage.

CORE CASES AND STATUTES

Case	About	Importance
Bernstein v. *Skyviews* [1978] 1 QB 479	The extent of land ownership above the property.	The ownership of land extends to the 'lower stratum' to a reasonable height necessary to enjoy the property and to be able to bring a claim in trespass.
Kelsen v. *Imperial Tobacco* [1957] 2 QB 334	The overhanging sign.	The correct claim would be for trespass not nuisance as for trespass there is no need to prove damage – trespass is actionable *per se*.
Anchor Brewhouse v. *Berkeley House* [1987] 2 EGLR 173	The arm of a crane overhanging a property.	Again – the claim for trespass would succeed where nuisance might fail.

Case	About	Importance
Waverley BC v. *Fletcher* [1995] QB 334	The medieval brooch found in the land.	Where objects are found in the land – then the landowner is the owner and not the finder.
Parker v. *British Airways* [1982] 1 QB 1004	A bracelet found in the BA passenger lounge.	Where the landowner has not expressed control over the land, objects found on the land rather than in the land belong to the finder.
Holland v. *Hodgson* (1872) LR 7 CP 328	Spinning loom attached to the mill floor.	Established the 'degree of annexation' and 'purpose of annexation' tests: the more firmly an object is fixed, the more likely it is to be a fixture; the more the purpose of annexation is to enhance the land, the more likely to be a fixture.
Berkeley v. *Poulett* [1977] 242 EG 39	Fixtures and fittings.	Scarman LJ preferring the degree test, but expressing concerns over its application.
Elitestone v. *Morris* [1997] 1 WLR 687	Bungalows resting on their own weight.	The new 'part and parcel' test is established: the more an object becomes integral to the land, the more it will be seen as a fixture.
Botham v. *TSB* (1997) 73 P & CR DI	109 objects – were they fixtures or fittings?	Trial judge – 108 were fixtures; Lord Justice Roch disagreed – a detailed application of the tests to distinguish between a fixture and a fitting.

Statute	About	Importance
LPA 1925, s. 62(1)	Sets down that fixtures will be deemed to pass with the land.	Anything deemed to be a fixture must be left in the property by the landowner.
LPA 1925, s. 62(4)	The exception to s. 62(1).	Fixtures can be 'listed' for removal in the conveyance documents.
LPA 1925, s. 205(i)(ix)	The definition of land.	This includes all corporeal and incorporeal rights: land, buildings, hedges, fences and also easements covenants and mortgages.
Treasure Act 1996	Defines treasure found in or on land and how it is dealt with – by the coroner.	'Treasure' must be handed over to the coroner's court but compensation may be payable to the owner of the land.

FURTHER READING

Botham v. *TSB Bank Plc* **[1996] EWCA Civ 549**
This judgment is worth reading in full – an excellent explanation of the law on fixtures and fittings and how the courts apply the 'annexation' and 'part and parcel' tests.

Friedman, M. *Capitalism and Freedom* **(University of Chicago Press: Chicago, 1962). http://plato. stanford.edu/entries/property/**
Land ownership as seen as an economic commodity – a very insightful article which set the scene for the Thatcherite 'right to buy' programme.

Heath, A. 'Thatcher's property-owning democracy needs to be rescued' http://www.cityam.com/ article/thatcher-s-property-owning-democracy-needs-be-rescued
An article explaining the explosion in home ownership – especially under Margaret Thatcher.

The Yorker, Socialist Society Column, 'Land ownership: it's a homes issue', April 2013, http://theyorker.co.uk/politics/york/ 13747-land-ownership-it-s-a-homes
This gives an interesting political overview of land ownership – especially from a more 'left-wing' perspective.

PART 2

Rights, interests and their protection

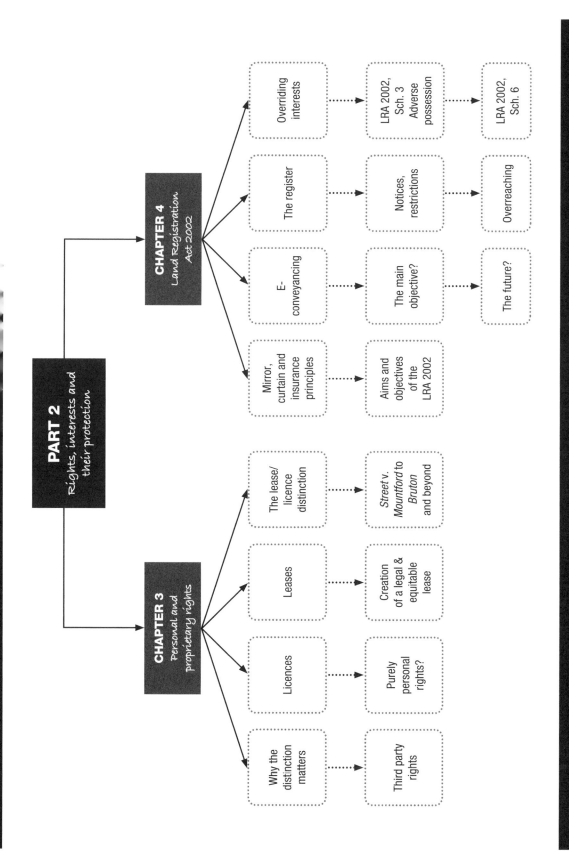

PART 2 INTRODUCTION

Part 2 of *Blueprints Land Law* begins to explain the key rights which owners may enjoy in relation to their own land, and also looks at the interests which third parties may have over your land. Part 2 will also explain how these rights and interests may be protected and as such become binding on successors in title (new owners) or lenders taking possession of a property. In Chapter 3 we will begin by looking at the vital differences between a personal right and a 'proprietary' right. We will use the main distinction of a **lease** and a **licence**, explaining that licences are generally contractual whereas leases are a 'property' right. You need to understand how a legal and an equitable lease is created and protected against third parties. We will also examine the key case of *Street* v. *Mountford*, which gives a modern definition of a lease, and look at whether the line between a lease and a licence has become blurred in recent years.

The Land Registration Act 2002 (LRA 2002) will be explained in Chapter 4. This is the thread which runs right through the study and practice of land law and is vitally important to understand as the whole subject of land law rests on the bedrock of the LRA 2002 – especially in relation to how proprietary rights may be recorded and protected to bind third parties. We will look at the principles underpinning the LRA 2002 – the mirror, curtain and insurance principles – and will also look at the 'revolution' that is electronic conveyancing (or **e-conveyancing**). We will also look in detail at the register – and you will need to understand how 'notices' and 'restrictions' can be entered to protect certain proprietary rights. It is also essential, though, to fully understand the 'crack in the mirror' known as 'overriding interests' – interests which though unrecorded and unwritten may still bind a new purchaser. Chapter 4 will finish with a detailed overview of 'squatting' – more correctly, in land law terminology, the law of **adverse possession**.

CHAPTER 3

Personal and proprietary rights

BLUEPRINT

Personal and proprietary rights

KEY QUESTIONS

LEGISLATION

- Law of Property Act 1925
- Rent Act 1977
- Land Registration Act 2002

CONTEXT

- The Rent Act 1977 gave tenants special rights – security and fair rent.
- Landlords began calling agreements 'licences'.
- The Housing Act 1996 created the Assured Shorthold Tenancy with little protection for tenants.

CONCEPTS

- Alienability
- Legal and equitable
- Overriding interests

- Does the distinction between a lease and a licence really matter after the Housing Act 1996?
- Was *Bruton* correctly decided?
- Is there such a thing as a 'non-proprietary lease'?

- Is the definition of a lease now clear?
- What is the difference between a legal and an equitable lease?
- Can licences ever bind third parties?

CASES

- *Lloyd* v. *Dugdale* [2000]
- *Street* v. *Mountford* [1985]
- *Bruton* v. *London Quadrant Housing Trust* [2000]

REFORM

- Is future case law likely to follow *Bruton*?
- Is there a need for a new Landlord and Tenant Act?

SPECIAL CHARACTERISTICS

- The definition of a lease: exclusive possession; for a term; at a rent
- The *Facchini* exceptions [where exclusive possession will remain a licence]

CRITICAL ISSUES

Setting the scene

A 'right' can in simple terms be defined as giving you permission to do something or to allow you to be somewhere in particular. The payment of fees to a University gives a student the right to enter the campus buildings, and to use the facilities. This contractual right ('a licence') can of course be taken away if fees are not paid or are outstanding. If fees are paid, then this 'right' is a purely personal right and gives a student no 'ownership' of University land. Compare this to the student paying rent to a landlord for a lease of a flat for one year with the right to keep out all others. This would be seen by land law as more than just a personal contract, rather a right in and over the property itself – a proprietary right. It is vital to understand the key differences between rights that are purely personal and a right in or over the land. The distinction becomes fundamental when third parties get involved. The general rule is that proprietary rights are capable of binding third parties whereas personal rights are not. If I allow you to stay in my house over the summer rent-free, this would generally be seen as a licence, and as such if I sell my house during the summer my purchaser may not have to let you stay. However, if I grant you a lease, then the new owner may be bound by your proprietary right to stay until the end of that lease.

WHY THE DISTINCTION MATTERS – THIRD PARTIES

CORNERSTONE

Alienability

Whether a right is purely personal or is proprietary is vital in relation to one of the fundamental principles underpinning land law – **alienability**. The concept of alienability means that the owner of a property should be able to sell without any hidden rights getting in the way of that sale. The best way for you to start to understand this topic is to look at *why* the difference matters.

APPLICATION

Peter owns a freehold property and has granted a five-year lease to Simon of a one bedroom flat at the top of the building. Andy comes along and wishes to buy the property from Peter. If Simon has a *proprietary right*, rather than just a personal agreement with Peter, the new purchaser Andy may not be able to easily remove Simon from the building. He may be bound by the existing lease. As such, it is vital to establish whether a proprietary right exists or whether that right is a purely personal right – a licence.

It is also important to understand that having a proprietary right does not necessarily mean that the right is a 'legal' right. It may of course be an 'equitable' right. This distinction is vital in relation to the effect those rights may have on third parties.

INTERSECTION

As discussed in Chapter 1, proprietary rights in the land can be legal or equitable, and the rights capable of being legal are listed at section 1 of the Law of Property Act 1925. These include leasehold estates, or 'terms of years absolute'. Chapter 1 also explained how leases can be equitable, but whether legal or equitable, leases are rights in the land itself – *proprietary rights*. As illustrated in Chapter 1, legal rights will 'bind the world' whereas equitable rights bind everyone except 'equity's darling' – the *bona fide* purchaser for value without notice.

It is important to realise that a lease is also *still* a contract, and as such there is an overlap here with contract law. A simple contract is *usually* a purely personal right, and due to the rule of privity (see *Tweddle* v. *Atkinson* (1861)), can only be enforced by the parties directly involved in the agreement (unless the Contract (Rights of Third Parties) Act 1999 applies). However, in land law, a lease is more than just a contract as it is also proprietary in nature.

> **Take note**
> Make sure that you fully understand why the 'personal/proprietary' distinction matters, as this is absolutely fundamental to you successfully mastering land law – the thread running through the entire subject is the ability to recognise various proprietary rights compared to purely personal ones.

LICENCES

In relation to land law, the distinction between a lease and a licence is vital as generally speaking only those with leases, i.e. tenants, will be able to enjoy the protection of that right against third parties such as new purchasers or lenders taking possession. They can also rely on various statutory protections such as those under the Rent Act 1977, the Housing Act 1988 and the Landlord and Tenant Act 1954. The Rent Act and Housing Act deal with residential leases; the LTA 1954 deals with business leases.

However, if the right is only a 'mere licence' or mere permission to be on the land, this prevents them from being sued in trespass but does not create any interest in the land that might protect them. In *Thomas* v. *Sorrell* (1673) Vaughan LJ stated that a licence 'properly passeth no interest' other than to stop the licensee being called a trespasser.

Traditionally, licences are 'merely personal obligations, and not an interest in the land' and as such will not be binding on a third party such as a new purchaser (*King* v. *David Allen* [1916]).

In *Errington* v. *Errington* [1952] and later in *Binion* v. *Evans* [1972] Lord Denning suggested that it may be 'utterly inequitable' to remove the licensee in situations where the licence is 'coupled with an equity' and as such equity should step in to give a proprietary remedy that may bind the new purchaser. Really though, it was always the 'equitable right' that was binding on the third party

> **Take note**
> As with other areas of law, try to learn the line of case law in chronological order as it gives structure and clarity when you need to explain the development of the law on licences. Once you have understood that a licence is generally only a personal right, the next step is to understand how leases are created.

– never the licence. However, Denning suggested that the licence itself could in these 'equitable' circumstances, be binding.

However, in *Ashburn Anstalt* v. *Arnold* [1989], and later confirmed in *Lloyd* v. *Dugdale* [2000], the Court of Appeal referred to Denning's 'heresy' and re-stated the traditional viewpoint that a licence is non-proprietary and will not generally bind third parties.

LEASES – CREATION OF A LEGAL AND EQUITABLE LEASE

A lease can be created either expressly or impliedly.

Express creation

A lease can be created by **deed**, by a *written agreement* or even verbally (as explained below).

Implied creation

Even where there is no deed; written or verbal agreement, if a person enters land belonging to another and begins to pay rent on a periodic basis (weekly, monthly, quarterly) and this is accepted, where there is also a clear and mutual intention of the parties to create a tenancy relationship, then an implied tenancy arises (*Javad* v. *Aqil* [1991]).

As with general contract law, the usual contractual presumptions apply. For example, in a commercial situation there is a rebuttable presumption that the arrangement is intended to be legally binding whereas in a family/friendship arrangement the presumption is the opposite. Evidence will be needed to rebut the presumptions in both cases – remember cases such as *Jones* v. *Padavatton* [1969] where no contract was found to exist between mother and daughter.

A legal lease

Whether express or implied, a lease will only be a legal estate in land if created in accordance with section 52(1) or 54(2) of the LPA 1925 (see Figure 3.1).

INTERSECTION

If the lease is a legal lease of *over seven years*, it must be registered (Land Registration Act 2002). If a legal lease is *less* than seven years, it may be binding as an *overriding interest* under LRA 2002, Sch. 3, para. 1 – this is explained further in Chapter 4.

Section 52(1) – all conveyances of land must be by *deed*.
Section 54(2) – a legal lease can be created by writing which isn't a deed, or even *verbally* if:

- the lease is 'in possession' – i.e. takes effect immediately and not in the future
- it does not exceed three years

- it must be at the 'best rent' – i.e. market value
- no 'fine' or premium is payable in return for a reduction in the rent – i.e. no money paid up front to reduce the rent paid.

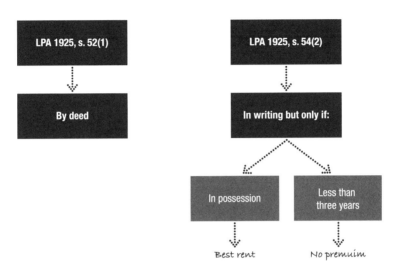

Figure 3.1 Legal lease

What is a deed?

A document will be a **deed** if it satisfies section 1 of the Law of Property (Miscellaneous Provisions) Act 1989 (in force 31 July 1990).

LP(MP)A 1989, section 1(1)–(5) defines how a deed is created:

- No longer necessary for a deed to be written on a particular substance or 'sealed' (s. 1(1)).
- It will only be a deed if the document makes clear on its face that it is intended to be a deed by the parties to it and it is validly executed as a deed by those parties (s. 1(2)).
- It is validly executed if and only if it is signed by the party in the presence of a witness or witnesses and delivered as a deed by him or an authorised person (s. 1(3)).
- It is presumed to be 'delivered' by an 'authorised person' if that person is a solicitor, licensed conveyancer, a certified notary, an agent or employee of the solicitor, conveyancer or notary in the course of the transaction to create an interest in land (s. 1(5)).

> **Take note**
> It may be a good idea for you to create a table to show the different requirements for a legal lease as this will impact on how that lease is protected against a third party.

The Council for Licensed Conveyancers ('the CLC') was established under the provisions of the Administration of Justice Act 1985 as the regulatory body for the profession of licensed conveyancers. These licensed conveyancers are specialist property lawyers who work on behalf of clients specifically dealing with the buying or selling of property. They deal with all matters involved in a property transaction.

Equitable lease

If there is an agreement for a lease of over three years, which is created in writing and not created by deed, or there is an agreement to create a lease in the future, this falls outside section 54(2) of the LPA 1925 and as such gives the tenant an equitable interest in the land.

However, the equitable lease *must* contain the following as a minimum:

(a) an accurate description of the property

(b) the parties to the lease

(c) the price or consideration (usually the rent)

(d) the commencement date of the lease

(e) the duration (term) of the lease.

If the agreement was entered into after 27 September 1989, then section 2 of the LP(MP)A 1989 applies, which allows for an agreement to create a lease to be enforced as long as a legally binding contract is in force *and* the contract:

- must be in writing;
- must incorporate all the expressly agreed terms (s. 2(1)); or
- may incorporate terms in another document (s. 2(2)); and
- must be signed by or on behalf of the parties (s. 2(3)).

APPLICATION

Peter signs an agreement for a five-year lease that states he will take possession of a property owned by Simon in six months' time. This is therefore an equitable lease of over three years and the above provisions apply. He must also register the lease as an 'estate contract' notice on Simon's 'register'. This type of equitable lease is also called a 'reversionary lease'.

INTERSECTION

The 'register' is the 'Official Copy of the Register' that contains all the relevant information needed by a new buyer. This is discussed in Chapter 4.

Differences between a legal lease and an 'equitable' agreement for a lease

(a) Certain rights do not pass to an equitable tenant: LPA 1925, s. 62 (As it is not a conveyance under s. 62, buildings, land, fixtures, rights and easements may not pass to the equitable tenant.)

(b) An agreement for a lease, in order to be protected against third party interests *will need to be registered*:

   (i) in unregistered land as a Class C(iv) land charge (*estate contract*) in the Land Charges Register;

   (ii) in registered land as a notice in the register. Even though a legal lease of under seven years will act as an overriding interest under the Land Registration Act 2002 (protection without the need to register), an agreement for a lease will not (see Figure 3.2).

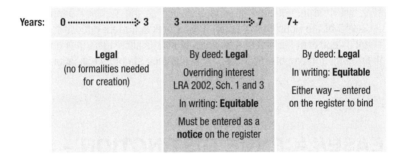

Years:	0 ·············> 3	3 ·············> 7	7+
	Legal (no formalities needed for creation)	By deed: **Legal** Overriding interest LRA 2002, Sch. 1 and 3 In writing: **Equitable** Must be entered as a **notice** on the register	By deed: **Legal** In writing: **Equitable** Either way – entered on the register to bind

Figure 3.2 Lease protection timeline

INTERSECTION ....

Even if the lease in itself is not an overriding interest due to it being equitable rather than legal, if the tenant is in *actual occupation* they will still be protected as having an **overriding interest** under Schedule 3, paragraph 2 of the Act (Chapter 4).

As stated above, in order for a lease for more than three years to be legal it must be created by deed (LPA 1925, s. 52). However:

- if the tenant takes possession and pays rent, an *implied periodic tenancy* may be created; or

- an equitable lease may be created following the rule in *Walsh* v. *Lonsdale* (1882). If there is a contract to create a lease that follows the requirements of LP(MP)A 1989, s. 2 then the courts may, at their discretion, order the equitable remedy of specific performance to enforce 'that which ought to be done'.

INTERSECTION

'That which ought to be done' is one of the equitable maxims referred to in Chapter 1. This means that if a landlord or tenant is trying to ask the court for an equitable remedy, this will only succeed where the party 'comes with clean hands' (*Coatsworth* v. *Johnson* (1886)).

It should be noted that an equitable lease prevails over an implied periodic legal tenancy (*Walsh* v. *Lonsdale*) and as such will need to be protected as indicated earlier.

It has been argued by commentators such as Dixon and Pascoe (see below) that as protected tenancies have largely been consigned to history with the introduction of the Assured Shorthold Tenancy (Housing Act 1996), the lease/licence distinction is now not as significant. However, with the introduction of schemes such as the Tenancy Deposit Scheme (under ss. 212–215 of the Housing Act 2004), which makes it more difficult for a landlord to keep a tenant's deposit at the end of a tenancy, landlords once again may be tempted to try calling their rental agreements 'licences' to escape their statutory obligations.

REFLECTION

THE LEASE/LICENCE DISTINCTION – *STREET V. MOUNTFORD* THROUGH TO THE *'BRUTON* TENANCY'

Landlords have often attempted to 'create' or 'label' an agreement a **licence**, where in the eyes of the law the agreement is really a **lease** and as such would enjoy the various protections as illustrated above.

However, the Rent Act 1977 gave two extensive benefits to tenants under a *lease*. These were *fair rent* and also *security of* **tenure**. Respectively, these meant that the tenant had the right to have their rent assessed by a rent officer and also they had the right not to be evicted by the landlord without following common law and/or statutory procedure. So, in order to get around their obligations under this statute, landlords began to call their agreements 'licences'.

The courts have often acted vigilantly to detect such 'sham devices' and stated that the label given to the agreement will not be conclusive (*Addiscombe Garden Estates* v. *Crabbe* [1957]). However, in *Somma* v. *Hazlehurst* [1978] it was held that the parties' intentions are paramount – if both parties have signed a 'licence agreement' then it will be seen as a licence and the courts will not intervene.

This viewpoint stood firm until the key case of *Street* v. *Mountford* [1985]:

CORNERSTONE

The Ratio in *Street* v. *Mountford*

On 7 March 1983, Mrs Mountford entered into an agreement described as a *licence* by which Mr Street granted her the right to occupy two furnished rooms in a house at No. 5 & 6, St Clements Gardens, Boscombe for £37 a week. The agreement contained ten 'rules' which were to be observed by Mrs Mountford. No one apart from her was to sleep in the rooms. The landlord, Mr Street, was entitled to enter the rooms '*from time to time*' to inspect their condition, to empty meters, and to carry out repairs. Mr Street provided neither attendance nor services and only reserved these *limited rights* of inspection. Mrs Mountford proceeded to register a fair rent under the Rent Act 1977 and Mr Street applied to the county court for a declaration that the occupancy was a licence. The court at first instance declared she was a tenant; however, the Court of Appeal held she was a licensee (following **Somma**). This was reversed in the House of Lords.

In the House of Lords, the case came before Lord Templeman, who famously stated that 'a five pronged implement for manual digging is a fork', even if the manufacturer decides to call it a spade.

Lord Templeman stated categorically that landlords should not be able to circumvent their duties under statute simply by the label given to the agreement. He stated that the *context* not the title of the agreement is paramount.

Essentials of a lease

Lord Templeman in *Street* v. *Mountford* [1985] stated that there will be a lease if there is:

(a) exclusive possession

(b) for a term

(c) at a rent.

(See Figure 3.3).

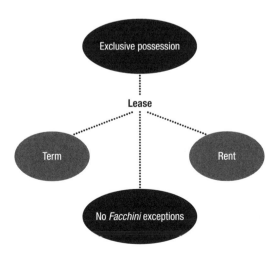

Figure 3.3 Essentials of a lease

(a) Exclusive possession

Lord Templeman referred to exclusive possession as the tenant being able to 'keep out strangers and keep out the landlord' apart from limited access to view and repair. Street had of course limited his own access.

Cases such as *Appah* v. *Parncliffe* [1964] and *Allan* v. *Liverpool Overseers* [1874] were also referred to by Lord Templeman to differentiate mere lodgers, stating that an occupier is a lodger if 'the landlord provides attendance or services' where the landlord has 'unrestricted access to and use of the premises'. As such, a lodger will be *a licensee* and not a tenant under a lease.

If the occupant has exclusive possession, he or she may have a lease unless certain exceptions apply. These are generally known as the *Facchini* exceptions, taken from *Facchini* v. *Bryson* [1952] presided over by Lord Denning:

- family arrangements: *Cobb* v. *Lane* [1952] where a sister allowed her brother to live rent-free;
- acts of kindness and generosity *Booker* v. *Palmer* [1942] where evacuees were allowed to stay rent-free throughout the war;
- employment relationships: *Norris* v. *Checksfield* [1991] – employer and employee.

The above situations, therefore, may give rise to a licence even though there may be exclusive possession. The fact that these arrangements are presumed to be licences can, however, be rebutted through evidence and, as such, a family arrangement could *still* be a lease.

Multiple-occupancy

Landlords have also tried to circumvent the statutory protections afforded to leaseholders by stating that the property is occupied by two or more people, with the landlord reserving the right to replace one occupier for another, introduce further occupiers or use the whole or part of the property for himself. This would arguably lead to 'non-exclusive possession' and create licences rather than leases.

INTERSECTION

However, if there are two or more tenants and the '*four unities*' are present there will be a **joint tenancy** (see Chapter 6) in existence.

Take note

It is possible for a number of tenants to have 'exclusive possession' of the whole property (a joint tenancy) or simply have exclusive possession of their own room. Always look for these possibilities in any problem question you face.

In *Antoniades* v. *Villiers* [1990], a couple who occupied an attic flat comprised of a bedroom, a bed-sitting room, a kitchen and a bathroom, where they both signed identical agreements at the same time, held a lease not a licence even though the landlord called it a licence, due to the fact that he reserved the right to share with the couple or allow others to do so. The House of Lords referred to this clause as a sham – the flat was far too small for sharing between strangers and as such the landlord was attempting to avoid the statutory protections.

In *A.G. Securities* v. *Vaughan* [1990], the arrangement concerning a four-bedroom flat where the multiple occupiers all signed different agreements at different times with a clause allowing the landlord company to nominate replacement occupiers was a licence as the four unities were absent and there was no suggestion of a sham.

(b) Term

The definition of a lease can be found at section 205(1)(xxvii) of the LPA 1925 as a '**term of years absolute**', but this also means that a lease can be for *any fixed term* or be a *periodic tenancy* providing the term is certain and definite or can be made certain. In *Lace* v. *Chantler* [1944] an agreement that a property should be let 'furnished for the duration' of the Second World War was void as the term was uncertain (in 1944). In *Prudential Assurance* v. *London Residual Body* [1992] a 'lease' for a strip of land 'until the land was required for road widening' was also void for uncertainty.

It is also important to understand that a lease can be a periodic tenancy – for example, a weekly, monthly or yearly tenancy. This is capable of being made certain in that either party can **create certainty** by giving notice to quit. It is the ability to give the notice by either party that creates the certainty needed.

Also, if there is a 'tenancy for life' at common law, certainty can be provided by reference to section 194(6) of the LPA 1925, which the law treats as a 90-year lease terminable on the death of the tenant. This has recently been confirmed in *Berrisford* v. *Mexfield Housing Corporation* [2011].

(c) Rent

In the LPA 1925, section 205(1)(xxvii), there is an express reference to a *term of years* with or without rent, and this point is referred to in *Ashburn Anstalt* v. *Arnold* [1989] where Fox LJ questions Lord Templeman's definition in *Street* v. *Mountford* in relation to the need for rent. It would seem from the statutory definition that rent is *not* a necessary ingredient of a lease, but the definition from the House of Lords stands as good law, mainly due to the fact that rent is a usual component of a lease as it is the necessary consideration for the contract. Lord Templeman also argued in response to Fox LJ that he (Lord Templeman) was sitting in the Lords whereas Fox LJ was only sitting in the Court of Appeal!

> **Take note**
>
> Although it is vital to be able to cite the ratio of *Street* v. *Mountford* along with the *Facchini* exceptions, it is also crucial to be able to complete the topic by looking at the confusion caused by the case of *Bruton*.

The '*Bruton* tenancy'

In relation to *Street* v. *Mountford*, it seemed that the definition of a lease set down by Lord Templeman would stand only in relation to private residential leases as the case related to the Rent Act which only relates to such tenancies.

However, the distinction between lease and licence post-*Street* seems to have been blurred by way of a number of cases where the *Street* definition has been applied in an extremely broad manner.

In *Family Housing Association* v. *Jones* [1990] a homeless person was given a flat for a weekly charge and the agreement was described as a 'licence'. The agreement specifically stated that there was no exclusive possession. However, the Court of Appeal decided that on the facts the defendant *did* have exclusive possession and Jones did have a lease, even though the entire arrangement was based on a licence agreement between the Housing Association and the local authority.

The landmark case of *Bruton* v. *London and Quadrant Housing Trust* [2000] followed the decision in *Jones* but caused great controversy and legal and academic debate that still rages a decade or more later.

CORNERSTONE

The *Ratio* in *Bruton*

London and Quadrant Housing Trust held various properties on licence from Lambeth Council. These properties were to provide accommodation for the homeless. Each individual occupier (of which Mr Bruton was one) entered into their own licence agreement with LQHT.

Later the Trust were accused by Bruton of not carrying out their landlord obligations of repair under section 11 of the Landlord and Tenant Act 1985, and Bruton claimed that he had a lease following the definition in *Street* in an attempt to get the Trust to carry out these repairs.

The main stumbling block for Bruton was the fact that the Trust did not have a lease itself. As such, legally, they simply could not grant a lease to Bruton. In strict legal terms, it is generally impossible for a person with simply a personal right to grant another a proprietary right over the land (other than **estoppel**, which was not accepted here as an argument – see Chapter 7). The Court of Appeal held that therefore this was a licence. They stated that a lease cannot be 'carved out' of a licence – only out of an existing proprietary right.

However, the House of Lords reversed this decision. Lord Hoffmann stated that Bruton had exclusive possession, for a term at a rent, and, therefore, had a lease following *Street*.

According to Lord Hoffmann, the fact that the Trust could not actually *grant* a lease was not fatal to Bruton's claim to be a tenant. Lord Hoffmann stated that Bruton had a '*non-proprietary lease*' for the purposes of forcing the Trust to carry out their repairs, without giving Bruton a right in the land itself! Academics and judges (see Pawlowski, Pascoe and Hinjosa below) have of course since argued that this was a policy decision, as a 'non-proprietary lease' is really a licence! As such it seems that Lord Hoffmann, at least temporarily, created a contractual tenancy that may be binding, rather than a 'non-proprietary lease'.

REFLECTION

However, cases such as *Kay* v. *Lambeth* [2004] and *London Borough of Islington* v. *Green and O'Shea* [2005] have both since suggested that such a 'contractual licence' may not be binding on the freeholder where the freeholder has only granted a licence. What is clear, is that the definition of a lease from *Street* v. *Mountford* stands as good law, and has been applied much more widely than Lord Templeman may have intended.

KEY POINTS

- The distinction between personal and proprietary rights is important due to the traditionally non-binding effect of a personal right on a third party.
- Historically, the view was that a licence – mere permission to be on the land – prevented you from being a trespasser but did not give you any ownership rights.
- The law seemed to change in the 1950s and 1970s due to Lord Denning, who found that certain licences *could* bind a new owner.
- Judicial viewpoint later changed – licences and leases are distinct; the traditional viewpoint returned – licences are purely contractual.
- The '*Bruton* tenancy' seems to have confused matters once again – the distinction between lease and licence is not quite so clear in the early part of the 21st century.

CORE CASES AND STATUTES

Case	About	Importance
Thomas v. *Sorrell* (1673) Vaugh 330	Non-proprietary rights.	This is the first case which established that a licence is only a personal right. This was, and still is, the orthodox view.
King v. *David Allen* [1916] 2 AC 54	Licence to put up advertisements.	This case in the early 20th century reinforced the traditional view. It confirmed that licences are purely personal and non-proprietary rights.
Errington v. *Errington* [1952] 1 KB 290 and *Binions* v. *Evans* [1972] Ch 359	Contractual licence coupled with an equitable right.	These two cases, both presided over by Lord Denning, added much confusion, stating that a licence could be proprietary in nature – where it was equitable to allow such a licence to bind third parties.
Ashburn Anstalt v. *Arnold* [1989] 1 Ch 1 and *Lloyd* v. *Dugdale* [2002] 2 P & CR 13	The binding nature of a licence agreement on third parties.	These two cases post-*Street* have once again confirmed that licences can *never* bind third parties and are purely personal rights.
Javad v. *Aqil* [1991] 1 WLR 1007	A tenancy where there was no set time period but rent paid periodically.	This case illustrates that certainty can be created by the payment of rent in a 'periodic tenancy'.
Walsh v. *Lonsdale* (1882) LR 21	An argument between landlord and tenant as to whether there was an 'equitable lease' or a periodic tenancy.	This very important case illustrates that an 'equitable lease' will always prevail over a periodic tenancy.

→

Case	About	Importance
Somma v. *Hazlehurst* [1978] 2 All ER 1011	An agreement was labelled a 'licence' by the parties.	This case, though overruled by *Street*, is important as it shows the position *before Street*: if the parties had signed the agreement, the 'label' was conclusive.
Street v. *Mountford* [1985] AC 809	The seminal case regarding the labelling of an agreement a 'licence'.	This case is the **key** case in this topic as this was Lord Templeman's ruling that if the three components are present, the agreement is a lease. This is vital as, even today, this judgment is used to establish a lease in a commercial or residential context.
Facchini v. *Bryson* [1952] 1 TLR 1386	The case presided over by Lord Denning where exceptions to the rule of exclusive possession were given.	Again, this case is important as it gives the exceptions that, if present, mean that even with exclusive possession there may only be a licence.
Antoniades v. *Villiers* [1990] and *AG Securities* v. *Vaughan* [1988] 1 AC 417	Both cases refer to the 'four unities' and where there is shared occupancy.	These two cases are used widely to illustrate a 'sham' agreement. If there is no 'sham' and the landlord can legitimately reserve the right to move other tenants in to the property then there is no joint tenancy.
Lace v. *Chantler* [1944] KB 368	An attempt at creating a tenancy 'for the duration of the war'.	Again, this case illustrates one of the three components: a lease must be for a 'certain' term.
Ashburn Anstalt v. *Arnold* [1989] 1 Ch 1	This time, Fox LJ disputed the need for 'rent' as a component of a lease.	The case illustrates that rent is a necessary component, as a lease is still a contract and rent acts as consideration.
Bruton v. *London and Quadrant Housing Trust* [2000] 1 AC 406	Mr Bruton claimed a lease in order to force the Housing Trust to repair the property – *but* the Trust only had a licence not a superior lease.	This very important and highly controversial case was where Lord Hoffmann 'blurred the lines' and stated that Bruton had a 'non-proprietary lease' that was binding on the Trust – due to the three components in *Street* being present – this case is vital today as it demonstrates how widely *Street* has been applied.

Statute	About	Importance
Law of Property Act 1925, s. 1	Proprietary rights.	Rights capable of being legal are listed here.
Contract (Rights of Third Parties) Act 1999	In contract law – the rights that third parties may have on the contract.	The exception to the doctrine of privity.
Rent Act 1977	Rights of a tenant.	Especially relevant to *Street* v. *Mountford* [1985] – the right to claim fair rent.
Land Registration Act 2002	Deals with the registration of land and interests in and over land.	Relevant to the protection of a lease either in its own right or as a notice or an overriding interest – this is the **key** statute in relation to the whole of land law in the 21st century.

FURTHER READING

Bright, S. 'Leases, Exclusive Possession and Estates' (2000) 116 LQR 7
Examines the nature of a lease and provides a clear explanation of 'exclusive possession'.

Hinjosa, J.-P. 'On Property, Leases, Licences, Horses and Carts' (2005) 69 Conv 114
This article gives a detailed critique of the *Bruton* case and suggests that Lord Hoffmann artificially created a 'non-proprietary lease' for policy reasons.

Pascoe, S. '*Street* v. *Mountford* gone too far – in *Bruton* v. *London*

***Quadrant Housing Trust*' [1999] *Journal of Housing Law* 87**
Pascoe gives an excellent overview of the confusion caused by the *Bruton* case and suggests that *Street* was never envisaged to have such a broad application.

Pawlowski, M. 'The *Bruton* Tenancy – Clarity or More Confusion?' (2005) 69 Conv 262
Again, a leading article on the confusion caused by Lord Hoffmann. Pawlowski is one of the more vocal critics of the decision in *Bruton* and gives a solid explanation of the lack of clarity post-*Bruton*.

CHAPTER 4

The Land Registration Act 2002

BLUEPRINT

The Land Registration Act 2002

LEGISLATION

- Law of Property Act 1925
- Land Registration Act 1925/2002

CONTEXT

- The introduction of the LRA 2002.
- The aim of e-conveyancing.
- The 100% reflection of reality by the register as a 'mirror'.
- The ability to take land through adverse possession.

CONCEPTS

- Registered and unregistered conveyancing
- The official copy of the register
- Notices
- Restrictions
- Overreaching
- Interests which override
- Alteration/rectification/indemnification
- Adverse possession

- Should there be any hidden interests – should it be that only registered interests bind third parties?
- Is adverse possession a breach of human rights – should a landowner's title ever be taken?
- Is the LRA 2002 revolutionary or evolutionary?

- What is the fundamental difference between registered and unregistered conveyancing?
- How did the LRA 2002 re-enforce the 'mirror principle'?
- What are 'interests which override' and why does this 'crack' in the mirror remain?

CASES

- *William & Glyn's Bank* v. *Boland* [1981]
- *City of London Building Society* v. *Flegg* [1988]
- *Abbey National* v. *Cann* [1991]
- *Chhokar* v. *Chhokar* [1984]
- *Buckinghamshire County Council* v. *Moran* [1990]
- *Pye* v. *Graham* [2001]

REFORM

- Did the LRA 2002 go far enough – why do we still have a 'crack' in the mirror?
- Will e-conveyancing ever really happen?

SPECIAL CHARACTERISTICS

- The entry of notices in the charges section of the Register
- Unregistered interests which are still capable of binding as 'overriding'
- The register can be altered or rectified and an indemnity paid
- Adverse possession – title can be 'taken' if an adverse possessor follows the procedure at Schedule 6 LRA 2002

CRITICAL ISSUES

Setting the scene

Secure land tenure and property rights are essential for the stable economy of countries and effective land registration is the basis for long-term global economic growth. HM Land Registry's 150 year history has contributed to one of the most vibrant and confident property markets in the world. (Malcolm Dawson, Chief Land Registrar, UN Economic Commission for Europe Conference 2012 (see T. Lilleystone, below).)

This bold statement made by the Chief Land Registrar illustrates the great emphasis placed on *Registration of title* rather than simple 'ownership' and 'possession' of land. The statement also begins to illustrate exactly why the Land Registration Act 1925 and its 'revolutionary' replacement, the Land Registration Act 2002, came into force.

As suggested by Ian Clarke, a barrister at Selborne Chambers, the driving force behind the concept of registration was to 'make the register as inclusive as possible' whilst trying to 'overcome . . . the implications of feudal tenure' (see below). The Law Commission in their Consultative Document prior to the drafting of the Land Registration Act 2002 suggested that land registration had a somewhat 'tortuous history' but it was 'highly desirable' that it should be allowed to 'develop according to principles that reflect both the nature and the potential of Land Registration' (see below). These principles – namely the *mirror*, *curtain* and *insurance* principles – were not creatures of the Land Registration Act 2002. In fact, they already existed as the foundation underpinning the Land Registration Act 1925. The Land Registration Act 2002, however, sought to improve on the LRA 1925 which has been described by the Law Commission as 'badly drafted and lacking in clarity'. Martin Dixon (see below) explains that its replacement, the LRA 2002, was 'received with much critical acclaim' and is a 'work of monumental importance and monumental effort'. However, Dixon points out that the LRA 2002 is clearly 'transaction driven' with reform being 'bent deliberately and methodically towards the goal of e-conveyancing'.

The aim of this chapter is therefore to explain the background to the Land Registration Act 2002, and to explain and illustrate how this Act is the 'thread of continuity' which runs through the centre of the study and practice of land law. Without an understanding of the workings of the LRA 2002, it is impossible to understand how proprietary rights can be protected in registered land, especially against third parties. After all, according to Dixon (citing Land Registry figures), the LRA 2002 is said to regulate 'over £2000 billion worth of property'. As Clarke points out, whether the Act is in fact 'revolutionary or evolutionary' is perhaps an 'unnecessary question' to ask, as the changes introduced by the LRA 2002 are indeed 'profound and far-reaching'.

AIMS AND OBJECTIVES: MIRROR, CURTAIN AND INSURANCE PRINCIPLES

As explained in Chapter 1, prior to 1925, land was generally 'unregistered' and as such the method of 'traditional' conveyancing was used. This potentially involved searching through a large number of documents, searching back through title deeds (at least 15 years) and also checking documents such as marriage certificates and probate after death, to ensure that the seller was legally entitled to transfer the property. This could, and indeed did, cause problems where a 'gap' in ownership appeared.

APPLICATION

Emilia Jones and Finn Matthews buy a property together in 1897. Both names are recorded on the title deeds (the land is *unregistered*). In 1910, Max wishes to buy the property. The contract for sale names Emilia Matthews and Finn Matthews as the legal owners. Max would not be able to rely on the names on the contract as being the true legal owners as the current title deeds show the same forenames but different surnames. Max would need to see a copy of the marriage certificate (assuming a marriage has taken place between Emilia and Finn between 1897 and 1910). In an alternative scenario, if the contract for sale only states the name of Emilia Jones as the seller, Max would need to find out what had happened to Finn – maybe the two have separated, or maybe Finn has died. If the latter is true, Max would need proof of death and need to take a look at the probate documents which would show what has happened to Finn's share. Hence, if a property has changed hands a number of times over a 15-year period, it would always be a tricky process for the buyer to establish 'good root of title' without any ownership issues. The 'beauty' of registered land is that, in terms of ownership and third party rights, there is just the one document to check – the Official Copy of the Register – guaranteed as accurate by the State.

The system of 'registered land' was first introduced in Australia in 1858, generally credited to the work of Sir Robert Torrens, who saw a way in which conveyancing could be made more straightforward, and where once registered at the Land Registry, title would be guaranteed as accurate by the State. This method of 'title by registration' was then adopted by many Commonwealth countries, including, of course, England and Wales. The Torrens system could also be said to have introduced the three key principles underpinning registered land – the mirror, the curtain and the insurance principles.

(i) The mirror principle

As suggested earlier, the mirror principle suggests that the register (the Official Copy of the Register) should accurately reflect reality. As such, when a potential buyer examines the register of a particular property, the identity of the owner and all other rights enjoyed by third parties should appear on the register. This does not of course mean that the potential purchaser should rely entirely on the register. It is still advisable (and under Schedules 1 and 3 to the LRA 2002 still necessary) to physically inspect the land. The reason for this is that there are still a number of 'hidden rights' which under the LRA 1925 were known as 'overriding interests' and which under the LRA 2002 remain as 'interests which override' the register. These 'hidden' rights have been referred to as the 'crack in the mirror' and will be explained in full below. Under the LRA 2002, however, these 'interests which override' have been reduced, mainly to reinforce the mirror principle and also to pave the way for the onset of **e-conveyancing** (see below).

(ii) The curtain principle

It should be recalled that the common law only recognises legal rights rather than equitable and, as such, the common law position is that the new purchaser need only concern himself with the legal ownership of the property. The legal owners can, of course, also be trustees, holding the property on trust for certain beneficiaries. It is the beneficiaries, then, who are said to be 'hidden' behind the 'curtain' – it is not necessary or indeed, in the interests of 'alienability', desirable that a new purchaser should concern themselves with the rights of equitable beneficiaries. The LRA 2002 does not allow beneficiaries to place a 'notice' on the register that will be binding on a buyer, and prevent a sale. The statutory mechanism of 'overreaching' (see below) allows a purchaser to deal only with the legal owners, and on payment of purchase money to at least two trustees, the proprietary rights of any beneficiaries in occupation 'behind the curtain' will be 'swept away' and replaced with a money payment by the legal owners. This will happen whether the new buyer is aware of the 'hidden' beneficiaries or not. The beneficiaries may place a 'restriction' on the register (see below) or attempt to invoke the Trusts of Land and Appointment of Trustees Act 1996 (TOLATA 1996) (see Chapters 5 and 6) but this generally cannot prevent the sale (see Figure 4.1).

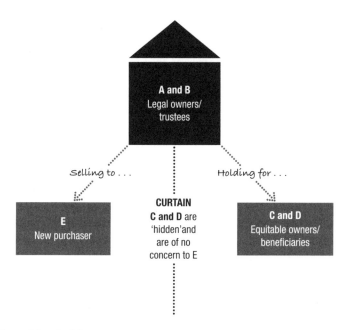

Figure 4.1 The curtain principle

(iii) The insurance principle

As suggested above, 'insurance' is one of the key factors which differentiate registered conveyancing from 'traditional' unregistered conveyancing. The register is 'guaranteed' by the State as accurate, and is capable of being *rectified* or *altered* if an error has been made, especially by the Land Registry. It also allows for '*indemnity*' or compensation to be paid where losses are suffered due to such an error. This is governed by Schedule 4 (for alteration) and Schedule 8 (for indemnity).

Alteration (Schedule 4)

Schedule 4, paragraphs 2 and 5 state that the court (para. 2) or the Registrar (para. 5) have jurisdiction to alter the register to:

(a) correct a mistake;

(b) bring the register up to date; and

(c) to give effect to any estate, right or interest excepted from the effect of registration (this only applies where a registered proprietor was registered with a title which is less than absolute).

Paragraph 5 also adds a further right given to the Registrar which is:

(d) to remove superfluous entries.

As such the register can be altered to correct mistakes (para. 5(a)), to remove a person incorrectly named and registered as the proprietor (para. 5(a) or (b)), where there has been fraud, or, more technically, where an implied easement (by **prescription**) has been established (see Chapter 8) and where an overriding interest has overridden a registered disposition (see below) (para. 5(c)). However, it should be noted that the register cannot be altered against a proprietor *in possession* 'unless he has by fraud or by lack of proper care caused or substantially contributed to the mistake or if for any other reason it would be unjust for the alteration not to be made' (Sch. 4, para. 3(2)(a) and (b)).

Rectification

It is important to understand that **rectification** is a *type* of alteration – but specifically an alteration which involves the correction of a mistake *and* prejudicially affects the title of the registered proprietor (para. 1(a) and (b)). As such all 'rectifications' are 'alterations' but not all 'alterations' are classified as 'rectifications'. It is a little like saying that all Mars Bars are chocolate but not all chocolate is a Mars Bar!

Indemnity (Schedule 8)

As explained above, one of the key distinguishing factors between registered and unregistered conveyancing is that the Register (in registered land) is *guaranteed as accurate by the State*. As such, an indemnity is paid, by the State (from the public purse), to someone who suffers a loss because a rectification needs to be made, or who suffers a loss because a rectification is refused (Sch. 8). An indemnity may also be paid where an 'official search' has been completed by the Land Registry in error, or where there is an error on an Official Copy of the Register (para. (1)(c) and (d)). Of course, no indemnity is paid where the claimant has acted fraudulently or negligently (para. 5).

> **Take note**
>
> Where an alteration takes place to record an overriding interest, this is not a rectification because the registered proprietor has not suffered a loss because of the alteration – the owner was always bound by the overriding interest. Any losses are due to the purchase of a property with an existing interest.

In relation to the amount that can be claimed (the quantum), at Schedule 8, paragraph 6 it states that where a rectification is ordered, the amount payable must not exceed the value of the lost interest at the time 'immediately before rectification of the register' and if rectification is refused, then the indemnity paid will not exceed the value of the lost interest *at the time the mistake was made*. This may, of course, be significantly less where property prices have increased since the mistake was made.

(iv) E-conveyancing

The Law Commission in its report prior to the introduction of the LRA 2002, states quite clearly that the introduction of electronic conveyancing is 'likely to be the most revolutionary reform' to conveyancing in England and Wales 'that has yet taken place'. The Commission goes on to clarify that there have been many reforms, including:

- the introduction of compulsory registration in England and Wales since 1990;
- the register itself being an 'open public document' that can be searched without the permission (or knowledge) of the owner; and
- computerisation of the register and on-line searches.

However, they refer to e-conveyancing as 'the most significant change'. Martin Dixon argues that the introduction of e-conveyancing aims to bring the land registration system 'into the modern age' but also points out that, even without the end objective of e-conveyancing being realised, many of the changes under the LRA 2002 'stand alone' and will 'change the face' of registered conveyancing 'before the first byte of e-conveyancing'.

At sections 91–93 of the LRA 2002, the provisions for e-conveyancing are set down, and allow for a future statutory instrument to specify further details but it is clear at section 93(2) that a transfer of land (once e-conveyancing has been fully introduced) will only be effective 'if it is made by means of a document in electronic form'. This suggests that when e-conveyancing is 'rolled out' nationally, then failure to use the e-conveyancing method will mean that there is an overall failure to dispose of the land.

If e-conveyancing does finally become a reality, then one key effect will be the 'closing' of what is referred to as the 'registration gap'. In order to understand what that means, it is necessary to explain the conveyancing transaction (see Figure 4.2). The first stage is that the buyer and seller **exchange contracts**. At this point, a deposit is paid and a legally binding contract is in force, but there is no change in ownership as such. Secondly, the parties move to **completion** where the outstanding purchase funds are transferred and keys are handed over. At that point the buyer, where relevant, must pay Stamp Duty Land Tax, and, once paid, the buyer is then and only then able to **register** their name as legal owner. In theory there can be a delay of up to two months between completion and registration, where technically speaking the seller is still the legal owner, holding the property on trust for the buyer who, until registration, has equitable title only. This means that again, in theory, before registration has occurred the seller still retains the rights of a legal owner. One of the key driving forces behind e-conveyancing is the closing of this 'registration gap' as completion, payment of stamp duty and registration of title will all happen simultaneously at the touch of a button.

Take note

It should be noted, however, that in July 2011, Malcom Dawson, the Chief Land Registrar announced a 'halt' to the development of the e-conveyancing trial due to factors such as cost and risk of lost data. He stated: 'Over a six year period we have invested £41 million to successfully deliver a suite of e-services including portal, e-security and business gateway. However, following the feedback it is clearly better to halt development of e-transfers now, before significant further sums are expended, than to continue to develop a product we are not confident our customers will use.'

However, this 'halt' seems to have been temporary and, following further consultation, the programme is said still to be 'on track' with a 'staged release' over time, once again following Australia's lead!

Current: (Before e-conveyancing)

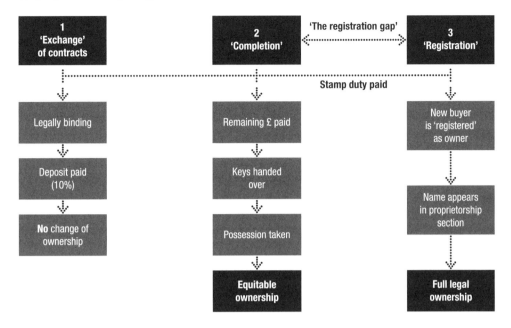

Aim of e-conveyancing: Stages 2 and 3 will happen at the same time – the 'registration gap' is closed

Figure 4.2 The conveyancing transaction

THE 'REGISTER' AND ITS THREE SECTIONS

As explained above, when a purchaser of land which is already registered makes initial enquiries about purchasing that land, they will be able to see one single document called the Official Copy of the Register. It is this 'state guaranteed' document which sets out the ownership of the property and all other 'registrable interests' such as easements, mortgages and covenants. This register is a 'tripartite' register and is split into the Property, Proprietorship, and Charges sections.
   See Figure 1.2 (Chapter 1).

Property section

This section gives a description of the property and its address and gives a reference to the 'title plan' which is an Ordnance Survey plan showing the land and its boundaries. It will also state that the land is either freehold or leasehold. It can also highlight legal easements (see Chapter 8).

Proprietorship section

This section names the legal owners. It will also state whether the title is 'absolute', 'good leasehold', 'possessory' or 'qualified'. *Absolute title* is given when there are seemingly no other claims on the land other than those interests that are 'entered' on the register or possible interests that override the register (see below). *Good leasehold* guarantees that the land is held on a valid lease, and assumes that the landlord has absolute 'freehold' title. If it is clear that the landlord does have registered absolute title then the tenant will be given *absolute leasehold* title. *Possessory title* can be given by the Registry if the deeds are missing (in previously unregistered land) or, more usually, when a 'squatter' has successfully claimed 'adverse possession' (see below). *Qualified title* is rarely given, but may be given by the Registrar conditionally, where there is a doubt over the ownership claim.

The proprietorship section may also contain 'restrictions' (LRA 2002, s. 40) entered by trustees and/or beneficiaries which highlight the existence of a trust (see below).

Charges section

This section will contain 'notices' (LRA 2002, ss. 32–35) of what are technically known as '**minor interests**' such as mortgages or covenants.

Notices and restrictions

Notices

As stated above, 'notices' are entered in the 'charges section' of the register and are governed by sections 32–35 of the LRA 2002.

There are two types of notice – an agreed notice (s. 34) and a unilateral notice (s. 35). The former is where the application to enter the interest has been made by the registered proprietor, or where the proprietor has given consent to the 'applicant' (such as a neighbour). A unilateral notice is when the applicant asks the Registrar to enter an interest against the title of the registered proprietor consulting the owner. Under section 35 of the LRA 2002, the Registrar will then contact the proprietor to see whether the owner wishes to apply for cancellation of the notice. The applicant then has 15 days to respond to the application to cancel, and if there is no response, the notice will be cancelled (under s. 36).

Restrictions

There are a number of 'restrictions' that may be placed in the 'proprietorship section' of the register as an attempt to limit the proprietor in his dealing with the land. For example, the Serious Organised Crime Agency (SOCA) can place such a restriction on the property register of a convicted drug dealer – pending an investigation under the Proceeds of Crime Act 2008 where it is suspected that the property has been purchased with 'drug money' or there is possible money laundering about to take place. There can also be a restriction placed on the register by a 'trustee in bankruptcy' (see Chapter 6) to prevent a bankrupt from trying to sell their property. The holder of an 'option to purchase' estate

---

Take note

The entry of a notice on the register does not mean that interest is valid in itself. It would still be necessary, especially where there is litigation, to establish first that the interest exists – for example, if there was a dispute over an 'easement' (see Chapter 8) it would need to be established that the interest is capable of being an easement. The entry on the register of the easement secures its priority as an interest once it has been established that the interest is valid in itself. If, for example, the easement turns out to be only a licence, then the fact that it is 'protected' as an easement by a notice on the register means nothing.

It is vital to understand that the register is about the priority and protection of rights and not the substantive creation of those rights. In land law, it is essential to establish that the proprietary right has been validly **created**, and then to see if that right has been **protected**.

contract can also place a restriction on the register to prevent the owner breaching the 'option' contract (see *Midland Bank* v. *Green* in Chapter 1).

However, the most usual form of restriction can be placed on the register by a beneficiary under a trust of land. As stated above, this will simply follow the wording of the 'overreaching' mechanism found at sections 2 and 27 of the LPA 1925. This will state that there can be 'no disposition of land without payment to at least two trustees'. However, it should be noted that this only really sends out a 'warning' to a prospective buyer that overreaching is *necessary* – it will not necessarily stop the sale from taking place.

OVERREACHING

As stated above, the common law only recognises the rights of the legal owners. In order to be able to dispose of their property as freely as possible, the common law recognises that any hindrances or obstacles should be kept to a bare minimum. The situation could therefore be complicated by a trust being in operation where legal owners are holding the property on trust for beneficiaries. The 'curtain principle' (as explained above) suggests that the new purchaser should not be 'concerned with trusts' and as such the LPA 1925 at sections 2 and 27 sets down a statutory mechanism known as **overreaching** (see Figure 4.3). If the purchaser of a legal estate pays the purchase price to at least two trustees (remember – there can be a maximum of four) or to a 'trust corporation' then the proprietary rights of the beneficiaries are 'swept away' and replaced by a 'monetary interest' – meaning that the legal owners should pay money to the beneficiaries in line with their equitable 'share'. In the case of *HSBC* v. *Dyche* [2010] it was stated that the trustees do have a duty to 'act in good faith' but generally, if the purchase price (or a mortgage advance by a lender) is paid to at least two of the trustees, overreaching will occur on purchase or repossession. There are two key cases which highlight the need for two trustees. The first of these is *Williams & Glyn's Bank* v. *Boland* [1981] where Mr Boland was the sole legal owner, with Mrs Boland a beneficiary under a trust due to her contributions to the purchase price (see Chapters 5 and 6). When Mr Boland signed for a second mortgage and subsequently defaulted, the bank began possession proceedings. Mrs Boland successfully argued that her proprietary interest had not been overreached as Mr Boland was the sole trustee. As such, Mrs Boland successfully argued that her right to remain in the property was intact.

Conversely, the case of *City of London Building Society* v. *Flegg* [1988] demonstrates that even with an 'overriding interest', beneficial rights can be overreached provided that the purchase money (or mortgage advance) is paid to at least two of the trustees:

APPLICATION

A young couple, the Maxwell-Browns, bought a property aptly called 'Bleak House' with a mortgage of £16,000 and with a contribution to the purchase price by the wife's parents, the Fleggs, of £18,000 with the understanding that the Fleggs would live in the house with the Maxwell-Browns, but as equitable owners – only the Maxwell-Browns were named as legal owners. After a while, the couple defaulted on their mortgage and the lender commenced possession proceedings. Although the Fleggs could successfully argue a constructive trust due to purchase price contributions (see Chapters 5 and 6), their proprietary rights had been overreached by the lender who had secured the two trustees' signatures necessary for overreaching to be successfully invoked.

It is a little less clear as to what happens when the beneficiaries' rights are not overreached (as with Mrs Boland). If the rights of the beneficiary are still intact and especially if the beneficiary is in actual occupation, then an overriding interest of 'actual occupation' will rank in priority before the possessing bank or new owner (as with **Boland** and also **Tizard** (see Chapter 1)). It may also be possible for a beneficiary who is in occupation and has not been overreached to invoke TOLATA 1996, section 14 (see Chapter 6 for details) to ask for a further sale of the property or perhaps to partition the property (as in *Chun* v. *Ho* [2003] (see Chapter 6)).

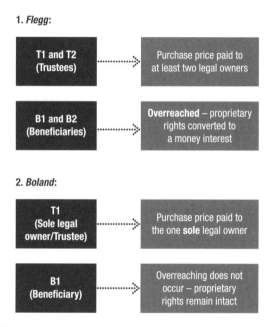

Figure 4.3 Overreaching

THE 'CRACK IN THE MIRROR' – 'INTERESTS WHICH OVERRIDE THE REGISTER'

Even though the key objective of the LRA 2002 was to pave the way for e-conveyancing, as Dixon suggests, many of the provisions *stand alone* irrespective of the aim of achieving 100 per cent electronic conveyancing. Many of these provisions are aimed at '100 per cent registration' to enable conveyancing to be more straightforward and more transparent. The LRA 2002 at section 4 sets down a 'list' of 'triggers' for **first registration** – in other words, events which *must* give rise to first registration. The key provisions are highlighted in bold:

APPLICATION

LRA 2002, section 4

4 When title must be registered

(1) The requirement of registration applies on the occurrence of any of the following events –

(a) **the transfer of a qualifying estate –**

   (i) **for valuable or other consideration, by way of gift or in pursuance of an order of any court, or**

   (ii) **by means of an assent (including a vesting assent);**

(b) the transfer of an unregistered legal estate in land in circumstances where section 171A of the Housing Act 1985 (c. 68) applies (disposal by landlord which leads to a person no longer being a secure tenant);

(c) the grant out of a qualifying estate of an estate in land –

   (i) **for a term of years absolute of more than seven years from the date of the grant,** and

   (ii) for valuable or other consideration, by way of gift or in pursuance of an order of any court;

(d) **the grant out of a qualifying estate of an estate in land for a term of years absolute to take effect in possession after the end of the period of three months beginning with the date of the grant;**

(e) the grant of a lease in pursuance of Part 5 of the Housing Act 1985 (the right to buy) out of an unregistered legal estate in land;

(f) the grant of a lease out of an unregistered legal estate in land in such circumstances as are mentioned in paragraph (b);

(g) **the creation of a protected first legal mortgage of a qualifying estate.**

As can be seen above, any transfer of property, whether purchased or by way of a gift or inherited after death (assent) will trigger registration of the property as registered land. The same is also true for a lease of over seven years or a lease of any length but which does not take effect for more than three months from the date of the grant of that lease (a so-called reversionary lease). All of these events trigger first registration and the Official Copy of the Register would then 'mirror' these interests clearly.

It should also be noted that sections 6 and 7 of the LRA 2002 place the obligation to register firmly in the hands of the new owner, and failure to register within two months (see above) will have the effect of creating a trust where the original owner will hold the property on trust for the purchaser (see the issue of the 'registration gap' above).

As explained above, the majority of land is *already* registered, and as such, the LRA 2002 needs mainly to be applied to '*subsequent dispositions*' of registered title – in other words, the sale or lease of land already registered. At section 27, there is a list of 'dispositions' that must be registered, and these follow the 'events' at section 4. The list includes:

> ### Take note
> Under the LRA 1925, any lease of over 21 years needed to registered. The LRA 2002 has reduced that to a lease of over seven – this means that far more leases will be registered than were so under the LRA 1925 – this once again illustrates the attempt to 'mirror' reality more accurately through the register. Section 118 of the LRA 2002 makes provision that in the future this may be reduced further to a lease of over three years rather than seven – but this is not yet in force.

- any transfer of land (s. 27(2)(a));
- the grant of a lease of more than seven years (s. 27(2)(b)(i));
- a reversionary lease (s. 27(2)(b)(ii));
- an express legal easement (s. 27(2)(d)); and
- a legal mortgage (s. 27(2)(f)).

At section 29 of the LRA 2002 – known as the priority rule – the new 'purchaser for value' is said to take the property freely, other than being potentially bound by:

- *pre-existing rights which appear on the register; and*
- *interests which override registered dispositions.*

Notices such as mortgages, covenants, easements and leases are therefore likely to appear on the register – and as such the mirror reflects brightly. However, there are a number of interests which are 'unregistrable' – and yet seen as so important, perhaps socially and economically, that they remain potentially binding even though they cannot and do not appear on the register. These are the '*cracks in the mirror*' – now known as 'interests which override' the register.

Interests which override

The concept of 'overriding interests', once again, is not an 'invention' of the LRA 2002. Overriding interests played a major role in the LRA 1925, at section 70(1)(g), and much of the case law used to 'flesh out' the new provisions in the LRA 2002 was based around the old section 70(1)(g) provisions. However, it is vital to note that section 70(1)(g) along with the rest of the LRA 1925 has been replaced entirely by the provisions of the LRA 2002. The relevant provisions relating to the 'rules' on 'interests which override' can be found in Schedule 1 and Schedule 3 to the LRA 2002. It should be noted also that Schedule 1 deals with interests which override in relation to **first registration** of unregistered land, and, as stated at the outset of this book, unregistered land will not be analysed in any detail. As such, in any modern study of land law, only the workings of Schedule 3 are relevant and vital.

CORNERSTONE

LRA 2002, Schedule 3

SCHEDULE 3 UNREGISTERED INTERESTS WHICH OVERRIDE REGISTERED DISPOSITION

Leasehold estates in land

1. A leasehold estate in land granted for a term not exceeding seven years from the date of the grant, except for –
   (a) a lease the grant of which falls within section 4(1)(d), (e) or (f);
   (b) a lease the grant of which constitutes a registrable disposition.

Interests of persons in actual occupation

2. An interest belonging at the time of the disposition to a person in actual occupation, so far as relating to land of which he is in actual occupation, except for –
   (a) an interest under a settlement under the Settled Land Act 1925 (c. 18);

(b) an interest of a person of whom inquiry was made before the disposition and who failed to disclose the right when he could reasonably have been expected to do so;

(c) an interest –
  (i) which belongs to a person whose occupation would not have been obvious on a reasonably careful inspection of the land at the time of the disposition, and
  (ii) of which the person to whom the disposition is made does not have actual knowledge at that time;

(d) a leasehold estate in land granted to take effect in possession after the end of the period of three months beginning with the date of the grant and which has not taken effect in possession at the time of the disposition.

Easements and profits a prendre

3. (1) A legal easement or profit a prendre, except for an easement, or a profit a prendre which is not registered under the Commons Registration Act 1965 (c. 64), which at the time of the disposition –
  (a) is not within the actual knowledge of the person to whom the disposition is made, and
  (b) would not have been obvious on a reasonably careful inspection of the land over which the easement or profit is exercisable.

(2) The exception in sub-paragraph (1) does not apply if the person entitled to the easement or profit proves that it has been exercised in the period of one year ending with the day of the disposition.

Source: from Schedule 3 LRA 2002, http://www.landregistry.gov.uk/professional/law-and-practice/act-and-rules, Land Registry, Crown copyright

It is generally accepted, therefore, that there are three main interests which, if established, will override any pre-existing rights appearing on the register, and in terms of priority, these 'overriding interests' will rank in priority to bind a new owner or lender taking possession. Simply put, these are:

(i) **a legal lease of less than seven years (see Chapter 3)**

(ii) **the proprietary rights of a person in actual occupation**

(iii) **an implied legal easement.**

(i) A legal lease of less than seven years

First, it should be noted that the word 'granted' in Schedule 3, paragraph 1 refers to a 'legal' lease rather than equitable. It will be a 'legal' lease if it is between three and seven years and created by deed (see Chapter 3) though a lease of less than three years is 'legal' regardless of the formalities of its creation. Secondly, it should also be noted that the exceptions referred to at paragraph 1 are 'reversionary leases' (see above) and leases of a 'discontinuous' nature – such as a time share. These kinds of leases, along with all equitable leases and leases over seven years *must* be registered to bind a third party.

APPLICATION

Richard buys a registered property 'The Tower' from Edward. At the top of The Tower is a self-contained two-bedroom flat occupied by Elizabeth and Anne. They are there by way of a five-year lease granted by Edward before selling The Tower to Richard. The lease does not appear on the register of The Tower. Due to the fact that this is a legal lease of less than seven years, Elizabeth and Anne benefit from an 'unregistered interest which overrides' under Sch. 3, para. 1 and as such Richard will be bound by the remaining term of their lease.

(ii) The proprietary rights of a person in actual occupation

It is important to note, as stated above, that this section replaces the old section 70(1)(g) of the LRA 1925, though the case law and general principles still apply. It is also very important to understand that this section protects *any* proprietary right the person in actual occupation already enjoys – it does not necessarily protect the right *of* actual occupation. The first place to start is paragraph 2 of Schedule 3 itself. This states that a person in actual occupation will lose their rights if, when asked, they fail to disclose their rights; or it is not obvious on a reasonably careful inspection of the land that the person is in occupation when the new owner has no *actual* knowledge of them being there. However, it is case law which 'puts flesh on the bones' of the statutory provisions. The main case law 'rules' are as follows:

The person must have a proprietary interest to begin with: *National Provincial* v. *Ainsworth* [1965]. Hence a person must be able to establish their rights – such as a right as a beneficiary or with an equitable lease. A licence will not satisfy this test, and as such a person under a licence will not be able to claim an overriding interest of actual occupation.

The person must be in actual occupation at the time of the transfer (completion) as well as at the time of registration – being in actual occupation at the time of registration is too late. In *Abbey National* v. *Cann* [1991] Mr Cann purchased a property, completion of which took place on 13 August. Mrs Cann (Mr Cann's mother) was to live in the property under a constructive trust (hence she had a proprietary right). However, even though her furniture and her removal men were present at the property some 35 minutes before the transfer was completed on 13 August, Mrs Cann was not present. Lord Oliver in the House of Lords stated that for there to be actual occupation it must be at the time of the transfer with 'some degree of permanence and continuity which would rule out mere fleeting presence'. Being present at the time of registration is too late.

Take note

As above, with the coming into practice of e-conveyancing, this registration gap will be closed. If e-conveyancing had been in place for Mrs Cann, the outcome may well have been different!

In the case of *Chhokar* v. *Chhokar* [1984] Mr Chhokar was the sole legal owner of a property with Mrs Chhokar being there as a beneficiary under a trust. Mr Chhokar wanted to sell the property (they were about to start divorce proceedings) and so he waited until his wife went into hospital to give birth to their baby, at which point he showed his friend Mr Parmar around the property, having hidden *most* of his wife's belongings in cupboards, and sold it to him while Mrs Chhokar was 'away'. Mrs Chhokar returned home to find Mr Parmar and the locks changed! Mr Chhokar argued that she was not in actual occupation at the time of the transfer. The court disagreed. They stated that to be in 'actual occupation' does not need actual presence at the time of transfer, just 'evidence of your physical presence' coupled with an 'intention to return'. This was echoed in the case of *Thompson* v. *Foy* [2010] and *Link Lending* v. *Bustard* [2010].

It should also be noted that a person can be in actual occupation through their *agents*, such as Mrs Rosset's builders in *Lloyds Bank* v. *Rosset* [1991] though the presence of the children of the owner will not in itself give rise to a successful claim of actual occupation by the owner (*Hypo-Mortgage Services* v. *Robinson* [1997]).

APPLICATION

Richard buys a registered property 'The Tower' from Edward. This time, at the top of The Tower is a self-contained two-bedroom flat occupied by Elizabeth and Anne. This time, though, they are there by way of a nine-year lease granted by Edward before selling The Tower to Richard. The lease does not appear on the register of The Tower. As this is a lease of more than seven years it needs to be registered to bind as an equitable lease (it can't be 'legal' as it is not registered). However, it is still a proprietary right, and as such Elizabeth and Anne can claim actual occupation using the lease as a trigger to claim under Sch. 3, para. 2 and as such Richard will still be bound by the remaining term of their lease.

(iii) An implied legal easement

As explained earlier, an express legal easement must be entered on the register to be binding. This is not the case with an 'implied' easement. Once an easement has been established (see Chapter 8 – *Re Ellenborough Park*) it can be said to be 'implied' if it is created through necessity; common intention; the operation of the rule in *Wheeldon* v. *Burroughs*; by way of section 62 of the LPA 1925 or by pre-scription (see Chapter 8 for substantive detail). If the right amounts to an implied easement, then unless the easement is attached to an equitable lease, for example, that implied easement will be deemed to be 'legal' – mainly due to the fact that it could be written in a deed – and as such may be protected under Schedule 3, paragraph 3. This paragraph sets down that such an easement will be binding if the new owner has knowledge of the easement at the time of the disposition; or that the easement was obvious on a reasonably careful inspection of the land; or that the person claiming the easement can show that they have been using the easement at any time in the last year. This last provision clearly demonstrates the 'power' of such overriding interests – it would not be too difficult for a claimant to show that they had used the easement at some point in the last 12 months.

APPLICATION

Richard buys a registered property 'The Tower' from Edward. This time, Henry, who was Edward's neighbour, claims that Edward gave him the right to tie his horse to a post on what is now Richard's land. There is nothing in writing, however, but it can be established that Henry has absolutely nowhere else to tie his horse, and as such has an easement by necessity. He can easily establish that he has tied his horse to this post for the last six months, and as such can claim an overriding interest of the implied easement under Sch. 3, para. 3 and as such Richard will be bound by the easement and must allow Edward to continue using the post to tie his horse.

Other remaining overriding interests – the transition period

Also at Schedule 3, at paragraphs 10–14, can be found a list of other overriding interests which were originally governed by section 70(1)(a) of the LRA 1925. These include such interests as 'manorial rights'; 'sea walls' and 'chancel repairs'. These interests were given a 10-year transitional period, and, as such, ceased to be overriding interests in October 2013. They can still be protected but will need to be entered on the register as a notice. Perhaps the most salutary of lessons can be learned from the story of the Wallbanks:

APPLICATION

Andrew Wallbank was a church warden serving in his local parish. The farm owned by the Wallbanks was land that had been worked by the family for decades, serving as the source of their farming livelihood and, it was hoped, the couple's pension. Gail Wallbank's father bought the land to farm in Aston Cantlow in 1970. A clause in the deeds noted an ancient lay rector liability: The Act of Valor Ecclesiasticus of 1535, as amended by the Chancel Repairs Act of 1932. This was queried by the previous owner in 1968 and the then vicar and Parochial Church Council (PCC) were told by Coventry Diocese's legal advisers that the liability had no weight in law. But in 1990 the PCC of Aston Cantlow wrote demanding money for repair to the chancel (this is the part of a church at the altar end). The couple offered to donate a field, worth more than £21,000, which had the potential for development or community use and would make the church eligible to receive grants. This offer was rejected.

So the Wallbanks had no option but to fight the demands, incurring vast legal costs. The High Court found the couple liable for the chancel repair costs, but the Appeal Court overturned this, ruling that the law was unjust and contravened the couple's human rights, declaring that the Wallbanks should be released of the obligation.

The PCC appealed to the House of Lords, and the couple were forced to remortgage their house to pay legal fees. The House of Lords, though not condoning this law and the implementation of it, ruled that PCCs are not public bodies and are therefore *exempt* from adhering to the Human Rights Act 1998 (HRA 1998). To decide the final repair bill amount, the case went back to the High Court, where Mr Wallbank was forced to represent himself as they had run out of money to pay the legal fees.

The judgment found them liable for a bill for repairs totalling £186,986, plus VAT and costs, which will bring the total up to approximately £250,000 – in addition to the £200,000 they've spent over the years fighting the case (see chancelrepair.org below).

As stated above, these arguably archaic interests are no longer 'overriding' – but once again go some way to illustrate the potential 'bindingness' and effect on the owner of a property subject to these rights.

ADVERSE POSSESSION: THE CHANGE IN PROCEDURE IN THE LAND REGISTRATION ACT 2002

One final area of land law which the LRA 2002 has attempted to restrict to further strengthen the reflective nature of the 'mirror' is that of **adverse possession**. The media tends to refer to 'squatters' (see below) and reports are often printed detailing the work of various 'squatter rights' pressure groups. However, it is vital from a land law perspective to understand that 'adverse possession' is far more than simple 'squatting'. It would be true to say that 'squatters' may eventually make a claim under the law on 'adverse possession' – but there is far more to being an 'adverse possessor' than there is a squatter. As the title suggests, an 'adverse possessor' must 'take' the land as their own by essentially displacing the rights of the 'paper' owner. There is also a strict timeframe in place as to when the 'adverse possessor' may claim the title of property – and though the LRA 2002 has not changed the substantive requirements of establishing that you are an adverse possessor, it has changed the procedure by which a claim is made. The LRA 2002, with its change of procedure detailed under Schedule 6, has made it far more difficult for an adverse possessor on registered land to succeed in being awarded the title of the land by the Registrar. Also, since 1 September 2012, a new law – section 144 of the Legal Aid, Sentencing and Punishment of Offenders Act 2012 – has made it a criminal offence to be a 'squatter' on residential property. It is as yet unclear as to how this sits with the law on claiming title as an adverse possessor under Schedule 6 to the LRA 2002. It would seem that it may now be even more unlikely for a 'squatter' to get to the necessary '10-year point' which would then allow a claim under the LRA 2002. As section 144 is also retrospective, it is also unclear as to whether, even if the adverse possessor does reach 10 years, they will be arrested at the point of making a legitimate claim under the LRA 2002 – only time will tell.

The traditional definition of 'adverse possession', then, is 'the acquisition of land simply by possessing it without assent or dissent of the owner' (Lord Denning in *Wallis's Cayton Bay Holiday Camp Ltd* v. *Shell-Mex and BP Ltd* (1974)). The controversy, of course, has always been, and remains to be, that just because a property is left empty and abandoned for a number of years, the 'paper owner' should not be penalised by losing his title. For example, a property owner may own a property but then win the 'Euromillions' jackpot and decide to take off to the Cayman Islands for the next 15 years! Why, then, if their property is simply locked up and left unoccupied, should a 'squatter' arrive and, after the requisite time period, be allowed to take the land? According to the LRA 2002, they are perfectly entitled to do so.

There are many social and economic reasons why the law on adverse possession exists. First, it is arguably more desirable for a property not to stand empty and abandoned for many years – it could start to fall apart and damage may be done to other property or to people passing by. Secondly, if whole neighbourhoods decided to move to the Cayman Islands, then not a single property in that locality would be 'saleable' and as such the housing market would start to stagnate. Social reasoning also suggests that it is better for the homeless to be housed in abandoned properties than to be left on the street.

CONTEXT

The other 'side of the coin', though, is that an owner has the right to do as he pleases with his property – and that includes abandonment. It seems harsh and contrary to the tenets of 'ownership' but the law suggests otherwise – it has been said that 'those who go to sleep on their claims should not be assisted to recover their property' (*RB Policies at Lloyds* v. *Butler* [1950]).

As such Parliament acted, and the Limitation Act 1980 (LA 1980), section 15(1) states that no action to recover land can be brought after 12 years from the date the right of action accrued. This means that traditionally, prior to the enactment of the LRA 2002, if a 'squatter' had taken possession of land for a full 12 years, then the 'squatter' can at that point claim title, and the Registrar was bound to award title. The original owner would be dispossessed of the title to their land. It should be noted that this is *still the law in relation to unregistered land* – only the procedural rules for registered land were changed by LRA 2002. However, it is worth looking at the 'old law' briefly to set the context for the changes fashioned by the LRA 2002.

The law prior to the Land Registration Act 2002

(Please note that this is still the law for unregistered land.)

The LA 1980 did *not* give title to the 'squatter' *per se*: as explained above, it merely extinguished the rights of the paper owner. Prior to the LRA 2002, the adverse possessor became entitled to the land after 12 years – the paper owner was then time barred to make a claim (*Fairweather* v. *St Marylebone Property* [1963]). In registered land *prior to the LRA 2002*, the paper owner after 12 years was said to hold the property on trust for the adverse possessor who could then apply for possessory title which may then be upgraded by the Registrar to absolute title (LRA 1925, s. 75).

As such the paper owner would need to act *within* the 12 years to remove the 'squatter'. It should also be noted that from day 1 the 'squatter had proprietary rights under *section 70(1)(f) of the LRA 1925* as an overriding interest which could bind a future purchaser. However, this does not appear in the LRA 2002, hence there is no longer an overriding interest from day 1. The proprietary right *now* only comes into existence at the 10-year point (under the LRA 2002) when the right to claim exists.

It was the case, and still is, that the 'clock starts ticking' as soon as the paper owner had either been *dispossessed* or had *discontinued* possession and the adverse possessor had '*taken the land to the exclusion of all others*'.

Substantively, there was and still is a **two-stage test** to determine as to whether a 'squatter' is actually an 'adverse possessor':

(i) The paper owner must be dispossessed or have discontinued possession

As Lord Denning stated, a 'squatter' may be on the land, but 'Possession is not enough . . . it must be adverse possession. The true owner must have discontinued possession and another taken adversely to him' (Lord Denning – *Wallis Cayton Bay Holiday Camp* v. *Shell Mex* [1975]).

Therefore there needs to be strong evidence that the paper owner has indeed been dispossessed. The early case law, namely *Leigh* v. *Jack* (1879), suggested that it is *not* adverse possession where land is left unoccupied but there is evidence that the paper owner intends to use it again in the future. In *Cayton*, Denning suggested that leaving the land unused gives an '*implied licence*' to the squatter, but that licence can of course always be revoked by the owner if they return. However, in the Court of Appeal, this idea of 'return' was effectively consigned to history. In *Buckingham County Council* v. *Moran* [1990], Slade LJ stated that the law in *Leigh* was 'too broad' and it was wrong to 'suggest that an owner who retains land with a view to using it in the future can NEVER be dispossessed'. Slade LJ suggested that if there is an *intention* by the adverse possessor to '*possess the land to the exclusion of all others*' then it may amount to dispossession. Hence the second test became vital . . .

(ii) The adverse possessor must take the land to the exclusion of all others

The adverse possessor therefore needs to demonstrate *factual possession* and *animus possidendi* – the *intention to possess with the exclusion of all others*. The line of cases demonstrates how this principle works. In *Powell* v. *McFarlane* [1977] grazing a cow, cutting hay and repairing fences did not succeed. There needed to be 'clear and affirmative evidence' of the intention to possess and exclude. Neither did the claim succeed in *Boosey* v. *Davis* (1989) where grazing goats and clearing shrubs was not seen as evidence of the requisite intention. Similarly, in *Stacey* v. *Gardner* [1994] the installing an incinerator on the landlord's land, with a lack of fences or boundaries also failed. In *Basildon Council* v. *Charge* [1996], where geese, vegetables and wood were simply kept on the land, the Court of Appeal stated there needed to be 'cogent and compelling evidence of a single degree of occupation and physical control of the land uninterrupted by others'.

It is also important to understand that an acknowledgement of the ownership of the paper owner will defeat a claim in adverse possession. In *Morrice* v. *Evans* [1989] the claimant failed in his claim as he had stopped using the greenhouse when asked to do so by the owner. Also, in *Lambeth Borough Council* v. *Archangel* [2001] the claimant referred to the 'possessed land' in a letter to the Council as 'Lambeth's property', hence his fail claimed. The key to a successful claim for substantive adverse possession is therefore evidence of 'exclusion'. It was stated in *Lambeth Borough Council* v. *Blackburn* [2001] that all factors are crucial but it is 'exclusion of others' that is likely to be the conclusive factor. In *Moran*, Slade LJ relied on a statement in *Seddon* v. *Smith* [1987] which suggested that 'enclosure is the strongest possible evidence of adverse possession'. Slade went on to suggest that 'locks and chains and a gate' amounted to 'a final and unequivocal demonstration of the defendant's intention to possess the land'.

CORNERSTONE

Pye v. Graham [2001]

The Grahams were farmers who owned land next to Pye – a property developer. Pye was not using the land, and was waiting for planning permission to build. The Grahams were then given a licence to graze animals and cut hay, but in 1985 the licence was revoked. They continued to use the land. In 1997 they registered a claim stating that they now owned the land as adverse possessors (12 years' uninterrupted use). Pye objected and litigation began.

At first instance the Grahams won, though the court expressed its disquiet as the land was valuable. Pye appealed, and the Court of Appeal reversed the decision, stating that the Grahams had stated in evidence that they 'hoped' to get a new licence – implying they recognised Pye's rights as owner. However, the Lords reversed the Court of Appeal, stating that the Grahams had dispossessed the paper owner and showed *physical custody* with an *intention to exclude* the world at large including Pye.

Physical control would of course depend on the facts, but they argued that there was enough evidence here – it was therefore immaterial that they recognised Pye's rights and as such there was no need to show an intention to own the land permanently, it was only necessary to show that they had an intention to possess and exclude for the requisite period of time (here, 12 years). As such, the Lords applied cases such as *Moran*, and *Leigh* v. *Jack* was formally overruled. (Note: Pye later launched an unsuccessful human rights challenge in *Pye* v. *UK* [2007] – the Grand Chamber, albeit by a small majority, stated that English law on adverse possession does not *quite* breach Protocol 1 of the European Convention on Human Rights (the right not to have property taken without compensation) as the law is needed to balance the rights of the owner with the right of the State to protect its housing market. See below for the full judgment of the ECtHR.)

Procedural change under the Land Registration Act 2002

It is, of course, important to note that for unregistered land, the 12-year rule still applies. The 12-year rule also still applies if the adverse possessor has been in 'adverse possession' for a *full* 12 years prior to 13 October 2003 (the date the LRA 2002 came into force) and *remains in possession* after that date. If *any* time less than 12 years has been spent in possession before the Act came into force, then the new '10-year' regime comes into play. In registered land, once again as a way to further the 'mirror principle', it became far more difficult for the adverse possessor to get title.

··· **APPLICATION**

Scenario 1: Lecter takes 'adverse possession' of an abandoned property belonging to Crawford in September 1991. In late October 2003, Lecter claims title to the property. He has been there undisturbed and excluding all others for over 12 years prior to 13 October 2003 (LRA 2002). He will be given title by the Registrar.

Scenario 2: Lecter takes 'adverse possession' of the same property in January 1992. If he claims title in late October 2003, he will have been there for 11 years and 9 months before the LRA 2002 came into force, and 3 months after it came into force. On claiming title in October 2003, the Registrar will contact the paper owner, Crawford, who will then have two years to remove Lecter.

Scenario 3: Lecter takes 'adverse possession' of the same property in October 2000. He can now claim adverse possession (as he has been there for over 10 years) but the Registrar will contact the paper owner as in scenario 2.

Scenario 4: Lecter takes 'adverse possession' of the same property in October 2009. He cannot claim adverse possession until he has been there for 10 years – so the paper owner must act to remove him before that point. Now, of course, it is also a criminal offence – so Lecter may be arrested (as indeed he could be retrospectively in scenario 3 if he is still present).

Part 9 of the Land Registration Act 2002 and Schedule 6

Part 9, sections 96–98 of the LRA 2002 states categorically that section 15 of the LA 1980 does *not* apply to registered land, so no longer will the paper owner automatically lose their rights after 12 years. At Schedule 6, paragraph 1 it states that after *10 years* the adverse possessor may apply to the Registrar claiming title. The claimant will need to prove that they have been *in possession to the exclusion of others* (as above) and is still there at the time of the application. At paragraph 2 it states that the Registrar will then *inform the paper owner and any other interested parties*, at which point the paper owner must take steps to recover the land within two years. At paragraph 3, it states that the adverse possessor will succeed after 10 years *if*:

- an estoppel has arisen,
- for some other reason, or
- where boundaries have been mistaken.

It the claim is rejected at the 10-year stage by the Registrar, the adverse possessor can apply after a further two years (para. 6) but not if possession or eviction proceedings have already commenced. If successful, of course, the adverse possessor will be awarded title.

So is the LRA 2002 '*revolutionary*' or simply '*evolutionary*'?

KEY POINTS

- After the LRA 1925, land was conveyed using the 'traditional', unregistered method – with reference to title deeds and other evidentiary documents dating back at least 15 years – *or* using the 'new' registered system introduced by Torrens in Australia.
- The aims of the Torrens 'registered' system were to further the key principles of registered conveyancing – the mirror, the curtain and the insurance principles.
- The mirror principle states that the 'register' should reflect reality – there should be no hidden rights – though the 'crack' remained due to 'overriding interests'. The curtain principle suggests that a new buyer should not have to concern himself with beneficiaries – dealing only with the legal owner. The insurance principle allows the State to guarantee the accuracy of the register, correcting it and/or paying an indemnity where errors are made.
- The LRA 2002 replaced the LRA 1925 in its entirety – and aimed to pave the way for e-conveyancing by reducing the number of 'overriding interests' and increasing the 'triggers' for first registration.
- The key remaining 'interests which override' can be found at Schedules 1 and 3 to the LRA 2002 – short legal leases; the rights of a person in actual occupation; and implied legal easements. Section 29 of the LRA 2002 states that a new buyer will be bound only by pre-existing interests which appear on the register as 'notices' or by those 'unregistered interests which override'.
- A beneficiary can place a 'restriction' on the Register in the proprietorship section – but this simply warns a prospective buyer that the statutory mechanism of overreaching may need to be used to replace the equitable proprietary rights of the beneficiaries with a money payment. Overreaching can only occur when the purchase money is paid to at least two legal owners/trustees (*Boland* and *Flegg*).
- The LRA 2002 has also procedurally changed the rules on 'adverse possession' – making it more difficult for a 'squatter' to claim title – strengthening the 'mirror principle' further. The adverse possessor must now take the land exclusively for 10 years, make a claim to the Registrar, who will then contact the paper owner. The 'old' regime of taking title automatically after 12 years has been consigned to unregistered land only. It is also now a criminal offence to 'squat' on residential land.

CORE CASES AND STATUTES

Case	About	Importance
Williams & Glyn's Bank v. *Boland* [1981] AC 487	The effect of a single owner on the mechanism of overreaching.	Where there is a sole legal owner (trustee) – overreaching cannot occur.
City of London Building Society v. *Flegg* [1988] AC 54	The Maxwell-Browns and the parents – the Fleggs; the purchase of 'Bleak House'.	Where there are two legal owners, the rights of the beneficiaries will be overreached – even with an existing overriding interest.
National Provincial v. *Ainsworth* [1965] AC 1175	Personal v. Proprietary rights in relation to actual occupation.	Only an existing proprietary right can act as a trigger for a claim of actual occupation under Sch 1 or 3.
Abbey National v. *Cann* [1991] 1 AC 56	Mrs Cann's furniture arrived 35 minutes after the transfer.	The person must be in 'actual occupation' at the time of the transfer – not just the time of registration.
Chhokar v. *Chhokar* [1984] FLR 313	Husband sells property to friend while his wife is in hospital giving birth.	Actual occupation needs 'evidence of physical presence' coupled with an intention to return.
Link Lending v. *Bustard* [2010] EWCA Civ 424	Susan Bustard was sectioned (in a psychiatric unit).	As above – she was still in actual occupation following the *ratio* in *Chhokar* and *Thompson* v. *Foy* [2010].
Buckingham County Council v. *Moran* [1990] Ch 623	'Locks, gates and chains' as evidence of adverse possession.	In order to claim adverse possession, the claimant must show evidence of the dispossession of the paper owner – taking the land to the exclusion of all others.
Pye v. *Graham* [2001] 1 AC 419 *Pye* v. *UK* (2008) 46 EHRR 45	The Grahams stayed on Pye's land 12 years after the licence had been revoked. *Pye* v. *UK* – the human rights argument.	The fact that the owner may use the land in the future does not stop a claim for adverse possession if exclusion can be demonstrated for the requisite time period – *Leigh* v. *Jack* overruled. In the ECtHR the human rights argument failed.

Statute	About	Importance
LRA 1925, s. 70(1)(g))	Sets down the old rules on the overriding interest of actual occupation.	Now repealed – but the case law is largely based on this section.
LRA 2002, s. 4	List of triggers for first registration.	As s. 27 below.
LRA 2002, s. 27	List of dispositions which must be registered.	Transfer of land; lease of over seven years; express legal easement; legal mortgage.
LRA 2002, s. 29	The priority rule.	A new buyer (or lender in possession) is bound only by pre-existing interests on the register or unregistered interests which override.
LRA 2002, ss. 32–35	Notices.	'Minor interests' can be placed on the register as 'notices' in the charges section – either agreed or unilateral.
LRA 2002, ss. 91–93	E-conveyancing.	Sets down the regime for e-conveyancing.
LRA 2002, Sch. 3	Unregistered interests which override the register.	Legal leases of less than seven years; actual occupation; implied legal easements.
LRA 2002, Sch. 4	Alteration.	The register can be altered/rectified.
LRA 2002, Sch. 6	Adverse possession.	Sets down the 'new' registered land regime for claiming adverse possession.
LRA 2002, Sch. 8	Insurance/indemnity.	The State may compensate where there has been an error and the register needs alteration or where the legal owner has suffered a loss (rectification).
Legal Aid, Sentencing and Punishment of Offenders Act 2012, s. 144	Criminalisation of squatters.	It is now a criminal offence to 'squat' on residential land: it is unclear how this may affect a claim for adverse possession under the LRA 2002 if the claimant gets to 10 years without being arrested!

FURTHER READING

Bowcott, O. 'First Squatter jailed under new law', *The Guardian*, Thursday 27 September 2012 http://www.theguardian.com/society/2012/sep/27/first-squatter-jailed-new-law
A look at the new law criminalising squatters and its first 'victim'.

Clarke, I. 'The Land Registration Act 2002 – A Conveyancing Revolution?' (Selborne Chambers) www.selbornechambers.co.uk/library/050210.doc
Background to the LRA 2002 dealing with the key changes from its predecessor the LRA 1925.

Dixon, M. 'The Reform of Property Law and the Land Registration Act 2002: A Risk Assessment' (University of Cambridge, Faculty of Law) (2003) *Conveyancer and Property Lawyer*, 136–156, http://papers.ssrn.com/sol3/papers.cfm?abstract_id=911326
Dixon gives an excellent critical overview of the LRA 2002.

European Court of Human Rights: Grand Chamber Judgment, *J.A. PYE (OXFORD) LTD & J.A. PYE (OXFORD) LAND LTD v. UNITED KINGDOM* (application no. 44302/02) https://wcd.coe.int/ViewDoc.jsp?id=1176761&Site=COE
A very useful overview of the law on adverse possession as seen by the judges of the European Court of Human Rights – an interesting and illuminating account of why the law on adverse possession does not quite breach the ECHR Protocol 1.

Jenkins, S. 'How a church roof in Warwickshire cost a farmer in Wales £500,000', *The Telegraph*, 9 February

2007 http://www.theguardian.com/commentisfree/2007/feb/09/lords.religion; 'Chancel Repair Liability – The Wallbanks' Story' http://www.chancelrepair.org/2.html
Both of these articles tell the story of the Wallbanks and their overriding interest of chancel repairs – a critical analysis of the Law Lords decision and the law itself.

Land Registry 'Land Registration Act 2002: Land Registration Rules 2003' http://www.landregistry.gov.uk/professional/law-and-practice/act-and-rules
A practical guide to the workings of the LRA – useful especially in relation to overriding interests.

Land Registry 'Land Registration Act 2002: Law and Practice' http://www.landregistry.gov.uk/professional/law-and-practice
As above – an explanation of how the LRA operates.

Land Registry 'Report on responses to e-conveyancing secondary legislation' http://www.landregistry.gov.uk/__data/assets/pdf_file/0006/3102/econveyancing_cons.pdf
Background information on the introduction of e-conveyancing and the reasons for its creation.

The Law Commission *Land Registration For the Twenty First Century; A Consultative Document* http://lawcommission.justice.gov.uk/docs/lc254_land_registration_for_21st_century_consultative.pdf
This is the full consultation document prior to the LRA 2002 – it gives a superb overview of the aims and objectives of the LRA 2002.

Lilleystone, T. 'Law Society chief criticises delay in introduction of electronic Conveyancing', 22 October 2012 http://www.fridaysmove.com/property-law-blog/tonyl/law-society-chief-criticises-delay-introduction-electronic-conveyancing

A warning as to why e-conveyancing may not be as straightforward to implement as the Registry intended – issues of security and data protection are highlighted.

'The mirror cracked – the contradiction between the idea behind registered land and the concept of overriding interests', *The Law Society Gazette*, 19 January 1994 http://www.lawgazette.co.uk/news/the-mirror-cracked-contradiction-between-idea-behind-registered-land-and-concept-overriding-int

A critical account of 'overriding interests' – why they remain even after the LRA 2002 – the social and economic background as to why the Law Commission suggested that some overriding interests should remain.

PART 3

Trusts of land: joint ownership

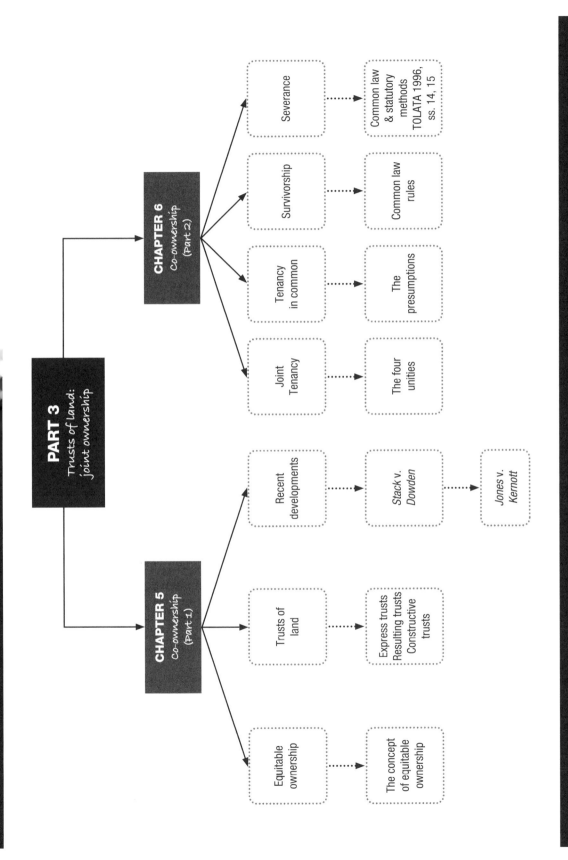

PART 3
Trusts of land: joint ownership

CHAPTER 5
Co-ownership (Part 1)

Equitable ownership → The concept of equitable ownership

Trusts of land → Express trusts Resulting trusts Constructive trusts

Recent developments → *Stack v. Dowden* → *Jones v. Kernott*

CHAPTER 6
Co-ownership (Part 2)

Joint Tenancy → The four unities

Tenancy in common → The presumptions

Survivorship → Common law rules

Severance → Common law & statutory methods TOLATA 1996, ss. 14, 15

PART 3 INTRODUCTION

Part 3 of *Blueprints Land Law* examines the relationship between joint owners of land and explains the concept of the '**trust** of land' which exists either expressly or impliedly every time we have more than one person owning either a legal or an **equitable interest** in a property. Part 3 is split into two chapters, 5 and 6, both dealing with the topic of co-ownership. Chapter 5 will begin by defining an 'equitable interest' and look at how that equitable interest is acquired and then quantified to determine each party's 'share' of the property. You will need to understand the '**express trust**' where the co-owners have defined and recorded their interest, but will also need to understand the '**resulting**' and '**constructive**' trust of land based essentially on contributions rather than an express agreement – especially difficult where the co-owners are unmarried couples. Chapter 5 will trace the development of the **common law** in this area from the case law of the 1970s and 1990s to the far more 'modern' approach taken by Baroness Hale in 2007 in *Stack* v. *Dowden*. The chapter will finish with a look at the very recent case law on co-ownership such as *Jones* v. *Kernott* from 2011.

In Chapter 6 we will begin by looking at the specific co-ownership relationships of '**joint tenancy**' and 'tenancy in common'. You will need to understand the important differences between these two types of co-ownership and why the difference matters – mainly due to the rules of 'survivorship'. We will also look in detail at the operation of 'severance' where a joint tenant can 'sever' their equitable 'share' to create a 'tenancy in common'. Where 'trustees' and 'beneficiaries' – that is, legal and equitable owners – are in dispute over a property, or a lender is threatening possession, then the Trusts of Land and Appointment of Trustees Act 1996 (TOLATA 1996) may come into play, and Chapter 6 will finish with an explanation as to how this Act may be applied.

CHAPTER 5

Co-ownership (Part 1)

BLUEPRINT

Co-ownership (Part 1)

LEGISLATION

- Law of Property Act 1925
- Trusts of Land and Appointment of Trustees Act 1996

CONTEXT

- All property bought by more than 1 person is subject to a trust.
- All trusts have trustees and beneficiaries - this can be expressly declared or implied through 'common intention'.
- 2 million unmarried couples living in the UK.

CONCEPTS

- Resulting and constructive trusts
- Equitable interests
- Acquisition
- Quantification
- Common intention – express and implied

- Who was right – Baroness Hale or Lord Neuberger – flexibility or certainty?
- Should the courts 'imply, infer or impute' common intention?
- If there is no express declaration – shouldn't equity always follow the law?

- What is the fundamental difference between a resulting and constructive trust?
- Is there a distinction between a constructive trust and proprietary estoppel?
- Was Baroness Hale right in *Stack* – should we be following a holistic approach?

CASES

- *Stack* v. *Dowden* [2007]
- *Pettitt* v. *Pettitt* [1970]
- *Eves* v. *Eves* [1975]
- *Lloyds Bank* v. *Rossett* [1991]
- *Oxley* v. *Hiscock* [2004]
- *Laskar* v. *Laskar* [2008]
- *Jones* v. *Kernott* [2011]

REFORM

- Should the Law Com Report 307 become law – do we need legislation to clarify the position for unmarried partners?

SPECIAL CHARACTERISTICS

- The 'real' difference between a constructive and resulting trust
- The meaning of 'common intention'

CRITICAL ISSUES

Setting the scene

When a property is owned outright by a sole owner, clearly that person owns the legal title of that property (see Chapter 1). However, the situation becomes far more complicated, certainly in land law terms, when two or more people buy a property together. This is known as 'concurrent ownership' and land law refers to them as co-owners. Rather confusingly, they are also referred to as 'joint tenants' (see Chapter 6) and they also carry the 'burden' of being trustees of that land – holding the land on trust for each other and any further beneficiaries.

The correct terminology, since the introduction of the Trusts of Land and Appointment of Trustees Act 1996 (TOLATA 1996 – see also Chapter 6), is that whenever there is co-ownership, there is a *trust of land* created – either *expressly* stated in the conveyance or on Land Registry Forms (the Form JO) or *implied* by way of a resulting or constructive trust. This chapter will seek to explain these types of trust – how and when they are created and the implications these trusts of land hold for both trustee and beneficiary.

It is also important to realise that there are a number of different possibilities available in any co-ownership relationship. A married couple, let's say Rebecca and Keith, buy a property together. Both names are on the title, and both contribute equally. It can be said that they are both co-owners at law (as joint tenants) and in equity – as they are holding as trustees for each other, also being, therefore, the beneficiaries. It could also be the case, though, that only Rebecca's name is on the register as legal owner. Is Keith just a lodger? Clearly that would not be the usual scenario in a 'relationship situation'. The couple may have declared a trust expressly setting out each person's 'real value' as Professor Martin Dixon calls the equitable interest. They may have also filled out a Land Registry form (Form JO) which also sets out their 'real' equitable interest. However, they may have not done either of the above – in which case there may be an implied trust in operation – even if the couple have no idea that this is the case.

This is *relatively* unproblematic if indeed Keith and Rebecca are married – we have legislation (see below) to assist us in the event of an unfortunate marital breakdown or a default in mortgage payments and a forced sale. Where the couple is unmarried no such legislation exists, and as such the computation of each person's equitable share becomes even more complex. The purpose of this chapter is to try to explain the effect of a 'trust of land' in any given co-ownership scenario. Since the 'holistic approach' taken by Baroness Hale in *Stack* v. *Dowden* [2007] the acquisition and quantification of the equitable interest behind a trust is perhaps, according to Lord Neuberger's view in *Stack*, 'difficult, subjective and uncertain'. According to Baroness Hale, though, the law in relation to co-owners has rightly 'moved on', with, as Martin Dixon suggests, 'our most senior judges (being) determined to introduce more flexibility'.

THE CONCEPT OF CO-OWNERSHIP – RECOGNITION OF EQUITABLE INTERESTS

CORNERSTONE

Legal and equitable ownership of land

It is one of the key principles of land law, and also one of the key areas of confusion, that there is a fundamental difference between legal and equitable ownership. In a co-ownership scenario, the legal owner (also the trustee) is the person whose name appears in the proprietorship section of the register. However, this is merely the 'title-holder' because, as Professor Martin Dixon points out (see Further Reading), it is the equitable interest that is the 'real value' in the property. The common law does not recognise an equitable (beneficiary) interest, focusing only on the legal title. This of course allows for certainty and clarity but lacks flexibility and also fails to recognise the 'relevant intentions of the parties' and can at times 'unconscionably frustrate their legitimate expectations' (Gray and Gray – see below).

As such, equity will play a positive role in at least trying to prevent 'unconscionable dealings' between the parties in relation to shared ownership. One way equity 'steps in' is through the doctrine of proprietary estoppel (see Chapter 7) and there is an obvious overlap between estoppel and implied trusts which will be analysed later in this chapter. Other than estoppel, equity may intervene through the equitable imposition of an implied trust – either *resulting* or *constructive* – in order to avoid unconscionable dealings in co-owned property. It is also very pertinent to point out that there is statutory assistance here to avoid the formalities of land transfer – as section 53(2) of the LPA 1925 sets down that land transfer formalities are not necessary when such implied trusts are in operation. The question arises as to whether an implied trust is based on a resulting or a constructive trust – and in order to understand the difference, we need to trace back through the historical case law surrounding these devices to try to understand the basis for such an informal transfer of land. As the court commented in *Springette* v. *Defoe* [1992], the law does not simply 'allow property rights to be affected by telepathy'.

TRUSTS OF LAND

As explained above, whenever there is co-ownership, there is a *trust of land* created – either expressly stated in the conveyance or on Land Registry Forms (the Form JO) or implied by way of a *resulting* or *constructive trust*. Co-ownership is, of course, usually the model when two people purchase property within a relationship (spouses; partners; civil partners) but property can also be co-owned commercially within a business relationship. In either situation, co-ownership will create this trust of land (no longer referred to as a '*trust for sale*' since the Trusts of Land and Appointment of Trustees Act 1996, section 1 – see Chapter 6). As such there will be always be a trustee–beneficiary relationship in existence, and although this has no real meaning whilst the co-owners live in 'perfect harmony', the extent of their legal (trustee) and equitable (beneficiary) interests become vital if the property is repossessed, sold or there is a dispute over ownership.

As suggested above, if the co-owners are married, then legislation such as the Family Law Act 1996 (as amended) and the Matrimonial Causes Act 1973 set down basic rules for the division of property on divorce. However, if there is no divorce or if the co-owners are not married in the first place, then the situation as to the quantification (and in some cases the acquisition itself) of the equitable interest in the property is far more complex. Baroness Hale in the key case of *Stack* v. *Dowden* [2007] and the Law Commission in its 2007 report on *Cohabitation: The Final Consequences of Relationship Breakdown* (Law Com. No. 307), both seem to state quite categorically that the common law in relation to property and trusts can only go so far. The law on resulting and constructive trusts, especially in relation to quantification of an equitable interest, has been, as Lord Walker suggested in *Stack*, 'potentially productive of injustice' and needs to be 'recast'.

Express trusts

The most straightforward way to ensure clarity when two or more parties take ownership of a property together is to declare a trust in writing, either before the purchase in the conveyance deed itself, or after the purchase following the requirements of the Law of Property Act 1925, section 53 (emphasis added):

CORNERSTONE

LPA 1925, section 53

53　Instruments required to be in writing

(1) Subject to the provision hereinafter contained with respect to the creation of interests in land by parol—

    (a) no interest in land can be created or disposed of except by writing signed by the person creating or conveying the same, or by his agent thereunto lawfully authorised in writing, or by will, or by operation of law;

    (b) *a declaration of trust respecting any land or any interest therein must be manifested and proved by some writing signed by some person who is able to declare such trust or by his will;*

    (c) a disposition of an equitable interest or trust subsisting at the time of the disposition, must be in writing signed by the person disposing of the same, or by his agent thereunto lawfully authorised in writing or by will.

(2) *This section does not affect the creation or operation of resulting, implied or constructive trusts.*

The parties are free to set down the extent of their equitable ownership in a declaration of trust deed: once 'witnessed, signed and delivered' as a deed, an express private trust of land will have been created. If the express trust has been validly created (without any fraud or mistake) then it is conclusive (*Goodman* v. *Gallant* [1986]).

Alternatively, since 1 November 2012, the co-owners are now able to lodge a Form JO (see Figure 5.1) with the Land Registry, in order to declare the beneficial interest in a property. However, there is a very brief window of opportunity here – the form must be lodged between exchange of contracts and completion of the transfer (see Chapter 2). According to Macdonald (see Further Reading below), the Form JO – put in place by the Registry following Baroness Hale's 'heavy hint' in *Stack* – is especially useful 'if one of the joint purchasers is not on the title', describing the Form JO as 'an important opportunity for those who do not intend equity to follow the law, or who have unusual arrangements about the equity'.

Land Registry
Trust Information

JO

This form may accompany an application in Form AP1, FR1 or ADV1 where:
- panel 9 of Form FR1 or ADV1 has not been completed and the applicant is more than one person, or
- the Form AP1 relates to a transfer (in Form AS1, AS3, TP1, TP2, TR1, TR2 or TR5) or a prescribed clauses lease (within rule 58A of the Land Registration Rules 2003) of a registered estate to more than one person (the Joint Owners), and
  - the declaration of trust panel in the transfer or lease has not been completed and/or the transfer has not been executed by the Joint Owners, and the estate transferred or leased is not a rentcharge, franchise, profit or manor.

Enter the same information as either in the transfer or lease to the Joint Owners or in panel 6 of Form ADV1. Leave blank if this form accompanies a Form FR1.	1	Title number(s) of the property:
Insert address including postcode (if any) or other description of the property as it appears either in the transfer or lease to the Joint Owners, in panel 3 of Form ADV1 or in panel 2 of Form FR1.	2	Property:
	3	Date:
Give full name(s) and address(es), as in either the transfer or lease to the Joint Owners, panels 6 and 7 of Forms ADV1 or panels 6 and 8 of Form FR1.	4	Joint Owners:

Complete either this or panel 6.

Place an 'X' in the appropriate box.

If completing the fourth box, insert details either of the trust or of the trust instrument under which the Joint Owners hold the property.

The registrar will enter a Form A restriction in the register if an 'X' is placed:
- in the second or third box, or
- in the fourth box, unless it is clear that the Joint Owners hold on trust for themselves alone as joint tenants.

If this panel is completed, each Joint Owner must sign.

Please refer to Land Registry's *Public Guide 18 – Joint property ownership* and *Practice Guide 24 – Private trusts of land* for further guidance. These guides are available on the website www.landregistry.gov.uk

5 ☐ The Joint Owners declare that they are to hold the property on trust for themselves alone as joint tenants

☐ The Joint Owners declare that they are to hold the property on trust for themselves alone as tenants in common in equal shares

☐ The Joint Owners declare that they hold the property on trust for themselves alone as tenants in common in the following unequal shares: (*complete*)

☐ The Joint Owners are to hold the property (*complete*):

Signature of each
of the Joint Owners   _____

_____

Date:

Figure 5.1 The Form JO
Source: from Land Registry, Crown copyright

<table>
<tr>
<td>6</td>
<td colspan="2">Under the term of a written declaration of trust
dated (*complete*)   the Joint Owners</td>
</tr>
<tr>
<td></td>
<td>☐</td>
<td>hold the property on trust as joint tenants for themselves alone</td>
</tr>
<tr>
<td></td>
<td>☐</td>
<td>do not hold the property on trust as joint tenants for themselves alone</td>
</tr>
</table>

If this panel is completed, a conveyancer must sign.

Signature of conveyancer _____

Date:

WARNING
If you dishonestly enter information or make a statement that you know is, or might be, untrue or misleading, and intend by doing so to make a gain for yourself or another person, or to cause loss or the risk of loss to another person, you may commit the offence of fraud under section 1 of the Fraud Act 2006, the maximum penalty for which is 10 years' imprisonment or an unlimited fine, or both.

Failure to complete this form with proper care may result in a loss of protection under the Land Registration Act 2002 if, as a result, a mistake is made in the register.

Under section 66 of the Land Registration Act 2002 most documents (including this form) kept by the registrar relating to an application to the registrar or referred to in the register are open to public inspection and copying. If you believe a document contains prejudicial information, you may apply for that part of the document to be made exempt using Form EX1, under rule 136 of the Land Registration Rules 2003.

Figure 5.1 (*continued*)

However, case law suggests that for whatever reason, express trusts, especially between couples, are far from the norm.

Resulting trusts

As stated above, where there is a lack of any express written agreement, equity intervenes to potentially impose an implied trust of land, historically, either a resulting or a constructive trust. The presumption of a resulting trust dates back to 1788 and *Dyer* v. *Dyer*: if a property is purchased by A with money solely from B, then a '*trust of the legal estate . . . results to the man who advances the purchase money*'. What happens in a scenario such as *Dyer* is that A holds the legal title, but on trust for B who is the beneficial owner. If A and B contribute equally, then traditionally at the time of acquisition, equity will find a 'presumed intention' that the co-owners have a 50/50 beneficial interest, based solely on contribution to purchase price *at the time of purchase*. *Curley* v. *Parkes* [2004] clarifies that it must be by way of contribution to the purchase at the time of transfer, contributions to mortgage payments will not generate a resulting trust (though they may generate a constructive trust). In order for the resulting trust to operate, there must be evidence of the 'common intention' of both parties at the time of purchase that 'B' should take a beneficial share of the property and that evidence will be based on contributions to the purchase where there is a lack of words.

....APPLICATION

Springette v. *Defoe* [1992]

The common intention must be founded on evidence such as would support a finding that there is an implied or constructive trust for the parties in proportions to the purchase price. The court does not as yet sit, as under a palm tree, to exercise a general discretion to do what the man in the street, on a general overview of the case, might regard as fair . . . (Dillon LJ)

However, since the case of *Stack* v. *Dowden* it seems that other than in purchases for investment reasons rather than as a home (see *Laskar* v. *Laskar* later), as Baroness Hale suggests, 'it is now clear that the constructive trust is generally the more appropriate tool of analysis in most matrimonial cases'.

Constructive trusts

Even though the 'policy' behind a constructive trust is still to prevent unconscionable dealing, seminal cases such as *Lloyds Bank* v. *Rosset* [1991] and more recently *Stack* v. *Dowden* [2007] set down that for a constructive trust to arise there must be evidence of common intention and detrimental reliance by the 'injured' party. The key difference between a resulting and a constructive trust, however, is that the common intention can be evidenced *at any time*, not just at the time of purchase.

INTERSECTION

In Chapter 7 the equitable doctrine of proprietary estoppel is explained in full. It is obvious that there is an overlap between a constructive trust and a claim for proprietary estoppel. Estoppel requires the claimant to show that there has been a clear promise made in relation to land ownership; reliance on that promise; some detriment suffered; and overall that it would be unconscionable for the person making the promise to go back on their word and deny the proprietary interest promised (see *Gillett* v. *Holt* [2000]). If a constructive trust is to be imposed there must also have been detrimental reliance and unconscionability is still of course the central pillar – the subtle difference being that constructive trusts need evidence of common intention rather than evidence of what really can be described as a unilateral promise. The usual 'wording' of a promise in estoppel is along the lines of 'when I die all of this will be yours' whereas in a constructive trust, if words are used those words suggest current co-ownership rather than subsequent ('this house is yours as well as mine'). If words are not used, the 'common intention' is evidenced by contributions given and accepted by both parties. Post-*Stack*, due to the infinitely wider definition of 'contributions' it may of course now be possible to choose your route when claiming an equitable interest – either estoppel or constructive trust. It should be noted, however, that estoppel is usually viewed as the last resort, as the role of the court in estoppel claims is to 'do the minimum necessary to achieve justice' (see Chapter 7) whereas, with a constructive trust, the role of the court is to provide a remedy based on contributions – Baroness Hale would argue that this 'holistic approach' is far more likely to bring about a proportionate remedy.

In *Lloyds Bank* v. *Rosset* [1991], Lord Bridge identified two categories of constructive trust – the first based on express discussion, the second based on implied intention through conduct.

(i) Evidence – 'the express common intention constructive trust'

For the requirement of common intention to be satisfied, if the party claiming the interest can point to clear words promising co-ownership rights, then this should suffice. In *McKenzie* v. *McKenzie* [2003] it was stated that where such 'common intention can be proved or imputed . . . the technique of equity is to impose a constructive trust'. For the 'express common intention' trust to be successfully argued, there must be evidence of some 'agreement, arrangement or understanding reached' between the two parties that the 'property is to be shared beneficially' (Lord Bridge in *Lloyds Bank* v. *Rossett* [1991]). In *Springette* v. *Defoe* [1993] the court used precisely the same definition but added that this 'agreement, arrangement or understanding' must be based on 'evidence of express discussions . . . however imperfectly remembered and however imprecise their terms may have been'. However, the court added that there must be evidence of such a discussion, as 'trust law does not allow property rights to be affected by telepathy'. What is clear, however, is that this express intention may assist in arguing that an equitable interest has been *acquired* but may not assist greatly in terms of *quantification*. In *Oxley* v. *Hiscock* [2004] it was held that the parties do not need to have agreed the size of their beneficial interest. This can be done through the second 'category' of constructive trust – the 'implied or inferred [or maybe even imputed] common intention constructive trust'.

(ii) Evidence – 'the implied or inferred common intention constructive trust'

In the early 1970s, the implied 'common intention constructive trust' could only really be said to succeed if there had been substantial contributions to the purchase price or at least mortgage payments after purchase. Two cases affirmed this rather stringent approach. In *Pettitt* v. *Pettitt* [1970], a rare case where the husband was claiming an equitable share of a property solely owned by his wife, Lord Diplock ruled that it would be an 'abuse of legal technique' to allow the husband to succeed as contributing by way of minor decorations to the property did not give rise to a constructive trust. Similarly, in *Gissing* v. *Gissing* [1971] the wife's contribution of £220 towards furnishings and mowing the lawn did also not evidence common intention of a trust. Once again, Lord Diplock stated that where there was 'no initial contribution' to the purchase deposit and no other 'direct contribution to the mortgage instalments' the inference is that there was a common intention only to 'share the day-to-day expenses' and no more.

However, in 1975, Lord Denning 'created' the 'new model constructive trust', allowing such a trust to be based on broader contributions. In *Eves* v. *Eves* [1975] Mr Eves bought a property solely in his name. His reason was such that his girlfriend Janet was not yet 21 years of age. However, Janet worked 'extensively on the dirty and dilapidated house', as Lord Denning put it, whilst breaking up a patio 'wielding a 14lb sledgehammer'. This, Lord Denning stated, gave rise to a 25 per cent share in the property under the 'new model' constructive trust. Less than ten years later, however, the Court of Appeal returned to a more 'orthodox' approach in *Burns* v. *Burns* [1984]. The claimant had lived with Patrick Burns, unmarried, for 19 years, but had made no initial contribution or payments towards the mortgage. She had, however, brought up their children, acted as 'homemaker' and also paid towards household bills. Lord Justice Fox stated that 'the mere fact that the parties live together and do ordinary domestic tasks is . . . no indication . . . that they thereby intended to alter the existing property rights of either of them'.

This high threshold was followed by Lord Bridge in *Lloyds Bank* v. *Rosset* [1991] where, once again, the property was in the sole name of Mr Rosset. Mrs Rosset spent six months supervising the renovation of the property, managing the project and the builders. Mr Rosset then defaulted on a mortgage and the bank came seeking possession. At that point Mrs Rosset claimed an overriding interest as a person in actual occupation under the provisions of section 70(1)(g) of the Land Registration Act 1925.

INTERSECTION

A full discussion of the issue of overriding interests in *Rosset* can be found in Chapter 4. Actual occupation would now come under LRA 2002, Schedule 3, paragraph 2 – but the common law 'rule' for needing to have a pre-existing proprietary interest before being able to claim actual occupation was in place at the time of *Rosset*.

Even though Lord Bridge did concede that Mrs Rosset, either in her own right or through her builders, was in actual occupation, he held that she did not have a proprietary right to begin with and was therefore unable to claim such an overriding interest against the bank. He stated that, without an express agreement evidencing common intention, there needed to be evidence of clear common intention implied or inferred through conduct. He said that Mrs Rosset's efforts were 'the most natural thing in the world for any wife . . . irrespective of any expectation she might have of enjoying a beneficial interest in the property'. He went on to state quite categorically that 'direct contributions to purchase price . . . or . . . payment of mortgage instalments, will readily justify the inference necessary to the creation of a constructive trust . . . it is at least extremely doubtful *whether anything less will do*' (emphasis added).

In 1995, in *Midland Bank* v. *Cooke*, the Court of Appeal took a slightly broader approach in relation to quantification at least. Even though Mrs Cooke's direct contribution equated to just under 7 per cent, the Court of Appeal decided that the whole 'course of dealing' between the parties can be analysed and as such, using equitable principles, they found an implied common intention through her conduct (substantial financial contribution to bills, an earlier mortgage and evidence of sharing everything equally) that Mrs Cooke was entitled to a 50 per cent share in the property. However, it was not until 2004 that the *Rosset* 'narrow view' began to change more dramatically – especially in terms of quantification rather than acquisition of the equitable interest.

Recent developments – *Stack* v. *Dowden* [2007] to *Jones* v. *Kernott* [2011]

Generally speaking, much of the early case law was based on acquisition arguments as there was only one name on the register as legal owner – this was true in *Pettitt*, *Gissing* and *Rosset*. In *Oxley* v. *Hiscock* [2004] Mrs Oxley and Mr Hiscock bought a property together using just over 70 per cent of Hiscock's money and 30 per cent from Oxley. The legal title was in the sole name of Mr Hiscock. Both parties contributed to the maintenance and improvement of the property. When the relationship broke down, the Court of Appeal was asked to determine their equitable shares – hence the real question here was one of quantification. Chadwick LJ decided that it was equitable, where there is no evidence of actual discussion, to have 'regard to the whole course of dealing between them in relation to the property' and this includes 'the arrangements they make from time to time in order to meet the outgoings'. The result was a 60/40 split in favour of Mr Hiscock. He argued that a resulting trust mathematical approach should be avoided where possible in such cases as this. This seemed to pave the way for the 'holistic approach' that was about to be taken by Baroness Hale in *Stack* v. *Dowden* – a case where this time *both parties* were on the register as legal owners.

⊕ CORNERSTONE

The Case of *Stack* v. *Dowden*

The facts of the case are as follows:

Mr Stack and Ms Dowden began a relationship in 1975 and lived together as man and wife raising four children. They bought a property together, in joint names, with 65 per cent of the purchase price being paid from Dowden's building society account and with proceeds from the sale of a previous house owned solely by Dowden. The remaining 35 per cent came from a joint mortgage and two endowment policies – one of which was in Dowden's sole name. Over the years the parties kept separate bank accounts and saved and invested separately. The mortgage was eventually paid off with Dowden contributing around 60 per cent of the lump sum payments. On the breakdown of the relationship, Mr Stack argued that where there was no evidence of express discussion between the parties as to their equitable share, then 'equity follows the law' where there is a legal joint tenancy (see Chapter 6) and the share should be 50/50. The House of Lords imposed a constructive trust based on 'holisitic approach' and found in favour of Ms Dowden to the tune of 65/35.

The House of Lords did agree that the start point for quantification in a case where there are two or more legal owners is that 'equity follows the law' and the equitable interest should be shared equally. However, Lord Hoffmann suggested that a relationship such as the one in *Stack* is 'ambulatory', with the parties' intentions capable of changing and developing over time. Lord Walker 'respectfully doubted' the stringent approach taken in *Rosset*, stating that the 'law has moved on, and your Lordships should move it a little more in the same direction'. Lord Walker, along with Baroness Hale, was also keen to point out that the Law Commission was, in 2007, 'soon to come forward with proposals' for legislation in relation to the financial regulation of the breakdown of unmarried couples' relationships. This did come to fruition in the Law Commission Report *Cohabitation: The Financial Consequences of Relationship Breakdown* (No. 307, 31 July 2007) (see Further Reading below) where the Law Commission proposed a scheme for 'property adjustment' for unmarried partners. Recently, David Cameron's Alliance government announced that there were no plans to legislate. This has been heavily criticised, with the head of family law at the law firm Mishcon de Reya, Sandra Davis, commenting that 'the continued failure of Parliament to introduce legislation which protects the property interests of the two million cohabiting couples in this country is a disgrace' (see Further Reading below).

As such, it was left to Baroness Hale to state in *Stack* that in 'exceptional circumstances', where there are joint legal owners and no express declaration, equity does not need to 'follow the law' at all, but can rather find a way to justify awarding an 'equitable share' that falls either side of the 50/50 'default line'. Baroness Hale, at what is now referred to simply as 'paragraph 69', goes on to list the factors which may be taken into account:

CORNERSTONE

Stack v. *Dowden*, paragraph 69

69. In law, 'context is everything' and the domestic context is very different from the commercial world. Each case will turn on its own facts. Many more factors than financial contributions may be relevant to divining the parties' true intentions. These include: any advice or discussions at the time of the transfer which cast light upon their intentions then; the reasons why the home was acquired in their joint names; the reasons why (if it be the case) the survivor was authorised to give a receipt for the capital moneys; the purpose for which the home was acquired; the nature of the parties' relationship; whether they had children for whom they both had responsibility to provide a home; how the purchase was financed, both initially and subsequently; how the parties arranged their finances, whether separately or together or a bit of both; how they discharged the outgoings on the property and their other household expenses. When a couple are joint owners of the home and jointly liable for the mortgage, the inferences to be drawn from who pays for what may be very different from the inferences to be drawn when only one is owner of the home. The arithmetical calculation of how much was paid by each is also likely to be less important. It will be easier to draw the inference that they intended that each should contribute as much to the household as they reasonably could and that they would share the eventual benefit or burden equally. The parties' individual characters and personalities may also be a factor in deciding where their true intentions lay. In the cohabitation context, mercenary considerations may be more to the fore than they would be in marriage, but it should not be assumed that they always take pride of place over natural love and affection. At the end of the day, having taken all this into account, cases in which the joint legal owners are to be taken to have intended that their beneficial interests should be different from their legal interests will be very unusual.

Baroness Hale also states, at paragraph 70, that the list is 'not exhaustive'. She also stated that due to this 'holistic approach' there is no longer a place for a resulting trust application in marital or relationship situations. It should be noted that Lord Neuberger dissented vociferously, first disputing that the courts should be asked to 'impute' common intention, especially from a 'course of dealing'. He also disputed that the role of the resulting trust is consigned to history, and successfully proved in a later Court of Appeal case that there is still a place for the resulting trust, albeit in an 'investment' purchase by a couple rather than as a family home (*Laskar* v. *Laskar* [2008]). However, it seems that the 'holistic approach' hit a judicial nerve, as the '*Stack* approach' was followed in the Privy Council case of *Abbott* v. *Abbott* [2007] (also presided over by Baroness Hale) and in the 2008 Court of Appeal case of *Fowler* v. *Barron.* 'Exceptional facts' were also found in *Ritchie* v. *Ritchie* [2007] but not so in *Segal* v. *Pasram* [2007] where a 50/50 split was ordered. It is perhaps not surprising that Professor Dixon refers to the real legacy of *Stack* as being uncertainty – a case is 'exceptional' he states '. . . or not, as the judge chooses' (see Further Reading below).

The question of quantification where there are two legal owners arose again in what is now a leading case on the subject – *Jones* v. *Kernott* [2011] (see Further Reading below).

....**APPLICATION**

Jones v. *Kernott* [2011]

Leonard Kernott and Patricia Jones separated in 1993 after living together in their property in Thundersley, Essex, for eight years. The Supreme Court was asked whether the assets should be shared 50/50 or predominantly allocated to Ms Jones, who paid all of the mortgage for the past 13 years. Kernott moved out after the break-up, leaving Jones to pay the mortgage, maintain the house and raise the couple's two children. The court was told Kernott waited until his children were grown before making a claim on his old home in 2006. In 2008, a county court judge sitting in Southend ruled that Jones should get 90 per cent of the value of the house and her former partner 10 per cent. That decision was upheld by the High Court in London in 2009. In 2010 the Court of Appeal overturned the lower courts' rulings, deciding that Kernott was entitled to half the value of the house because the couple owned equal shares when they separated and neither had since done anything to change the situation.

The case then went on appeal to the Supreme Court in late 2011.

The judgment in the lower courts found in favour of Ms Jones 90 per cent to Mr Jones 10 per cent, following the 'exceptional circumstances' ratio set down in *Stack*. They found that this was a clear exception to the rule that 'equity follows the law' and found it relatively straightforward to depart from the presumption of 50/50 – even though Ms Jones gave evidence that she conceded that if the property had been sold when the relationship first broke down, Mr Kernott would, in her view, have been entitled to 50 per cent. The question for the Court of Appeal, therefore, was whether the 'common intention' had shifted away from 50/50 as a result of him leaving the marital home and not contributing to the mortgage or upkeep from 1993 when the relationship ended to 2008 at the start of the litigation. Wall LJ began the judgment in the Court of Appeal with a warning: 'This is a cautionary tale, which all unmarried couples who are contemplating the purchase of residential property as their home . . . should study.'

Wall LJ went on to find that the conduct of Mr Kernott did not amount to justification of a movement away from the common intention at the breakdown of the relationship that the equitable interests were equal. The result was that Wall LJ decided that a 50/50 split was fair, as there seemed to be a clear common intention that 'equity should follow the law'. He stated that 'the critical question is whether or not I can properly infer from the parties' conduct since separation a joint intention that, over time, the 50–50 split would be varied . . . Presumably, if the beneficial interests are "ambulatory" and the ambulation continues in the same direction, the appellant's interest in the property will at some point be extinguished.'

Take note

The judgment is well worth reading in full as, apart from giving a clear insight into the case itself, it also gives a very detailed overview of the entire development of the constructive trust (see Further Reading below).

However, the case went on final appeal to the Supreme Court in May 2011 with the eagerly awaited judgment given in November 2011. The leading judges were Lord Walker and, of course, Baroness Hale. It perhaps goes without saying that the Court of Appeal judgment was reversed and the 90/10 split reinstated.

It seems that unless and until the Law Commission's recommendations are taken up by Parliament, the *implied common intention constructive trust* will continue to be, as Lord Neuberger put it in *Stack*, 'difficult, subjective and uncertain'. It is perhaps true to suggest, as Baroness Hale has done in *Stack*, that the law should move on to respond to 'changing social and economic conditions . . . to ascertain the parties' shared intentions, actual, inferred or imputed'. However Neuberger's dissent suggests that 'fairness is not the appropriate yardstick' when dealing with property transactions, and to analyse 'the whole course of dealing . . . in relation to property is too imprecise'. It is also unclear as to whether the nature of common intention is indeed 'ambulatory'. In the recent Court of Appeal case of *Pankhania* v. *Chandegra* [2012], Mummery LJ in the Court of Appeal ruled that where there is an express declaration of trust between the parties, then the courts should only go behind the express declaration where there are 'valid legal reasons' to do so.

It still remains unclear, however, as to what these *valid legal reasons* might be, and when they may be applied. Perhaps, as Dixon suggests, these difficulties are exactly what '*Lord Bridge sought to avoid*' in **Rosset**. Perhaps we are torn between a judicial desire to 'move the law on' and the need for conveyancing clarity. As the Law Lords and many other key players in the realm of family law have suggested, maybe the only real answer for unmarried couples will be found in future legislation.

REFLECTION

KEY POINTS

- When two or more people own a property together, there is always a trust of land in existence. The legal owners with their names on the title are the trustees and may be holding on trust just for each other as beneficiaries, or for beneficiaries outside the legal title.
- This trust of land can be express, or implied through a resulting or constructive trust.
- The express trust can be written in the conveyance or expressly declared by deed after purchase. It can also be expressly stated on the Land Registry Form JO.
- If it is not express, then a trust can be implied: this can be by way of a resulting or a constructive trust. This falls outside section 53(1)(b) of the LPA 1925, and as such there is no need for formalities (s. 53(2)).
- A resulting trust was traditionally used in all co-ownership situations where there was a direct contribution to the purchase price at the time of purchase.
- Traditionally, a constructive trust could be imposed by the court when there were contributions to purchase price or mortgage payments – but the contributions needed to be substantial (*Pettitt*; *Gissing*; *Rosset*). However, these could be made at any time, including after purchase.
- The case of *Stack* v. *Dowden*, especially in relation to joint legal owners ascertaining the quantification of their equitable interest, set down that almost any contribution may allow the imposition of a constructive trust – using the 'holisitic approach' given by Baroness Hale. The 'common intention' of the parties can be implied, inferred or imputed from their 'holistic' conduct and may even be 'ambulatory' (changing over time). There was strong dissent by Neuberger L who disagreed that the courts can 'impute' and that there is no place for a resulting trust in a 'relationship purchase' (*Laskar*).
- *Stack* was effectively followed in *Abbott* and *Fowler* and importantly in *Jones* v. *Kernott* [2011].
- In the Court of Appeal in *Pankhania* a warning was given that the court should only look behind an express declaration to imply or infer that common intention has changed – if the intention was that 'equity follows the law' and it was 50/50 then it should generally remain so over the passing years.
- The Law Commission Report No. 307 (from July 2007) proposes a statutory framework for unmarried partners on the break-up of property. Perhaps only legislation will create the certainty that is lacking in the current common law.

CORE CASES AND STATUTES

Case	About	Importance
Pettitt v. *Pettitt* [1970] AC 777	Husband carries out minor improvements.	No constructive trust – there needs to be substantial contribution to purchase price or mortgage payments.
Gissing v. *Gissing* [1971] AC 886	Wife pays for furnishings and minor decorations.	As above.
Eves v. *Eves* [1975] 1 WLR 1338	Girlfriend 'wields a 14lb sledgehammer'.	A 'new model' constructive trust – according to Lord Denning.
Lloyds Bank v. *Rosset* [1991] 1 AC 107	Wife oversees building work.	No constructive trust – only doing what is 'natural for any wife' – Lord Bridge.
Oxley v. *Hiscock* [2005] Fam 211	Mrs Oxley contributed 30% – Hiscock 70%.	Chadwick LJ awarded 60/40 in favour of Hiscock – broader application of 'contributions' took into account the 'whole course of dealing'.
Stack v. *Dowden* [2007] 2 AC 432	Joint legal owners – equity should follow the law, 50/50 argued.	Baroness Hale – the law has moved on. Based on a holistic analysis, all and any contributions count towards the quantification of a constructive trust: 65/35 to Ms Dowden.
Abbott v. *Abbott* [2007] UKPC 53	Privy Council case on quantification.	Follows *Stack*.
Laskar v. *Laskar* [2008] 1 WLR 2695	Neuberger's dissent from *Stack* put to effect.	There is still a place for the resulting trust – in relationship investment purchases, however.
Jones v. *Kernott* [2011] UKSC 53	50/50 at the time of the relationship breakdown.	The reasons for moving behind an agreement must be 'exceptional' – but, following *Stack*, 90/10 to Ms Jones.
Pankhania v. *Chandegra* [2012] EWCA Civ 1438	50/50 at the start – can the court look behind an express declaration?	No – not unless there are 'valid legal reasons'.

Statute	About	Importance
LPA 1925, s. 53(1)(b)	Declarations of a trust of land.	Must be evidenced in writing.
LPA 1925, s. 53(2)	Constructive and resulting trusts.	No need for formalities.
TOLATA 1996, s. 1	This defines the relationship between co-owners.	Any co-owned land will be held as a 'trust of land', no longer a 'trust for sale'.

FURTHER READING

Bowcott, O. 'Supreme court rules on property rights for unmarried couples', *The Guardian*, Wednesday 9 November 2011 http://www.guardian.co.uk/law/2011/nov/09/court-rules-property-rights-unmarried
This gives an excellent overview of the judgment in *Jones* v. *Kernott* – explains why the Supreme Court awarded 90 per cent to Ms Jones.

Jones v. *Kernott* [2011] UKSC 53
http://www.supremecourt.gov.uk/docs/uksc_2010_0130_judgment.pdf
The entire judgment is a valuable read from beginning to end – a superb explanation of the development of the law in this area.

Land Registry 'Public Guide 18: Joint property ownership'

http://www.landregistry.gov.uk/public/guides/public-guide-18
This useful practice guide sets down the rules and relevant practice forms available for declaring a trust of land.

Law Commission Report *Cohabitation: The Financial Consequences of Relationship Breakdown* (No 307, 31 July 2007)
www.parliament.uk/briefing-papers/sn03372.pdf

MacDonald, S. 'Form JO – A Potentially Important Development'
http://familyproperty.org.uk/form-jo-a-potentially-important-development/
This gives an excellent overview of the new JO form available for joint owners – written by a family law barrister from private practice in the Midlands.

CHAPTER 6
Co-ownership (Part 2)

BLUEPRINT

Co-ownership (Part 2)

LEGISLATION

- Law of Property Act 1925
- Trusts of Land and Appointment of Trustees Act 1996

CONTEXT

- All property bought by more than 1 person is subject to a trust.
- All trusts have trustees and beneficiaries.
- Not all beneficiaries are also trustees – the context of the '5th' owner.

CONCEPTS

- Legal and equitable ownership
- Joint tenancy and tenancy in common
- Survivorship
- Severance
- The workings of TOLATA, ss.14 and 15

- Should co-ownership always be a joint tenancy – tenancy in common is always possible through severance after all?
- Is it correct that the last surviving joint tenant takes the property?
- Should beneficiaries have more power?

CASES

- *AG Securities* v. *Vaughan* [1990]
- *Goodman* v. *Gallant* [1986]
- *Williams* v. *Hensman* [1861]
- *Burgess* v. *Rawnsley* [1975]
- *Kinch* v. *Bullard* [1999]
- *First National* v. *Achampong* [2003]
- Re Citro [1991]

REFORM

- Does TOLATA go far enough – banks will nearly always win over the 'consequences of debt'.

SPECIAL CHARACTERISTICS

- The 'real' difference between joint tenancy and tenancy in common
- The doctrine of survivorship
- Severance by common law and by LPA, s. 36(2)

CRITICAL ISSUES

Setting the scene

When one person owns a property, generally that person owns the legal title of that property. In relation to land law, the only other people that are 'relevant' are any others who may have a claim on or over that property – such as adjacent landowners with possible easements or covenants or lenders who may have provided the money by way of a mortgage. However, what if Jim and Zoe buy a property together? If there is concurrent ownership by two or more people then land law refers to them as co-owners. Rather confusingly, they are referred to as 'tenants' – not because they have a lease, but because the term 'tenant' is derived from the 14th-century word 'tenaunt', which was in itself derived from the verb 'tenere' – 'to hold' (Chapter 5).

It is also true to say that whenever there is co-ownership, there is a *trust of land* created – either expressly stated in the conveyance or on Land Registry Forms (the Form JO); or implied by way of a resulting or constructive trust (see Chapter 5). Co-ownership is of course usually the norm when two people purchase property within a relationship (spouses; partners; civil partners) but it can also be by way of a business relationship in a commercial sense. In either situation, co-ownership will create this trust of land (no longer referred to as a *'trust for sale'* since the Trusts of Land and Appointment of Trustees Act 1996 (TOLATA 1996)). As such there will be a trustee–beneficiary relationship in existence, and although this has no real meaning whilst the co-owners live 'happily-ever-after', the existence of their legal (trustee) and equitable (beneficiary) interests become vital if the property is repossessed, sold or there is a dispute over ownership (see Chapter 5). This chapter will seek to explain the different types of co-ownership available – that of the **joint tenancy** and the *tenancy in common* – and illustrate the ramifications of such types of co-ownership. It will also explain the rules of severance and how TOLATA 1996 plays a vital role in the event of a dispute.

JOINT TENANCY AND TENANCY IN COMMON

CORNERSTONE

Legal and equitable ownership

It is absolutely vital to understand from the outset that there is a difference between legal and equitable ownership. The 'paper owner' (legal owner and as such also the trustee) is the person whose name appears in the proprietorship section of the register – but this is really no more than the 'nominal' title. As Professor Martin Dixon points out (see Further Reading), it is the equitable interest that is the 'real value' in the property. The equitable interest, by way of the express or implied trust that is in existence, is the extent of the right the beneficiary has to enjoy and/or use the land. So, if Jim and Zoe buy a property together, and both names appear on the title, then they are said to be joint legal owners (or joint tenants at law) but are also holding the property on trust for each other as beneficiaries – and as such their equitable interest will be either as joint tenants or tenants in common. It should be noted that the legal title can only be held as *joint tenants* under section 1(6) of the LPA 1925 but as this legal co-ownership is only really nominal, it is the equitable interest that is the key – and that can be held as joint tenants or tenants in common. Once again, whilst the co-owners are in a state of harmony, and are still alive, the distinction is of minimal importance. However, on separation, sale, bankruptcy, repossession or death, the distinction becomes vitally important as the status of a joint tenancy or a tenancy in common will lead to a very different outcome in relation to each person's equitable interest. It should also be noted that there can be an infinite number of equitable owners (in theory), but a maximum of four legal co-owners, and where the property is purchased by more than four people together, the first four will be 'named' as the legal owners under section 34(2) of the Trustee Act 1925. It is also worth remembering that if there is only one legal owner, the beneficiaries' interests cannot be overreached (see Chapter 4).

It is therefore necessary to establish at the outset whether the co-owners are joint tenants in equity or tenants in common. In practice, a conveyancer will usually (if not always) ask the question to the prospective co-owners as to whether they wish to hold as joint tenants or tenants in common and this will be recorded on the conveyance document. A conveyancer or solicitor should be able to explain the consequences of each type of co-ownership, the key consequence being the operation of the rule of '*ius accrescendi*' or *survivorship* and this will be explained below. Essentially though, this means that if the co-owners are joint tenants in equity, they cannot leave their interest in a will – on death, the interest will automatically vest in the remaining joint tenant. If the co-owners are tenants in common, then survivorship rules do not operate and the parties are free to leave their interest in a will to whomever they choose. This will be explained in full below.

APPLICATION

Jim, Zoe, Ava, Jake and Elsa buy a property together. Their conveyancer fills in the relevant conveyance document and all but Elsa are named as the legal owners. The status of the co-ownership relationship is that all but Elsa are joint tenants at law (LPA 1925, s. 1(6)) and are therefore trustees holding for each other as beneficiaries and also holding as trustees for Elsa who only has a beneficial interest. All five are beneficial co-owners but may hold their equitable interests as joint tenants or tenants in common – there are, of course, rules which need to be applied to establish their equitable status – and these will now be explained (see Figure 6.1).

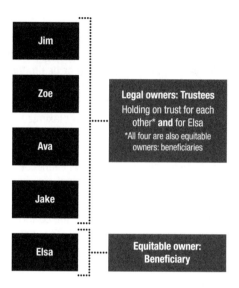

Figure 6.1 Legal and equitable co-ownership

Joint tenancy – the four unities

The defining feature of a joint tenancy is that the joint tenants own the entire property 'as one', with no distinct shares either equal or unequal. As stated by William Blackstone in his *Commentaries on the Laws of England* as far back as 1765, a joint tenancy is an estate which the law recognises as a 'thorough and intimate union of interest and possession' (see Further Reading below). This means that each joint tenant is entitled to the whole of the property. However, for a joint tenancy to exist, as Blackstone put it, the joint tenancy is 'derived from its unity, which is fourfold'. This is commonly known as the 'four unities', namely unity of *possession, interest, time* and *title* (see Figure 6.2). If a joint tenancy is to be established, these four unities must be present from the outset of the tenancy, as set down in the case of *AG Securities* v. *Vaughan* [1990]:

1. *Possession:* Essentially this means that the co-owners are entitled to possess the entire property. If boundaries or restrictions exist there cannot be a joint tenancy in operation. It is an 'undivided possession' as Blackstone stated.

2. *Interest:* This means that the co-owners have the same interest in the land. For example, if one of the joint tenants has a lease of 10 years, and the other has a lease of eight, it cannot be a joint tenancy. It also stands to reason that no single co-owner can sell the property unilaterally, as they do not own it unilaterally.

3. *Time:* This simply means that the interests of the co-owners vested at the same time – this will of course generally be at the time of the transfer of the property to the joint tenants.

4. *Title:* As above, the co-owners' title must be derived from the same conveyance or transfer of the land.

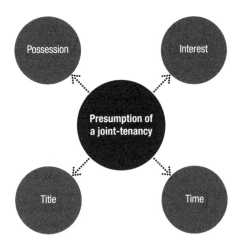

Figure 6.2 The four unities

The effect of the four unities being present is that it creates a *presumption* of a joint tenancy. It is important to understand that the existence of the four unities is only the start point. If there is a clear intention that the parties intended to hold the property in 'shares' – even equal shares – the tenants will be holding their equitable title as 'tenants in common' and not as joint tenants. As explained above, there can be no divisible share; all must own everything.

As such, if there are '*words of severance*' within the conveyance (in other words, any suggestion that the parties hold in shares), the equitable interest will be a tenancy in common regardless of the presence of the four unities. The words 'share and share alike' appeared in *Heathe* v. *Heathe* (1740); 'between' appeared in *Lashbrook* v. *Cock* (1816); and 'in equal shares' appeared in *Martin* v. *Martin* [1987]. These cases were held to be tenancies in common and not joint tenancies. Of course, if there are express words in the conveyance itself to suggest a joint tenancy, and the four unities are present, then generally, according to *Goodman* v. *Gallant* [1986], that will be conclusive. In *Roy* v. *Roy* [1996] the conveyance stated that the property was vested in the co-owners 'as Joint Tenants at law and in equity'. It is also a presumption, that where the four unities exist and there are no words of severance, then *equity follows the law*, and a joint tenancy at law will also be a joint tenancy in equity.

> **Take note**
>
> Remember that co-owners cannot hold the legal title as tenants in common – as the common law does not recognise the latter relationship (LPA 1925, s. 1(6)). It is only the equitable title that can be 'chosen' to be a joint tenancy or a tenancy in common.

INTERSECTION

A full discussion of the presumption of 'equity following the law' can be seen in the key case of *Stack* v. *Dowden* [2007], as discussed earlier in Chapter 5.

Tenancy in common – the presumptions

The only 'necessary' unity for a tenancy in common to exist is that of the unity of possession. Each tenant holds a notional, if yet undivided share of the property. As stated above, this can be an equal or unequal share, but the word 'share' should be used here, rather than the word 'interest' which is the more apposite description in a joint tenancy. All tenants in common must still have the right to entitlement of the property – the difference in a tenancy in common is that they hold in this notional fractional share. If there are no 'words of severance' in a conveyance to co-owners, and no express words suggesting a tenancy in common (or a joint tenancy), then equity allows certain presumptions to operate. It is true to say that common law has always favoured the joint tenancy, but in *McDowell* v. *Hirschfield Lipson & Romney* [1992] Stockdale J reminded the court of 'equity's dislike of the joint tenancy and its marked preference for the tenancy in common' for reasons of fairness. The presumptions (albeit rebuttable with appropriate and compelling evidence) operate as follows:

> **Take note**
>
> These presumptions, especially the latter in relation to business partners, clearly demonstrate that the fundamental operational difference between a joint tenancy and a tenancy in common is the application of the doctrine of survivorship.

1. Unequal purchase money contributions: *Bull* v. *Bull* [1955].
2. Joint mortgages: a presumption that each co-owner has an as yet undivided share.
3. Commercial assets in a partnership: due to the rule of survivorship (see below) this is presumed to be a tenancy in common – *Lake* v. *Craddock* (1732).
4. Business tenants: again, mainly due to the presumption that business associates will not want the survivorship rules to apply – *Malayan Credit Ltd* v. *Jack Chia* [1986].

Survivorship

The operation of the rule of survivorship only applies where there is a joint tenancy and *not* a tenancy in common. If a joint tenant dies, then the equitable interest belonging to the deceased joint tenant simply passes to the remaining joint tenants automatically. It was stated above that a joint tenant cannot therefore leave his interest in a will (*Gould* v. *Kemp* (1834)), and neither can it pass to their personal representatives or next of kin if the joint tenant dies intestate. Arguably, this makes conveyancing more straightforward, as there is no need for formal transfer as the property vests automatically in the remaining joint tenants. There is also a rather useful protective element, as if the deceased has creditors, then generally the creditors have no claim on the property. However, there is of course a risk taken by joint tenants, as the 'last man standing', or in legal terms the sole surviving joint tenant, takes the property absolutely! Stockdale J, in the *Romney* case above, likened the risk of survivorship in a joint tenancy to 'the well known gamble of double or quits' pointing out that each joint tenant 'ran the risk of dying first'!

'The Plane Crash Rule?'

Perhaps even more strangely, there is a quaint English law doctrine known as the *commorientes* rule, which states that if joint tenants die simultaneously and the order in which they died cannot therefore be ascertained, the general rule is that the property vests automatically in the estate of the *youngest* of the joint tenants, as 'the deaths are presumed to have occurred in order of age so that the younger is presumed to have survived the elder' (LPA 1925, s. 184).

As such, again as illustrated by Stockdale J, this 'risk' of survivorship has been cited as one of the reasons as to why equity with its inherent belief in fairness, prefers the tenancy in common. It is also one of the reasons why there are rules of *severance* which allow an equitable joint tenancy interest to be *severed* and, as if by magic, 'turned into' a tenancy in common share (see Figure 6.3).

SEVERANCE – COMMON LAW AND STATUTORY METHODS

CORNERSTONE

Severance of the equitable joint tenancy

It is absolutely vital to understand that the legal co-ownership status cannot be severed. Remember that this is really the nominal ownership not the 'real value' of the co-owners' estate. As such, when 'acts of severance' occur, the legal estate remains untouched. There can be no tenancy in common of the legal estate. This can be found at section 36(2) of the LPA 1925: 'No severance of a joint tenancy of a legal estate, so as to create a tenancy in common in land, shall be permissible . . . but this does not affect the right of a joint tenant to . . . sever a joint tenancy in an equitable interest.'

It is also crucial to understand that when the equitable interest is severed by one joint tenant unilaterally, it becomes a tenancy in common interest; the remaining joint tenants maintain their joint tenancy status, as the four unities have not been displaced. Think of it as removing a slice of a pie, that one slice may still be on the plate, but it is now distinct from the rest of the pie that is still intact. All acts of severance create an immediate tenancy in common interest due to the destruction of at least one of the four unities.

Before

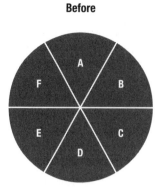

After

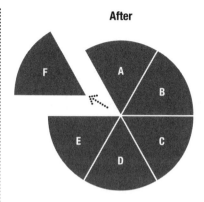

- **A, B, C and D** are legal joint tenants
- **A – D** hold on trust for themselves and **E and F**
- All six hold as joint tenants in equity (four unites and no contrary presumptions)

- **F** severs by common law methods in *Williams* v. *Hensman* or by LPA 1925, s. 36(2)
- **F's** share is now a 1/6 tenancy in common share
- **A – E** still have a 5/6 joint tenancy interest in the property

Figure 6.3 Before and after an act of severance

APPLICATION

Andrew, Bharda, Claire, Doda and Elsbeth all buy a property, each contributing 20 per cent. The first four, (A–D), hold the property as joint tenants at law on trust for each other and for Elsbeth, who has just a beneficial interest. All five, due to the four unities being present and a lack of any presumptions to the contrary, hold as joint tenants in equity. Elsbeth decides that she wishes to sell her equitable interest (20 per cent for the sake of simplicity) to Frederica. If the relevant method of severance (see below) has been used then Elsbeth drops out of the picture altogether. As soon as the severance occurs, Elsbeth's interest becomes a tenancy in common interest, and this tenancy in common interest is purchased by Frederica. Due to the fact that she now has a 20 per cent interest in the property along with the other four remaining co-owners, there is still co-ownership between the 'new' five co-owners. However, Frederica's status is as a tenant in common (due to the lack of four unities – time and title especially) whilst A–D still hold as joint tenants with their 20 per cent interests untouched. That of course means that A–D still operate under the survivorship doctrine, whereas Frederica is free to leave her 'share' in a will. It also means that Frederica will not benefit from automatic transfer of A–D's interests if any of them die.

If, however, going back to the original position, A–E all decide to sever 'mutually' (again, following one of the severance methods illustrated below), then all five will have tenancy in common interests – the joint tenancy between all five will be over.

As such, it is necessary to be able to identify the various methods of severance. There are three 'common law' methods (set down in the case of *Williams* v. *Hensman* (1861)) and one statutory method set down at section 36(2) of the LPA 1925.

Williams v. *Hensman* (1861) – the common law methods

(i) An act of any person interested operating upon his own share

This means that one of the joint tenants 'alienates' or transfers his share to another – either someone outside the existing co-owners or one or more of the original joint tenants. This will be seen as entering into a specifically enforceable contract to transfer the equitable interest (see *Walsh* v. *Lonsdale* in Chapter 2).

It is also true that partial alienation, such as taking an equitable mortgage of your interest, will also fall under this method of severance, as will being adjudicated bankrupt (as this has the effect of vesting your assets in the 'trustee in bankruptcy'). In *Re Dennis (a bankrupt)* [1995] the Court of Appeal held that bankruptcy severed the joint tenancy between husband and wife, and as such the wife could now leave her share in her will. The husband's creditors were free to claim against his now divided share.

> ### Take note
> Using this first method does not need the agreement of the other joint tenants – it is a unilateral act, but once complete it is final and irrevocable. Hence the serving of a summons at the commencement of litigation on fellow joint tenants, due to its finality and irrevocability, is another example of an act of severance using this first method (*Re Draper's Conveyance* [1967]).

(ii) Mutual agreement

By its very definition, this method requires *all* of the joint tenants to agree to sever the entire joint tenancy, turning it into a tenancy in common for all concerned. Of course, the intention of a common intention to sever must be communicated to all joint tenants and in *Burgess* v. *Rawnsley* [1975] Sir John Pennycuick stated that it is the 'indication of a common intention to sever' that allows severance through mutual agreement; the outcome of any evidenced negotiation is largely irrelevant. This evidence may be implied rather than in a written agreement, or in a simple draft agreement as in *Hunter* v. *Babbage* [1994].

(iii) Mutual conduct

Although on the face of it mutual conduct is not so different from mutual agreement, it is seen by the common law as a distinct method. This involves a 'course of dealing' between the co-owners – again, *all* of the co-owners. In *Burgess* Lord Denning distinguished the two methods by stating that a 'course of dealing' need not amount to an agreement as such; it is sufficient that such a course of dealing which demonstrates an intention to hold the property in shares is an act of severance. In *Hunter* v. *Babbage* John McDonnell QC disputes any real difference between the two methods, but states that the course of dealing must 'intimate that the interests of all were mutually treated as constituting a tenancy in common'.

APPLICATION

It would seem like the conduct of writing mutual wills leaving the interest to each other may act as severance by mutual conduct, even though technically 'shares' cannot be left in a will when co-owners are joint tenants. It would seem that the act of sitting down and writing the wills is the act of severance, as it demonstrates a common intention to sever (*Re Wilford's Estate* (1879)).

(iv) Murder

It goes without saying (hopefully!) that if one joint tenant murders the other then this does not amount to an act of severance and neither do the rules of survivorship apply (*Cleaver* v. *Mutual Reserve Fund*

Life Association [1892]). There is no authority in a case of manslaughter, however, but section 2(2) of the Forfeiture Act 1982 suggests that the court has discretion in situations such as a suicide pact (*Dunbar* v. *Plant* [1998]).

The statutory method – LPA 1925, section 36(2)

This is the most common and most straightforward way in which to sever a joint tenancy. In conveyancing terms, there is a Land Registry form known as the *Form SEV*: if it, or even a simple letter, is served on all remaining joint tenants, severance will occur. The notice to sever must therefore be in writing, can be a unilateral act and must be served on all remaining joint tenants. It must, however, demonstrate an immediate intention to sever, not a future desire. Wills, therefore, are excluded from the operation of section 36(2). Lawson LJ in *Harris* v. *Goddard* stated that under section 36(2) immediacy is vital. He stated that a 'notice in writing which expresses a desire to bring about the wanted result at some time in the future is not, in my judgment, a notice in writing within section 36(2)'.

It is also true to say that section 36(2) operates in conjunction with sections 196(4) and 196(3) of the LPA 1925, which set down the rules of service for such a notice and illustrate when that notice is deemed to be effective:

CORNERSTONE

LPA 1925, section 196(4)

Any notice . . . shall be sufficiently served, if it is sent by post in a registered letter . . . if that letter is not returned through the post-office undelivered; and that service shall be deemed to be made at the time at which the registered letter would in the ordinary course be delivered.

LPA 1925, section 196(3)

Note also that if the notice is sent by *ordinary post* then section 196(3) applies. This sets down that the notice is deemed to have been served if it is left at the last known address, deemed to be effective in line with normal postage times. As such, posting a notice with a first class stamp would be deemed to be served the next working morning. It is an irrebuttable presumption and the addressee cannot argue that it was never received. Neither does it need to be read by the addressee to be deemed as served.

There are two key cases which illustrate this method and how it operates. In *Re 88 Berkeley Road NW9* [1971], the two co-owners were joint tenants at law and in equity. A notice of severance was sent by one of the joint tenants to the other, and, even though the latter did not receive the notice, as it had been signed for by the severing tenant, it was deemed to have been served.

....**APPLICATION**

The 'tragic case' of *Kinch* v. *Bullard* [1999]

As Neuberger J (as he was then) suggested, this was indeed a 'tragic case' but one which illustrates the operation of section 36(2) perfectly. A man and his wife were living as joint tenants at law and in equity, but they were en route to a divorce. The wife was also sadly dying from a terminal illness and believed therefore that she would die before her husband. Her concern was that as joint tenants the survivorship rule would apply and, on her death, he would automatically take the entire property. She would be unable to leave any 'share' in a will. So, she decided that she would go to see her solicitor and send a notice of severance to her husband in order to convert her interest into a tenancy in common which she could then leave to family members. The solicitor duly posted a first-class stamped letter to the matrimonial home where they were both still living. However, just as the letter arrived on the Saturday morning, that very weekend the husband, before being able to read the notice, suffered a major heart attack and was taken to hospital. As Neuberger pointedly suggested, any good wife would rush to her husband's bedside, but the wife rushed home instead to intercept and destroy the letter of severance because she now, rightly, believed that the husband would die first, and if severance had not taken place she would take the property entirely!

The husband did in fact die 10 days later. The wife, having destroyed the letter, lived for the next five months believing that the severance had been 'cancelled', at which point she also died from her illness. The dispute then arose between the two executors (hence Kinch and Bullard) as to whether there had been valid severance or not.

Neuberger J pointed to section 196(3) of the LPA 1925 (as this was ordinary post) and stated clearly that once such a notice is deemed to have been served – and under section 196(3) this meant that the notice was served as soon as it 'hit the mat' regardless of the husband not having read the notice – then it is irrevocable. Once the deed has been done, he said, 'it cannot be undone' unless the letter is perhaps intercepted by the sender before it arrives or the wife had informed her husband that, even though the notice had been sent, she had changed her mind. However, arguably, this 'revocation' would also have needed to take place before the arrival of the letter.

Once severance has occurred, other than it being possible that an express agreement which states the contrary may be valid, the tenants in common hold in equal shares, even though they may have originally contributed unequally to the purchase (*Goodman* v. *Gallant* [1986]).

THE APPLICATION OF THE TRUSTS OF LAND AND APPOINTMENT OF TRUSTEES ACT 1996

Prior to the coming into force of the Trusts of Land and Appointment of Trustees Act 1996 (TOLATA 1996) on 1 January 1997, any land held under co-ownership was said to be held as a 'trust for sale' – the implication being that the co-owners were holding the property on trust with a duty to sell that property to realise the cash value, and, once sold, the proceeds of that sale would also be held on trust for the co-owners. However, as Lord Denning remarked in *Williams* v. *Williams* [1977], the idea of the 'trust for sale' was in effect a 'legal fiction' as he stated that 'nowadays . . . the house is bought as a home in which the family is to be brought up . . . not treated as property to be sold, nor as an investment to be realised for cash.'

Denning's view did not materialise as legislation until TOLATA 1996, where at section 1, the 'trust for sale' was replaced by a 'trust of land' defined as 'any property which consists of or includes land'. Any existing 'trusts for sale' were instantly 'converted' into 'trusts of land' (ss. 4 and 5) and the trust of land is imposed whether the trust was created expressly or impliedly. Hence the first point to make is that since TOLATA 1996 there is no longer a duty on any trustee/legal owner to sell the property.

The trustees, or joint tenants at law, have a number of key powers under TOLATA:

> **Take note**
>
> Selling to the beneficiaries confirms the old common law in Saunders v. Vautier (1841) (this can be found in the law of equity and trusts where, of course, there is an overlap with land law in this area).

1.   Sections 6 and 7: The trustees have the power of an 'absolute owner' – to sell, to lease, or to take a mortgage. They can also sell the land outright to beneficiaries of 'full age and capacity' where they are entitled to full ownership. The trustees can also partition the land under section 7 where the beneficiaries are 'of age and capacity' and are entitled to undivided shares in the land. The powers under sections 6 and 7 may be limited or expressly excluded, however, if the trust was created by a *disposition* (s. 8).

2.   Section 9: The trustees may also delegate their powers by 'power of attorney' to any beneficiary of 'age, capacity' and entitled to be in possession of the land.

3.   Section 11: This states that the trustees 'so far as practicable' consult the beneficiaries, and where 'consistent with general interest of the trust' give effect to those wishes. This does seem to suggest that TOLATA 1996, section 11 does protect the beneficiaries from an unwanted sale by the trustees, but really, this section is a duty merely to 'consult' – the threshold is set deliberately low to allow trustees to sell relatively freely and, of course, overreaching may always occur where the sale is by at least two trustees. (*City of London Building Society* v. *Flegg* [1988]). It is also true to state that consultation rights can also be expressly excluded (*Waller* v. *Waller* [1967]).

4.   Section 12: Allows entitled beneficiaries in possession of the land to occupy the land if the purposes of the trust include 'making the land available for occupation' or the land is already available, but not if the land is 'unavailable or unsuitable' for occupation. What is meant by 'unsuitable' is not clarified, and seems to be case-specific. Jonathan Parker LJ in *Chun* v. *Ho* [2003] stated that it must involve consideration of general situation and the 'personal characteristics, circumstances and requirements of the particular beneficiary'. The right to occupy can also be reasonably restricted or excluded where there are two or more beneficiaries with the right to occupy (see section 13).

5.   Section 13: This right to 'occupy' can be reasonably excluded or restricted or the trustees can impose conditions as to occupation. Also, at section 13(6) trustees also have the power to require a beneficiary in occupation to compensate other beneficiaries excluded or restricted under section 12. Under section 13(5) trustees can also impose conditions which compel payment of expenses by beneficiaries to cover the cost of repairs and improvements. This was previously dealt with by the common law in such cases as *Leigh* v. *Dickeson* (1884) and *Re Pavlou* [1993].

Disputes – sections 14 and 15

In any situation where there is a dispute between trustees and beneficiaries, then section 14 gives the power to 'any person who is a trustee or who has an interest in property subject to a trust of land [such as the beneficiaries; mortgagees; trustees in bankruptcy] to make an application to the court for an order under s14(2)'. The court can then make *any order* in relation to the powers of the trustee or make a declaration in relation to the beneficial interests. The factors which are considered by the court are listed at section 15 or, in the case of an application by a 'trustee in bankruptcy', the factors are listed at section 335A of the Insolvency Act 1986. The factors at section 15 are:

(a) the intentions of the person who created the trust;

(b) the purpose of the trust;

(c) the welfare of minors who occupy or might reasonably be expected to occupy;

(d) the interests of any secured creditors of any beneficiaries.

In *TSB* v. *Marshall* [1998], the first case which dealt with section 14, an order for possession and sale was granted as the section 15 factors were not satisfied – there was no evidence to suggest the purpose of the property was to provide a home for the *adult* children. In the key case of *Mortgage Corporation* v. *Shaire* [2001] Neuberger J referred explicitly to the development of the law under section 15 of TOLATA 1996. He stated that section 15 gives far more rights to beneficiaries than the previous 'primary purpose doctrine' under the now repealed section 30 of the LPA 1925. However, he also stated that section 15 allows the court to decide 'what weight to give to each factor' in a particular case. In *Shaire*, Neuberger left the parties to agree terms in a claim by the lender for possession. He made it clear, however, that if Mrs Shaire would not agree to favourable terms which would allow the lender to recover at least some of the debt (caused in no small part by Mrs Shaire's 'forging' partner) then he would order the sale.

> **Take note**
>
> It is normally not necessary for legal mortgagees (banks/ building societies) to apply under section 14 as there are already relevant statutory provisions under sections 101–105 of the LPA 1925. (See Mortgages – Chapter 10.) However, a lender may need to rely on section 14 if one of the co-owners has forged the signature of the other on the mortgage deed – only the forger's interest will then be bound by the mortgage charge (the forgery is in effect an act of severance). The lender may also need to apply section 14 if a mortgage is granted by a sole legal owner where a pre-existing beneficial interest is present and that person is in actual occupation (see Chapter 4).

It seems quite certain, especially from later cases, that in most situations, banks and lenders will be successful and will be allowed to realise their valuable commercial assets. In *Bank of Ireland* v. *Bell* [2001], another case where section 14 applied due to a forgery by one legal owner, despite the fact that the son of the marriage had great needs and the wife was suffering poor health, the Bank was successful. Peter Gibson LJ stated that, above all, 'powerful consideration is . . . whether the creditor is receiving proper recompense for being kept out of his money, repayment of which is over-due'. This was echoed in *First National Bank* v. *Achampong* [2003] where the Court of Appeal side-stepped the issue of a child with a mental disability and other occupying grandchildren in ordering a sale to prevent the lender 'waiting indefinitely for payment'. In *Pritchard Englefield* v. *Steinberg* [2004], Mrs Steinberg was granted two months' delay to find a buyer, even though this was highly improbable due to the buyer needing to purchase subject to Mrs Steinberg's right to occupy rent-free for life! Peter Smith J did allow this token two-month reprieve, but still ordered the sale should the two months expire without a buyer. A little more leniency was displayed by Park J in *Edwards* v. *Lloyds TSB* [2004] where a five-year postponement of the sale was ordered to account for the relatively small debt, two occupying minors and the proceeds of sale not being sufficient to allow Mrs Edwards to buy elsewhere at the time of the order. In 2010, in the case of *National Westminster* v. *Rushmer* it was decided that section 14 did not contravene Protocol 1 and Article 8 of the European Convention on Human Rights due to the discretion allowed through the application of section 15.

As stated above, where trustees in bankruptcy apply under section 14, the factors listed at section 335A of the Insolvency Act 1986 must be applied. These are similar to those at section 15 but include:

(a) the interests of the creditors;

(b) the residential nature of the property (where it is the home of the bankrupt or their partner);

(c) the conduct of the spouse or partner, so far as it may have contributed to the bankruptcy;

(d) the needs and resources of spouses and partners;

(e) the needs of any children; and

(f) any other circumstances of the case other than the needs of the bankrupt.

However, in *Re Citro* [1991] it was made perfectly clear by Nourse LJ that in cases where a spouse's needs will be weighed against a creditor in a situation of bankruptcy, 'the voice of the creditors will usually prevail . . . and a sale will be ordered within a short period'. Nourse LJ went on to clarify that even where the property is still the marital home, the 'voice of the spouse' will 'only prevail in exceptional circumstances'.

> How, then, would you define 'exceptional circumstances'? Nourse LJ in *Re Citro* argues that such factors as young children, schooling issues and a lack of money to buy elsewhere are simply 'melancholy consequences of debt'. He suggests that only perhaps when postponement of the sale does not cause 'any great hardship to any of the creditors' will a delay be ordered, pointing to the judgment in *Re Holliday* [1981], but states that even this 'went against the run of recent authorities'. In *Re Raval* [1998] the spouse's mental illness convinced the court to exercise its discretion, as did the spouse's disability in *Claughton* v. *Charalambous* [1999] but it seems abundantly clear that, as Stuart Isaacs QC stated in *Donohoe* v. *Ingram* [2006], *Re Citro* seems to suggest that 'only circumstances which were inherently unusual qualified as exceptional circumstances'.
>
> **REFLECTION**

As such, it is unarguable that TOLATA 1996 is useful in relation to a dispute between beneficiaries and trustees or any interested third parties, and if a beneficiary's rights remain intact then at least TOLATA may give them a chance to argue against, as Park J puts it in *Edwards*, 'severe consequences' of an owed debt, but the lender, especially in bankruptcy, will almost certainly prevail.

KEY POINTS

- When two or more people own a property together, there is always a trust of land in existence. The legal owners with their names on the title are the trustees and the equitable owners are beneficiaries under the trust.

- This trust of land can be express, or implied through a resulting or constructive trust – see Chapter 5.

- All co-owners hold the legal title as joint tenants but the equitable co-ownership can be held as joint tenants or tenants in common.

- There can be a maximum of four legal owners but, in theory at least, an indefinite number of beneficiaries. The relationship is also governed by TOLATA 1996.

- A joint tenancy in equity needs the existence of the four unities: possession, interest, time and title. Other presumptions may also apply, including 'equity follows the law', so that a legal joint tenancy points towards an equitable joint tenancy too. Equal purchase price and a 'family/matrimonial' relationship also suggest a joint tenancy.

- Words of severance or a business arrangement may point towards a tenancy in common – this is important due to the lack of survivorship operating in a tenancy in common. Shares may be left in a will or left open to a claim by creditors in a tenancy in common, but not in a joint tenancy.

- Survivorship allows joint tenants' interests to pass automatically to the remaining joint tenants.

- In order to avoid this, joint tenants may sever their equitable joint tenancy by the operation of the three methods in *Williams* v. *Hensman* (1861) or by notice under section 36(2) of the LPA 1925. When a notice of severance is deemed to be delivered it will be effective and irrevocable, converting the interest into a tenancy in common share (*Kinch* v. *Bullard*).

- Trustees and beneficiaries may be able to solve disputes by the application of the key sections of TOLATA 1996, especially sections 14 and 15 (section 335A of the Insolvency Act 1986 in place of section 15 factors in cases of bankruptcy).

- Beneficiaries should be aware that it is usually the bank or lender who will prevail, especially in a case of bankruptcy (*Re Citro*).

CORE CASES AND STATUTES

Case	About	Importance
AG Securities v. *Vaughan* [1990] 1 AC 417	Co-ownership of a property.	This case clarified the four unities needed for a joint tenancy to exist: possession; interest; time; and title.
Martin v. *Martin* [1987] P & CR 238	The words used in a conveyance may be a clear indication of co-ownership status.	Words of severance – 'in equal shares'; indicate a tenancy in common regardless of the four unities.
Goodman v. *Gallant* (1986) Fam 106 *Roy* v. *Roy* [1996] 1 FLR 541	'To X and Y – joint tenants at law and in equity'.	Words in a conveyance will be conclusive – if the interests are as one then the presumption is a joint tenancy.
Malayan Credit v. *Jack Chia* [1986] AC 549	A commercial agreement.	The presumption is that in a business arrangement it will be a tenancy in common as there is a presumption against the operation of survivorship.
Williams v. *Hensman* (1861) 1 John & H 546	Joint tenants wished to sever their co-ownership in equity.	This case sets down the three methods of common law severance – acting on your share/mutual agreement and mutual conduct.
Burgess v. *Rawnsley* [1975] Ch 429	Indication of a common intention to sever through negotiation.	This is an act of severance by mutual agreement – it must include all joint tenants.
Hunter v. *Babbage* (1995) 69 P & CR 548	Draft agreement to sever.	This is severance through mutual conduct.
Kinch v. *Bullard* [1999] 1 WLR 423	The unscrupulous wife who tried to rip up her letter of severance.	Once a letter has been served under section 36(2) of the LPA 1925 (and also LPA 1925, s. 196) it is effective from the moment it is deemed served – not when it is read.
First National Bank v. *Achampong* [2003] EWCA Civ 487	Attempt by a beneficiary to postpone sale by a lender.	Even with a mentally disabled child, the lender prevailed.
Re Citro [1991] Ch 142	Attempt by a bankrupt's family to postpone a sale.	The reasons for postponement must be 'exceptional' – not just the 'consequences of debt'.

Statute	About	Importance
LPA 1925, s. 1(6)	Legal title in co-ownership.	This section sets down that legal title can only be held as a joint tenancy.
Trustee Act 1925, s. 34(2)	Maximum number of legal joint tenants.	Four.
LPA 1925, s. 36(2)	The statutory method of severance – notice in writing.	It must be served on all remaining joint tenants and show an immediate intention to sever.
LPA 1925, s. 196	Once a notice is served it is deemed to be effective on arrival.	Section 196(3) and (4) set down that once a notice is deemed to have arrived through normal postage rules, it is irrevocable.
TOLATA 1996, ss. 12–15 Insolvency Act 1986 s. 335A	This governs the relationship between the trustee and beneficiary and any other interested party.	Sections 14 and 15 in particular allow an interested party to petition the court for a remedy in relation to their trustee power or their beneficial interest. Section 15 sets down the factors the courts will take into account (unless in a case of bankruptcy, where IA 1986, s. 335A factors apply).

FURTHER READING

Blackstone, W. 'Of Estates in Severalty, Joint-Tenancy, Coparcenary, and Common' in *Commentaries on the Laws of England*, Book 2, Chapter 12 http://ebooks.adelaide.edu.au/b/blackstone/william/comment/book2.12.html
This provides a thorough background to the law on co-ownership – from as far back as 1765!

Kinch v. _Bullard_ [1998] 4 All ER 650, 47 EG 140
Examines the nature of severance by notice – a clear explanation of the workings of LPA 1925, ss. 36(2) and 196.

Nicholls, A. 'Joint Tenants or Tenants in Common?' http://www.stephens-scown.co.uk/blog/2012/03/joint-tenants-or-tenants-in-common/ (Stephens Scown Solicitors)
A practical overview of the material differences between a joint tenancy and a tenancy in common and why they matter in conveyancing terms.

Pascoe, S. 'Section 15 of the Trusts of Land and Appointment of Trustees Act 1996 – A Change in the Law?' [2000] Conv 315
This gives a detailed overview of TOLATA 1996 – especially the workings of s. 15 and the changes from LPA 1925, s. 30.

PART 4

Specific proprietary rights: proprietary estoppel; easements; covenants; and mortgages

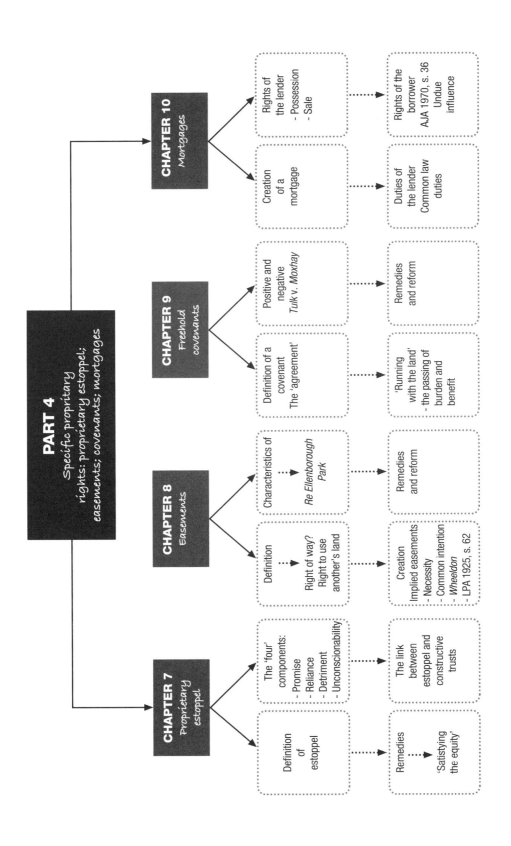

PART 4 INTRODUCTION

Part 4 of *Blueprints Land Law* brings the subject of land law to its conclusion by examining in detail four of the specific substantive proprietary rights: Chapter 7 will deal with **proprietary estoppel**; Chapter 8 with **easements**; Chapter 9 with **covenants**; and Chapter 10 with **mortgages**.

First, in Chapter 7, you will learn that the statutory rule that all land must be transferred in writing is not quite true! Proprietary estoppel is a doctrine which allows a party to claim a proprietary right in the land based on a verbal promise! There must also be reliance on that promise, detriment or loss suffered and finally the court will assess whether it is 'unconscionable' or unfair to allow the person who made the promise of 'all of this will be yours', for example, to go back on that promise. The case law deals with each of the four components but you will learn how to make a judgement based on a 'holistic' approach looking at all four of the components 'in the round'. You will also see how section 116 of the LRA 2002 allows for a proprietary estoppel right to be 'backdated' to the time of the promise and the detrimental reliance, which may assist a claimant to rank in priority before a new owner or a lender. Controversial – but fascinating!

Chapter 8 will deal with the law on easements, first explaining how what might seem like a very informal agreement to 'walk across my land' may well turn out to be a binding proprietary right. You will learn how to assess whether such an agreement is capable of being an easement and then also look at how that easement was created – expressly or impliedly. This area of land law, along with covenants in Chapter 9, is subject to a recent Law Commission report recommending reform, so the chapter will finish with an overview of this report.

Chapter 9 follows the pattern of Chapter 8, but deals with an agreement between landowners which normally restricts the use of your own land rather than allows the use of your neighbour's (as with an easement). This agreement, again, if common law and statutory rules are applied successfully, will result in a 'restrictive covenant' which may bind new owners. You will look at how covenants are created and protected by way of a notice on the register, and, again, look at the proposals for reform of this rather convoluted area of land law.

Finally, Chapter 10 finishes the book with an explanation of the law of mortgages. You will learn how a mortgage is created and also how a lender may take possession and sell the property – especially where there has been default on the mortgage payments. You will also need to understand how a lender has certain common law duties – to get the best price possible for example – when selling the property. You will also learn that the rights of the lender are counterbalanced to a certain extent by the rights of the borrower – to ask for more time to pay the arrears for example, and also not to be unfairly prejudiced by certain 'clogs and fetters' such as unfair interest rates which may unconscionably prevent them from paying off their debt to the lender. Finally, you will also learn about the contractual doctrine of 'undue influence' in a mortgage context, where a mortgage may be set aside by the courts due to one of the parties to a mortgage having signed for the loan under 'undue influence', though the '*Etridge* guidelines' are designed to prevent the lender from losing out in this way. As with all chapters within each Part of the book, each chapter ends with a table of key cases and statutes; key points to learn and remember and a Further Reading list to give you scope to widen your study of land law.

CHAPTER 7
Proprietary estoppel

BLUEPRINT

Proprietary estoppel

LEGISLATION

- Law of Property Act 1925
- Land Registration Act 2002

CONTEXT

- Social rights based on a promise were deemed vital by the Law Commission.
- Some rights – like those based on a promise – may exist even without the awareness of the person enjoying that right.

CONCEPTS

- Proprietary estoppel
- Unconscionability
- Satisfying the equity

- Does proprietary estoppel circumvent statutory formalities, as according to Lord Scott?
- Is there now a distinction between estoppel in commercial and residential cases?
- Should land transfer be based on an informal promise?

- Is there a difference between a constructive trust and a proprietary estoppel right?
- Can the courts take into account any unconscionable behaviour before a promise was made?

CASES

- *Taylor Fashions* v. *Liverpool Victoria* [1982]
- *Gillett* v. *Holt* [2001]
- *Thorner* v. *Major* [2009]

SPECIAL CHARACTERISTICS

- Promise/reliance/detriment/unconscionability – the four stage test
- The judicial safeguard – the award by the courts can be all, or nothing
- Proprietary estoppel is a right that can rank in priority – LRA 2002, s. 116

REFORM

- Should Parliament legislate to remove proprietary estoppel?
- Will future cases be decided on the issue of unconscionability?

CRITICAL ISSUES

Setting the scene

In order for a transfer of land to take place, the transaction should be in writing and not simply verbal. All conveyances of land should be created by **deed** (LPA 1925, s. 52(1)) or at least in written form and signed (LP(MP)A 1989, s. 2). However, it is possible for the courts to find that a valid transfer has taken place verbally, *if* the equitable doctrine of proprietary estoppel can be argued successfully. This is almost identical to the doctrine of promissory estoppel in contract law. In a contract, there will generally only be a valid contract where there has been offer, acceptance and consideration – the latter being defined in simple terms as an exchange of value. Without these formalities, a contract will not be formed. The exception is where promissory estoppel may operate to prevent someone who has made a promise, which is then detrimentally relied upon, from going back on their promise if it would be unconscionable or unfair to allow them to do so. The same is true for promises related to land ownership, where, albeit somewhat controversially, a promise for the transfer of land is enforceable through the operation of proprietary estoppel, even though no formalities have been followed.

All that is needed, at least on the face of it, is for a promise to be given – 'All of this will be yours when I die'. If you rely on that promise, as evidenced by you moving out of your own property, for example, that reliance causes you to suffer some kind of detriment or loss (financial or otherwise), and it would be unconscionable to allow me to go back on my promise, then the equitable proprietary right of estoppel may be argued successfully.

DEFINITION OF ESTOPPEL AND ITS APPLICATION

CORNERSTONE

An equitable proprietary right

Proprietary estoppel allows a claimant to argue that they should have an interest in someone else's land, or even full ownership of that land, even though the formalities of land transfer were not carried out. Unlike its 'sister' doctrine of promissory estoppel in contract law, proprietary estoppel can be used as a 'sword' as well as a 'shield': that is, to bring a claim for a right in the land, rather than just to defend one. Due to recent cases such *Yeoman's Row* v. *Cobbe* [2008] UKHL 55 and *Thorner* v. *Major* [2009] UKHL 18 it seems that this doctrine still has a fundamental role to play in the area of land ownership and transfer. The best way for you to start to understand this topic is to look at the historical context of the doctrine.

Historically, the doctrine of proprietary estoppel can be traced back to the case of *Willmott* v. *Barber* (1880). In this case Fry J set down what came to be known as the 'five probanda' or constituent parts that must be present for a claim to be raised. Generally speaking, a claimant would only be able to bring a claim if the landowner had encouraged the claimant to rely on an assurance knowing full well that the claimant was mistaken in the belief that they would take the property, in full or in part. This could be seen as tantamount to fraud on the part of the landowner.

APPLICATION

Simon owns a freehold property and invites Sally to move in, telling her that if she renovates the barn and keeps the garden in good condition, when he dies 'all of this will be yours'. Nothing is written down. Sally moves in, spends time, money and effort on renovating the barn and spends many hours working on the landscaped garden. Simon later transfers the property to his cousin Jamie following the correct formalities. Sally *may* have a claim in proprietary estoppel, but under the 'five probanda' it may be difficult to prove the fraudulent element as set down by Fry J.

So, it is necessary to move forward over 100 years to the key case of *Taylors Fashions Ltd* v. *Liverpool Victoria Trustees Co Ltd* (1982). Here, Oliver J developed a far more flexible test, where a claim for estoppel can be raised successfully if there has been a promise made by the landowner, reliance and detriment based on that promise, and it would be 'unconscionable' to allow the landowner to go back on the promise. In the example above, Sally may now have a much better chance of success! (see Figure 7.1)

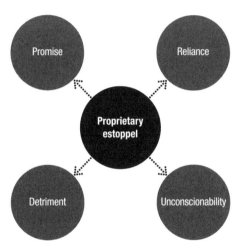

Figure 7.1 Proprietary estoppel

INTERSECTION

As discussed in Chapter 5, equitable rights in a property can also be based on a successful claim under a constructive trust, especially after the recent 'holistic approach' used by Lady Hale in the cases of *Stack* v. *Dowden* and *Jones* v. *Kernott*. The distinction between a constructive trust and proprietary estoppel has arguably been blurred by these recent cases, and this will be analysed later at the end of this chapter.

It is important to understand, therefore, that if these four key components can be made out, then a claim for proprietary estoppel can be raised, and possibly successfully argued. In the recent and now leading case of *Thorner* v. *Major* [2009], Lord Walker stated that other than looking holistically at the element of unconscionability, the starting point is to look at the 'representation or assurance made to the claimant' before going on to look at the reliance and the detriment. However, in the earlier key case of *Gillett* v. *Holt*, Walker LJ, as he was then, stated ([2001] Chat 225) that these component parts are not '*watertight*', but the 'relevant assurances may influence the issue of reliance, that reliance and detriment are often intertwined . . . [and] that equity is concerned to prevent unconscionable conduct . . . in the end the court must look at the matter in the round'.

The promise/assurance/representation

The first component is a promise, assurance or representation made by the landowner. This can be by silent acquiescence where the landowner stands by and allows the claimant to suffer a detriment based on an initial representation. In *Ramsden* v. *Dyson* (1866), a tenant who was promised a long lease built on the land. The landowner stood by and allowed the work to continue in full knowledge that the tenant would not in fact take the land. Lord Wensleydale explained that it was 'dishonest . . . to remain passive' and then profit at a later stage. In *Crabb* v. *Arun District Council* (1976) it was stated that the promise needed to be 'clear and unequivocal' in order for the claimant Crabb to begin to establish an estoppel. In *Yaxley* v. *Gotts* (2000) it was argued that an oral agreement between the two parties that Yaxley would take possession of the ground floor of a building owned by Gotts, in return for Yaxley's work renovating the property, was in breach of section 2 of the Law of Property (Miscellaneous Provisions) Act 1989, as nothing was committed to paper and signed. However, the Court of Appeal held that 'The circumstances in which section 2 has to be complied with are so various, and the scope of the doctrine of estoppel is so flexible, that any general assertion of section 2 as a "no-go area" for estoppel would be unsustainable.'

So it seemed at this point that a 'relatively clear' promise could give rise to a claim for proprietary estoppel. This could also be true where the promise was in relation to inheriting property under a will, even though a will can be revoked at any time before death, especially where the assurances are repeated many times.

CORNERSTONE

The *ratio* in *Gillett*

In the key case of *Gillett* v. *Holt* [2001] a wealthy farmer Mr Holt met a young 12-year-old boy Gillett, whilst Gillett was working as a golf caddy at Holt's golf club. Holt discovered that Gillett was interested in making a career in agriculture and invited the boy to live and work on his farm. Gillett worked for Holt for almost 40 years, and over a number of years, at family occasions such as over Christmas dinner, Holt repeatedly promised Gillett that after Holt died, Gillett would inherit the farm. Years later, the relationship between Gillett and Holt faltered and the estate was left in Holt's will to a Mr Wood. According to the Court of Appeal, 'the primary cause of the rift was the change in Mr Holt's affections' from Gillett to Wood' Walker LJ in his judgment lists a number of express promises made by Holt to Gillett and finds that the promises that Gillett would inherit the farm were indeed sufficiently certain to establish proprietary estoppel. (Note: the reliance and detriment will be explained below.)

It seemed, then, certainly in a domestic context, that a clear assurance could form the basis for an estoppel that would circumvent the formalities set down at section 2 of the LP(MP)A 1989 and even rank in priority ahead of a signed and executed will. However, the next key case, *Yeoman's Row Management Ltd* v. *Cobbe* [2008] made judges and academics start to think differently. Cobbe was an experienced property developer who verbally agreed to take possession of a property for £12 million in return for him obtaining planning permission for Yeoman's Row. Once Cobbe had spent time and money obtaining the relevant consents, Yeoman's Row then refused to sell at the agreed price. The Court of Appeal found in Cobbe's favour, but things were not so favourable in the House of Lords. Lord Walker stated that 'equitable estoppel is a flexible doctrine . . . but it is not a joker or wild card to be used whenever the court disapproves of the conduct of a litigant who seems to have the law on his side'.

Mr Cobbe was, according to Lord Walker, running a 'commercial risk, with his eyes open' and as such could not rely on the assurance given. Lord Scott, giving the leading judgment, went further, stating that estoppel requires 'clarity' as to the 'object' and the 'interest in the property'. He went on to say that if such clarity is lacking, proprietary estoppel will 'risk becoming unprincipled and therefore unpredictable, if it has not already become so'.

Lord Scott stated quite categorically that the doctrine of proprietary estoppel should be applied sparingly by the courts. He stated that:

> My present view, however, is that proprietary estoppel cannot be prayed in aid in order to render enforceable an agreement that statute has declared to be void. The proposition that an owner of land can be estopped from asserting that an agreement is void for want of compliance with the requirements of section 2 is, in my opinion, unacceptable. The assertion is no more than the statute provides. Equity can surely not contradict the statute.

You should be prepared to argue either in favour or against Lord Scott's view when you are asked to give an answer to a question on this particular topic.

REFLECTION

Lord Walker, however, pointed out that this requirement of almost total clarity as to the extent of the promise 'severely curtailed, or even virtually extinguished, the doctrine of proprietary estoppel'. The reality, however, was that just a few months later, the House of Lords 'resurrected' the doctrine by loosening the restraints imposed by Lord Scott in the now leading case of *Thorner* v. *Major* [2009]. Lord Hoffmann set the scene:

CORNERSTONE

The *ratio* in *Thorner* – estoppel 'reborn'?

The appellant David Thorner is a Somerset farmer who, for nearly 30 years, did substantial work without pay on the farm of his father's cousin Peter Thorner. The judge found that from 1990 until his death in 2005 Peter encouraged David to believe that he would inherit the farm and that David acted in reliance upon this assurance. In the event, however, Peter left no will. In these proceedings, David claims that by reason of the assurance and reliance, Peter's estate is estopped from denying that he has acquired the beneficial interest in the farm. The judge found the case proved but the Court of Appeal reversed him.

The issue was whether the assurance had the clarity that was deemed necessary under *Yeoman's Row*. Lord Hoffmann pointed out that 'the representation was never made expressly but was a matter of implication and inference from indirect statements and conduct.'

The Court of Appeal found against Thorner, as the promise was not of sufficient clarity. The Lords, however, reversed the decision of the Court of Appeal, Lord Walker finding that the assurance need only be 'unambiguous and must appear to have been intended to be taken seriously'.

It seems, therefore, that there may well be a distinction between commercial cases such as *Cobbe* and domestic cases such as *Thorner*. It may be true, as some academics such as McFarlane and Robertson argue, that the decision in *Thorner* has 'implicitly rejected the limits suggested in Cobbe' and 'allows proprietary estoppel to continue to perform its vital role of protecting those who reasonably rely on assurances' related to land ownership (McFarlane and Robertson (2009), 535).

REFLECTION

The reliance

There is, of course, a connection between reliance and detriment, and often these are dealt with by various texts as coming under the one heading of 'detrimental reliance'. However, it is clear that relying on a promise can be distinct from suffering detriment *because of* that reliance and, as seen above, it is necessary to analyse the two 'intertwined' issues in turn.

APPLICATION

As above, Simon, who owns a freehold property, invites Sally to move in, telling her that if she renovates the barn and keeps the garden in good condition, when he dies 'all of this will be yours'. Nothing is written down. Sally moves in, spends time, money and effort on renovating the barn and spends many hours working on the landscaped garden.

The reliance by Sally may be evidenced by her moving in to the property (her 'change of position'), as well as being evidenced by her efforts in carrying out the work. Reliance does not always have to be evidenced by financial loss. Also, Sally may be in love with Simon, and this may be one of the reasons she moved in – but, as we will learn in the next section, the promise only needs to be *one* of the reasons for her actions and not the sole inducement.

The key issue here is that of 'change of position'. If the claimant can establish that their position changed due to the assurance given, then the second of the *Taylors Fashions* components may be successfully argued. In *Pascoe* v. *Turner* [1979] Mrs Turner moved in to and renovated a property owned by her former partner Mr Pascoe, on the basis of an assurance that the house would be hers. The court held that, even though the claimant's actions could also have been based on her feelings for Pascoe, reliance on the promise was one of the reasons for her acting in the way she did. Turner was awarded title to the property.

In *Greasley* v. *Cooke* [1980], the maid Cooke was assured that she could remain in the property for life when she moved in with a family as a carer. Even though she then entered into a relationship with one of the family members, she continued unpaid to care for the family. Her partner died, and the heirs tried to evict Cooke, but Lord Denning found that her unpaid work was evidence that she had clearly relied on the assurances made. In *Wayling* v. *Jones* (1993) Wayling was held to have relied on the assurance by his partner Jones that he would leave him the business, as evidenced by the fact that Wayling worked for a minimal wage. The dual motive issue can be seen again in *Campbell* v. *Griffin* [2001], where Campbell cared for an elderly couple who promised to leave him their property for the remainder of his life. They died intestate, and Campbell claimed his right to stay in the property. Even though he stated categorically that he would have cared for them regardless of any assurance, the court found that he relied on the assurance, as the assurance was *one* reason for him staying. Returning to *Gillett* v. *Holt*, Gillett's reliance was clearly evidenced by his action of moving to and working on the farm, as well as being evidenced by the fact that he worked for many years at a low salary.

The detriment

Taking *Gillett* v. *Holt* once again, finding the detriment here was a potentially difficult matter. This is due in no small part to the fact that although over the years Gillett had worked for relatively little money, he had become independently wealthy due to investments he had made in the farm and its stock. Holt argued that Gillett had not therefore suffered any detriment. However, the court held that detriment was not only measured fiscally. Gillett had given up the chance of going to study at agricultural college and to better himself by going to work elsewhere. This was more than enough to establish detriment. It can be said, therefore, that the court performs a balancing act to make a decision as to the extent of any disadvantage or detriment. In *Sledmore* v. *Dalby* (1996) any detriment was completely outweighed by the advantages Dalby had enjoyed, such as living rent free. However, in the recent Privy Council case of *Henry* v. *Henry* [2010], in contrast to Dalby, even though Henry had also lived rent free, he had suffered a greater detriment through battling to provide for his family and giving up opportunities elsewhere on the strength of the assurances made.

> **Take note**
>
> Be aware that it is sometimes difficult to differentiate between reliance and detriment, and, as stated by Sir Jonathan Parker in the recent Privy Council case *Henry* v. *Henry* [2010], they are 'different concepts' but also 'often intertwined'. It is good practice, therefore, to analyse the two concepts together, but attempt to apply the case law independently. As such, a question on this topic would require you to look at reliance and detriment as above, as slightly separate issues.

The unconscionability

It is perhaps pertinent here to be reminded of the words of Walker LJ in *Gillett* v. *Holt*:

CORNERSTONE

Unconscionability

[The] fundamental principle that equity is concerned to prevent unconscionable conduct permeates all the elements of the doctrine. In the end the court must look at the matter in the round.

As such, the court will look at all three elements already discussed in this chapter. In answering a question on this topic, you need to follow the same structure to analyse the assurance, the reliance and the detriment. It will then be necessary to draw a conclusion as to whether it would be unconscionable to allow the landowner to go back on their promise.

INTERSECTION

There is, of course, a substantial overlap here with the equitable maxims explained in Chapter 1 and which form a major part of the 'rules' of equity. It is important to note that proprietary estoppel is an equitable doctrine and as such a lack of 'clean hands' may defeat any arguments a claimant has based on an assurance, reliance, detriment and unconscionability. This can be seen in *Williams* v. *Staite* [1979] where the claimants knew all along that they had no permission at all to build on the land. 'Delay' too can defeat a claim that the landowner acted unconscionably, regardless of the level of reliance and detriment.

Take note

You will often be asked to argue that, as has often been said (Lord Scott in *Cobbe*), proprietary estoppel circumvents statute and is 'unprincipled and unpredictable'. However, once you have explained the three key elements of a claim for estoppel, you can then go on and demonstrate what might be regarded as the judicial safeguard. Even if the court finds that an estoppel exists, the court has full discretion as to the award it allows the claimant. This can fall anywhere along the spectrum of remedies from full title on the one hand to a monetary award on the other and even to a decision that the 'equity has been satisfied'. No analysis of proprietary estoppel is complete without a discussion of a possible remedy.

In the key cases illustrated in this chapter, the claimants were able to argue successfully that the landowners had acted unconscionably, given the reliance and detriment based on promises such as those in *Gillett*, *Wayling*, *Campbell* and *Greasley*.

REMEDIES – THE POWER OF THE COURT TO 'SATISFY THE EQUITY'

The concept that the court must simply 'satisfy the equity' (see Figure 7.2) can be traced back to the case of *Dillwyn* v. *Llewelyn* (1862) where the transfer of a freehold from father to son was the only suitable remedy, as the expectations of the son could only be satisfied in this way. By way of contrast, in *Inwards* v. *Baker* [1965] Lord Denning awarded a life interest to a son who, like the son in *Dillwyn*, had built on land promised by his father. This time, however, 'the minimum necessary to achieve justice', as Denning stated, was to award such an interest and not full title as the son never really expected this to happen. In *Pascoe* v. *Turner* [1979] again, the court had discretion, but decided that full title was the only way to satisfy the equity given the facts. However, this 'expectation-based' approach is problematic as it tends to pre-assume the expectation of the claimant and also may be disproportionate in relation to any detriment suffered.

CORNERSTONE

Satisfying the equity

In *Jennings* v. *Rice* (2003), Walker LJ (again presiding) stated that the role of the court is to 'do what is necessary to avoid an unconscionable result, and a disproportionate remedy cannot be the right way of going about that'.

This echoed his view in *Gillett* that the court's objective is to 'do justice between the parties'.

Hence, the court will take into account all of the circumstances of each case, including weighing the detriment against possible advantages and looking at the unconscionability of the landowner. In *Pascoe*, Mrs Turner was awarded full title, as was the daughter in *Re Basham* [1986]. *Yaxley* and *Thorner* were both awarded rights in the land, the former a long lease of the renovated flat, the latter, the farm, buildings and other assets. *Gillett* was awarded the freehold of the farmhouse, land and £100,000 to compensate for land irrevocably transferred to Wood. *Campbell* and *Jennings*, based on proportionality, were awarded £35,000 and £200,000 respectively, as to transfer title would have been disproportionate given the facts. Dalby, as explained by Lord Justice Hobhouse, got nothing, as 'the effect of any equity . . . has long since been exhausted and no injustice has been done'.

Take note

Once you have explained the three key elements needed to bring a claim for proprietary estoppel, and also explained the role of the courts in making an award, it is now vital for you to demonstrate how such a right might be protected against a third party, such as a new purchaser or a bank taking possession. This is where we refer once again to the Land Registration Act 2002, section 116 as explained in Chapter 4.

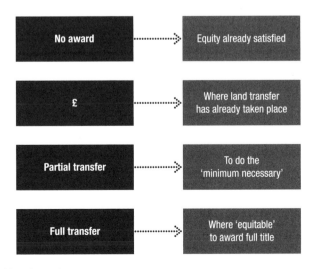

Figure 7.2 Satisfying the equity

PROTECTION OF AN ESTOPPEL RIGHT UNDER THE LAND REGISTRATON ACT 2002, SECTION 116

APPLICATION

As above, Simon, who owns a freehold property, invites Sally to move in, telling her that if she renovates the barn and keeps the garden in good condition, when he dies 'all of this will be yours'. Nothing is written down. Sally moves in, spends time, money and effort on renovating the barn and spends many hours working on the landscaped garden.

If Sally can establish proprietary estoppel through the assurance, the reliance and detriment, and it would be unconscionable for Simon to go back on his promise, under section 116 of the LRA 2002 Sally has an 'equity by estoppel' that would rank in priority from the 'time the equity arises' – meaning 'back-dated' to the time that she can establish the promise, the reliance and the detriment occurred. That way, Sally ranks in priority before a new buyer or a lender taking possession.

Since the introduction of the LRA 2002 (Chapter 4), estoppel rights can clearly be said to be proprietary rights in the land and rank in priority before rights created later in time. Under the LRA 2002, section 116 states:

CORNERSTONE

LRA 2002, section 116

116   Proprietary estoppel and mere equities

It is hereby declared for the avoidance of doubt that, in relation to registered land, each of the following –

(a) an equity by estoppel, and

(b) a mere equity,

has the effect from the time the equity arises as an interest capable of binding successors in title . . .'

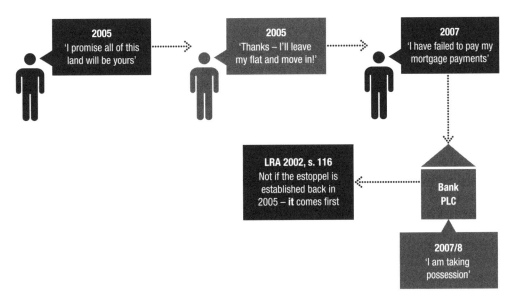

Figure 7.3 The operation of LRA 2002, s. 116

This means that there is no doubt at all that if proprietary estoppel is successfully claimed, this gives the claimant a 'pre-dated' right in the land itself. This point had been raised in *Lloyd* v. *Dugdale* [2001] and, as Professor Dixon states, 'estoppel rights are proprietary, and . . . can bind a purchaser of registered land as an interest that overrides through actual occupation . . .' (see Figure 7.3).

Take note

You should make sure that you explain, as discussed in Chapter 4, that under Schedule 3 to the LRA 2002, at paragraph 2, anyone who has a pre-existing proprietary right and is in discoverable actual occupation can use this 'interest which overrides' to defend against the registered proprietor if, for example, they are about to be evicted.

If the claimant can demonstrate a 'back-dated estoppel right' (LRA 2002, s. 116(a)) then this estoppel right will act as a trigger for the claim of 'actual occupation' and will rank in priority before any new owner.

Now you have understood how proprietary estoppel operates and protects the claimant against a third party, the final part of the equation is to briefly look at the link between estoppel and constructive trusts.

THE LINK BETWEEN ESTOPPEL AND CONSTRUCTIVE TRUSTS

Academics such as Professor Dixon and eminent judges such as Lord Walker have made it abundantly clear that there is an overlap between proprietary estoppel and constructive trusts. It is true to say that, after the 'holistic approach' taken by Lady Hale in *Stack* v. *Dowden*, claiming the latter is now much more all-embracing. It seems that almost any contribution by a claimant towards the well-being of the registered proprietor's property could now be seen as giving rise to a constructive trust. Both constructive trusts and estoppel are based on reliance, detriment and unconscionablity. In *Yaxley*, Walker LJ clearly states that 'there is much common ground between the doctrines of proprietary estoppel and the constructive trust'. He went one step further in *Jennings*, stating that the two doctrines are almost 'indistinguishable'.

INTERSECTION

There is now an abundance of recent case law surrounding the issue of the constructive trust (Chapter 5) so there is no need for repetition here. It is also vital to understand that if a claimant is successfully claiming beneficiary status under a constructive trust, then the doctrine of overreaching becomes a distinct possibility (Chapter 4). This is perhaps a key advantage of claiming estoppel rather than a constructive trust – it would seem that estoppel rights cannot be overreached – this mechanism only applies to beneficiaries under a trust.

There are also a number of other key distinctions. First, the constructive trust tends to assume an 'agreement' between the parties, rather than a unilateral assurance as in estoppel. Secondly, the estoppel right is effectively 'back-dated' from when the 'equity arises' (LRA 2002, s. 116) and the award can range from nothing to full title. The extent of ownership in a constructive trust now follows the rather tricky mathematical conundrum of quantification based on 'holistic contributions' as per Lady Hale in *Stack* and *Jones*. In relation to protection against third parties, a beneficiary under a constructive trust can place a restriction on the register (LRA 2002, s. 40) but this only serves to warn the purchaser that overreaching may be necessary if possible. An estoppel right, however, cannot be overreached. With an estoppel right, in theory it is possible to register this right as a notice, but it is far more likely that the claimant will have no idea they have such a right, but may well be able to use the right as a trigger for a claim under the LRA 2002, Schedule 3, paragraph 2, as an interest which overrides through actual occupation.

It may be worth noting that, given the confusion in relation to the quantification of equitable ownership in the recent cases of *Stack* and *Jones*, we may see claimants attempting to establish their equitable proprietary right through estoppel.

Pre-*Stack*, when equitable quantification was based on financial contributions to purchase and mortgage payments, it was a 'safer bet' for a claimant to follow the constructive trust route. Now, especially after the loosening of the reins in *Thorner*, we may be set for a return to a preference for an estoppel claim.

REFLECTION

KEY POINTS

- Generally speaking, for a transfer of land to take place, it must be in writing and not simply through a verbal agreement. The controversial exception to the rule is where the equitable doctrine of proprietary estoppel can be applied.

- Proprietary estoppel is an equitable right in the land itself, even with the absence of formalities. This is an echo of the 'sister' doctrine of promissory estoppel in contract law, where a contract may still be enforced without consideration.

- Traditionally, proprietary estoppel was based on fraud by the landowner, but the 20th century saw the focus change from fraud to 'unconscionability'.

- Key cases such as *Gillett* v. *Holt* [2001] suggest that the courts will look holistically at the facts of each case to establish whether there was 'a promise, reliance, detriment and unconscionability' before they find that a claim for proprietary estoppel succeeds.

- The role of the courts is to 'satisfy the equity' – to do the minimum necessary to achieve justice – but this leads to inconsistency of decision making.

- Recent case law suggests that there is a further distinction between commercial 'promises' and non-commercial, the former being more rigidly assessed.

CORE CASES AND STATUTES

Case	About	Importance
Willmott v. *Barber* (1880) LR 15 ChD 96	The five probanda.	This is the first case which established the doctrine of proprietary estoppel based on fraud by the landowner.
Taylors Fashions Ltd v. *Liverpool Victoria Trustees Co Ltd* [1982] 1 QB 133n	The four components of modern day estoppel: assurance; reliance; detriment; unconscionability.	This case in the later 20th century reintroduced the doctrine of proprietary estoppel and replaced the five probanda with the four key components that form the modern day test.
Gillett v. *Holt* [2001] Ch 210	Gillett goes to work for Farmer Holt for almost 40 years and is promised on numerous occasions that the farm will be his on the death of Holt. Holt then later leaves the estate to Wood.	The key case on estoppel that illustrates all four components. Gillett's claim was successful due to the repeated assurances by Holt alongside the reliance and the detriment.

→

Case	About	Importance
Yeoman's Row Management Ltd v. *Cobbe* [2008] 1 WLR 1752	A commercial agreement where Cobbe was promised he could buy the property for £12m in return for gaining planning permission and consents.	No estoppel in a high value commercial situation – Cobbe was an experienced developer and LP(MP)A 1989, s. 2 should not have been circumvented by an estoppel claim. It was thought briefly, though, that this would spell the end for claims for estoppel rights.
Thorner v. *Major* (2009) 1 WLR 776	The promise was 'clear enough' in this domestic situation.	This case illustrates that estoppel is far from dead – but there may be a distinction now between commercial and domestic cases.

Statute	About	Importance
LPA 1925, s. 52(1)	The need for a deed when transferring land.	This section sets down the formalities for a transfer of land by deed.
LP(MP)A 1989, s. 2	Sets down that land may be transferred equitably but in writing and with a signatory.	No need for a deed, but all conveyances of land must at least be in writing and signed – *not* verbal assurances. Proprietary estoppel arguably circumvents this.
LRA 2002, s. 116	Estoppel rights are proprietary in nature and are binding from when they arise.	This section confirms what was said in *Lloyd* v. *Dugdale* – that such rights are proprietary and are capable of binding third parties. Section 116 allows an overriding interest of actual occupation to be claimed.

FURTHER READING

Dixon, M. (2001) 'Proprietary Estoppel, Third Parties and Constructive Trusts. A Taste for the Future?: *Lloyd* v. *Dugdale* **[2002] EWCA Civ 1754' [2002] Conv 584**
Examines the nature of a proprietary estoppel and provides a clear comparison between estoppel and constructive trusts.

McFarlane, B. and Robertson, A. 'Apocalypse averted; proprietary estoppel in the House of Lords' [2009] LQR 125 (Oct) 535
This article gives a detailed critique of the recent case law of *Cobbe* and *Thorner*, and how *Thorner* 'saved' the doctrine of estoppel.

CHAPTER 8
Easements

BLUEPRINT

Easements

LEGISLATION

- Law of Property Act 1925
- Land Registration Act 2002

CONTEXT

- Neighbouring landowners' disputes.
- Hidden rights need protection.

CONCEPTS

- Legal and equitable easements
- Dominant and servient tenement
- The Rule in *Wheeldon* v. *Burrows*
- The Rule in LPA 1925, s. 62
- Prescription

- Was the decision by Gibson LJ in *Platt v. Crouch* correct?
- Is there a difference between an implied easement under *Wheeldon* v. *Burrows* and under LPA 1925, s. 62?

- Is the right to use a neighbour's pool an easement or purely personal?
- Was Lord Denning correct in *Crow* v. *Wood* – can there be an easement where money is spent by the servient landowner?

CASES

- *Re Ellenborough Park* [1956]
- *Hill* v. *Tupper* [1863]
- *Moncrieff* v. *Jamieson* [2007]
- *Wheeldon* v. *Burrows* [1879]
- *Platt* v. *Crouch* [2003]

REFORM

- Should Parliament legislate – The Law Commission Reform Paper 327 (2011)?
- Is the law on easements clear enough as it is?

SPECIAL CHARACTERISTICS

- The Ellenborough Park test:
  - Dominant and servient Land
  - The easement must benefit the land
  - The plots must be owned or occupied by different persons
- The easement must be capable of being an easement:
  - Implied easements and their creation
  - An overriding easement under Schedule 1 and 3 LRA 2002

CRITICAL ISSUES

Setting the scene

A number of years ago, I went to look at a house that was for sale. As I stepped into the back garden with the estate agent, I noticed a gate in the boundary fence with the adjacent property and a path leading from the gate that ran across the patio of 'my' house and across the garden. The path ended at a second gate that stood at the top of the garden and led directly to the main road. I asked the estate agent about this gate and questioned him as to the neighbour's access across 'my' land to the main road. His reply was that the neighbours 'might' want to use the gate to walk across 'my' garden to get to the main road more easily. I questioned the word 'might' and suggested to him that the access across 'my' land might be an **easement**. The estate agent rather quickly apologised, and admitted that, sure enough, it was an easement!

So what is the difference between 'might' want to walk across the garden and an easement to walk across? The answer is that an easement is a proprietary right in or over the land that is capable of binding a new owner – (me, in this case!) whereas the neighbour simply 'might' want to walk across suggests a merely personal right binding only through the contractual agreement (licence) with the seller of the property in whose garden I was standing. The fact that this easement could be binding on me as the new owner was enough to dissuade me from buying the property!

As such, the law of easements is a vital, if rather convoluted area of property law that, though subject to reform, is capable of binding third parties who are aware of the existing easement, either due to its existence on the register as a notice or as an overriding interest under LRA 2002, Schedule 3, paragraph 3. This chapter will define an easement, look at how an easement is created and protected and finally discuss proposed reforms to this area of land law.

DEFINITION OF AN EASEMENT

CORNERSTONE

A proprietary right

According to section 1(2)(a) of the LPA 1925, an easement is a proprietary right capable of being legal if the easement is for a fixed or certain length of time (term) or effectively 'for ever' (like a freehold estate) and it is created by deed. According to section 3 of the LPA 1925, an easement that is not a 'legal easement' can still be a proprietary right, but will operate as an equitable easement. The importance of this distinction is, as ever with land law, in its ability to bind a third party. Generally, a legal easement if it appears on the register, or under certain circumstances as an overriding interest, will be capable of binding a third party. An equitable easement, however, must be entered on the register as a notice in order to bind a third party; and, especially since the LRA 2002, if not, it will not operate as an overriding interest. Paragraph 3 of Schedules 1 and 3 to the LRA 2002 refers specifically to 'legal easements' as being capable of overriding. However, it is important to understand that only 'implied' legal easements can be overriding. This is due to section 27 of the LRA 2002 which states that any express easements created by deed must be registered or they remain equitable and as such are not binding unless they appear on the register. This will be discussed in detail later in the chapter.

The Land Registry describes an easement as a 'type of right which one person has over the land of another' (see Further Reading below). These rights can include: rights of way (though not a public right of way); a right to air and light (though only through a defined channel such as a pipe or a clearly defined window); a right to use a car parking space; a right to hang a sign on the side of a neighbour's wall; and even the right to use a toilet on a neighbour's land! However, certain criteria must be satisfied in order for a right to be seen as an easement. These criteria were set down in *Re Ellenborough Park* [1956] and will be discussed in detail below. If these criteria are not satisfied then these rights may be seen as purely personal rights – especially where money has changed hands in return for the right to use the land, as this would point to a contract between the two parties. According to the doctrine of privity, a contract is generally not binding on a third party such as a new owner, and as such if these rights can be classified as easements then a proprietary right is created. If registered under section 27 of the LRA 2002, this may then go on to bind a successor in title or a bank taking back possession following the priority rules under section 29 of the LRA 2002 (see Figure 8.1).

Take note

When analysing possible easements, the first stage is always to ascertain whether right's are personal or are capable of being easements in line with *Re Ellenborough Park*. The process is, as with most areas of law, quite formulaic, applying the four characteristics set down in the case, and applying the relevant case law. This will help you to identify as to whether certain rights fall within the criteria needed for an easement to be present before going on to analyse exactly how the right was created.

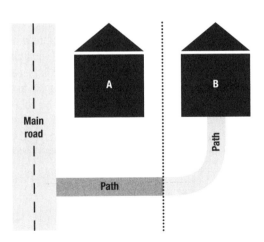

- **A** allows **B** to cross **A's** land
- The shaded path across **A's** land **could** be an **easement**

Figure 8.1 A typical easement

APPLICATION

Jason is granted an easement by his neighbour Paula, which was registered in line with section 27 of the LRA 2002. One month later, Jason sells his property to Hannah, and Paula sells her property to Freda. As the easement had already been registered at the time of the transfers of both pieces of land (it appears on the property register of both Jason and Paula) then due to the priority rules at section 29 of the LRA 2002, Freda will be bound (burdened) by the easement and Hannah will take the benefit.

It is true to say that an easement is a powerful and valuable proprietary right in or over another's land, and, if protected properly, will be capable of binding successors in title. However, the first stage of the test as to whether a right is capable of actually being classified as an easement is to apply the criteria set down in *Re Ellenborough Park*.

Characteristics of an easement (*Re Ellenborough Park* [1956])

The facts of the key case of *Re Ellenborough Park* are as follows:

CORNERSTONE

The facts

Ellenborough Park was a substantial area of parkland in Weston-super-Mare. In 1885, part of the land was sold for property development, with rights granted to the new owners to use and enjoy the remaining areas of the parkland. This was not an issue at all, until during the Second World War the land was taken by the War Office, with compensation due to be paid to the trustees of the original owners of the land. The question arose as to whether the rights to enjoy the parkland were proprietary and as such allowed for some of the compensation to be paid over to the new current owners in relation to their contributions to the upkeep of the park, or simply a personal licence which did not give rise to payment of any of the compensation. Evershed MR held that the right to enjoy the park was an easement not a licence. Evershed set down the four characteristics of an easement as the following:

1. There must be a dominant and servient tenement.
2. The easement must 'accommodate' the dominant tenement.
3. The two plots must be owned or occupied by different people.
4. The right must be capable of 'forming the subject matter of the grant'.

All four of these characteristics need to be understood and applied in full.

The dominant and servient tenement

It has been said in cases such as *Ackroyd* v. *Smith* (1850) that an easement cannot exist 'in gross'; in other words, an easement cannot exist without an estate in land to which the easement is connected. In *Banstead Downs Golf Club* v. *Customs and Excise* (1974) there was no easement for a member of the club to play golf on the club's course. The right was purely personal. The first characteristic in *Ellenborough* is therefore that there needs to be a 'dominant tenement' – land which is capable of taking the benefit of the easement, and a 'servient tenement' – land which grants the easement and as such carries the burden of that easement. These two pieces of land must be identifiable at the time of the grant as in the case of *London and Blenheim Estates* v. *Ladbroke Retail Parks* [1993] where no easement was present due to there being no dominant land at the time the easement was granted.

Benefiting the dominant land

In *Re Ellenborough*, Evershed MR referred to this second test as 'accommodating the dominant tenement', meaning simply that the right must clearly benefit the land itself rather than the owner. This second stage can be split into two 'sub-rules': first, that in order for the easement to benefit the land, the dominant and servient land must be sufficiently close enough geographically for the servient to confer a tangible benefit on the dominant land. Cases such as *Bailey* v. *Stephens* (1862) stated that where one property was in Northumberland with the other in Kent, this would not give rise to an easement. The second 'sub-rule' is that the easement must benefit the land itself and not just confer a personal benefit on the owner. The case of *Hill* v. *Tupper* (1863) conferred a purely personal advantage on the owner of a pleasure boat business to run canal boats down a river. Sir Edward Pollock CB stated quite categorically that the right given to the owner of the business by the canal company 'operates simply as a licence' and that no 'new species of burden' should be imposed. However, in the contrasting case of *Moody* v. *Steggles* (1879) (see Figure 8.2), Fry J held that the right to hang a pub sign on a neighbour's wall was an easement which was related not to the occupant of the business but to the 'business of the occupant'.

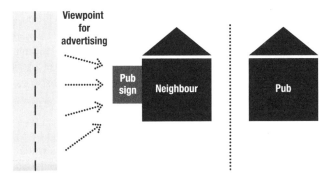

The sign benefits the pub business and not just the owner

Figure 8.2 *Moody* v. *Steggles* (1879)

Take note

It is, however, far, more uncertain as to whether an easement is possible when a right seems to give a 'recreational advantage' to the owner rather than a right attached to the land itself. You will often come across examples such as swimming pools or tennis courts. Is the right to use a neighbour's pool or tennis court an easement or, by virtue of its personal nature, simply a licence? In Californian law, an easement for the use of a pool, perhaps not unsurprisingly, does exist (Rose v. Peters (1943) 59 Cal) but in English law, this is far from certain. Lord Scott in Moncrieff v. Jamieson [2007] certainly suggested obiter that a swimming pool was purely recreational. However, you should note that in Re Ellenborough the use of the parkland was said to 'enhance the value' of the properties although, on the face of it, the use of the park simply gave a recreational advantage to the owners. Either way, you will also see that the use of a neighbour's pool may lead to extra expenditure on the part of the servient tenement in the form of extra maintenance, and this contradicts one of the rules under the fourth characteristic from Ellenborough (discussed below).

Different ownership or occupation of the two plots

It seems to be quite logical that the dominant and servient plots must be owned *or* occupied by different persons, as set down in *Roe* v. *Siddons* (1888). This can mean, of course, that both plots can be owned freehold by one person, provided that one of the plots has a tenant who also 'owns' the leasehold estate. The usual scenario here is therefore where one plot owner is the landlord and the other the tenant, as in *Borman* v. *Griffith* [1930].

The right must be 'capable' of being an easement

Lord Evershed in *Ellenborough* referred to this fourth characteristic as where the 'right alleged is capable of forming the subject matter of the grant', but he went on to state that this 'fourth and last condition is, at first sight perhaps not entirely clear'. He suggested that this fourth characteristic is more easily applied by reference to a number of 'sub-rules'. These rules include as to whether there is a capable grantor and grantee; whether the easement alleged is 'sufficiently certain'; whether the right is one of the traditionally accepted easements set down by the common law; whether the easement leads to positive expenditure on the part of the servient land; and whether the easement confers exclusive use on the dominant tenement.

Capable grantor and grantee

This means that there needs to be a person with legal title able to grant and able to receive the benefit of the easement. For example, if one of the parties has a licence then the right is not capable of being an easement.

INTERSECTION

As discussed in Chapter 3, a proprietary right cannot be 'carved out' of a mere licence as was the argument (unsuccessful) of the London and Quadrant Housing Trust in the *Bruton* case, where they argued that as licence holders they could not possibly grant a lease to Mr Bruton. The same is true of an easement – an easement cannot be given by someone with a mere licence, and neither can it be received.

Sufficiently certain

Traditionally, an easement needed to be written on a deed and be clear in its terms. As such, common law developed with this mind in relation to easements. In *Aldred's Case* (1610) the right to a view was seen as far too vague and intangible. In *Phipps* v. *Pears* [1965] there was no easement for 'protection against the weather', though in *Rees* v. *Skerrett* [2001] it was confirmed that there can be an easement of 'support' from an adjacent property where the demolition of the adjoining wall of that property will cause the destruction of the other. In *Webb* v. *Bird* (1863), although there is no easement of air *per se*, there can be an easement of air through a defined channel. Neither is there a right to light *per se* other than through a specific window as in *Colls* v. *Home & Colonial Stores* [1904]. The essentially tort law case of *Hunter* v. *Canary Wharf* [1997] also failed in its attempt to establish an easement of 'television signals' where Hunter's enjoyment of her TV was affected by the Canary Wharf tower being built! The case of *Browne* v. *Flower* [1911] demonstrates that the right to 'privacy' is also not capable of being an easement and the case of *Lawrence* v. *Fen Tigers* [2011] confirms that there is no easement of either 'noise' or 'silence'!

> **REFLECTION**
>
> The categories of easements, therefore, have been relatively restricted through the development of the common law, with the courts slow to allow 'incidents of a novel kind' to be 'attached to a property' as an easement (Lord Brougham in *Keppell* v. *Bailey* (1834)), even though it has also been suggested that categories of easement must 'alter and expand with the changes . . . of mankind' (*Dyce* v. *Lady James Hay* (1852)), hence the easement of the use of a lavatory in *Miller* v. *Emcer* (1956) and an easement of storage in *Wright* v. *Macadam* [1949]. Professor Martin Dixon is his book *Modern Land Law* seems to echo this view by suggesting that *Hunter* may have been decided differently if the TV signals were entering through a defined fibre-optic cable rather than through the traditional aerial.

Positive expenditure

The general rule is that there should be no positive expenditure on the part of the servient tenement, simply due to what could be argued as policy reasons, as in the case of *Regis* v. *Redman* [1956]. It would arguably be unfair for a servient tenement to grant an easement and then have to pay for the upkeep of that easement in favour of the dominant land. The *obiter* referred to above in *Moncrieff* seems to support this viewpoint. This was only contradicted in the case of *Crow* v. *Wood* [1971], where Lord Denning found an easement for the 'maintenance of a boundary fence' even though there was expenditure on the part of the servient tenement. This decision was roundly criticised, as it seemed that Denning was trying to find a way of avoiding a positive covenant which would not be binding on a third party (see Chapter 9) by creating a 'negative easement'.

Exclusive use by the dominant land

The general rule is that there can be an easement of a space such as that of a cellar for storage of coal (*Wright* v. *Macadam* [1949]) but not when that leads to a general exclusion of the servient tenement owner as in *Grigsby* v. *Melville* [1973] where the dominant tenement owner had exclusive use of the cellar space.

The line of case law in this final 'sub-rule' is almost entirely made up of car parking spaces. In *Copeland* v. *Greenhalf* [1952] the right to park was extensive and almost exclusive and as such was not seen as an easement. In *London & Blenheim Estates* v. *Ladbroke* it was stated that a non-specific parking space was

Take note

When analysing whether a right is capable of being an easement, it is crucial to work through all of the four characteristics and their 'sub-rules' from *Re Ellenborough*. If the alleged easement fails on any one of the above points, then the right will not be an easement. It may be an alternative proprietary right, such as a lease, or it may simply be a licence and as such will not bind a third party. However, that is only the start! Once you have established that a right is capable of being an easement, you now need to establish how that easement was created – expressly, or by one of the four main methods of implied creation.

capable of being an easement. Other cases such as *Newman* v. *Jones* (1982), *Batchelor* v. *Marlow* [2003] and *Moncrieff* v. *Jamieson* [2007] all suggest that the more exclusive the use by the servient tenement, the less likely it is that the right will be seen as an easement.

INTERSECTION

As discussed in Chapter 3, from the case of *Street* v. *Mountford* [1985], where there is exclusive possession, for a term and at a rent, the right is likely to be a lease rather than an easement. This is because the more exclusivity there might be, the more the right is tantamount to ownership and not *use* of the land (an easement is defined as the *use* of another's land and not the *ownership* of that land (*Reilly* v. *Booth* (1890)).

CREATION OF A LEGAL OR EQUITABLE EASEMENT

As explained above, an easement can be created expressly and, due to an easement being a proprietary interest in the land under s. 52(1) of the LPA 1925, this can be a 'legal easement' if created by deed (see Chapter 1), provided it is for a period equivalent to a freehold or leasehold estate ('for ever' or 'fixed term') (section 1(2) of the LPA 1925). It can also be created in writing under section 53(1)(a) of the LPA 1925 and the LP(MP)A 1989 (also Chapter 1) though this will result in an equitable easement being created. It is also an equitable easement if created by deed, but not for a fixed term or 'for ever'. It can, of course, also be created impliedly in one of a number of ways, and as explained above, with these implied easements deemed by the law as being 'legal' rather than equitable. The significance, as explained in the opening Cornerstone above, is that an equitable easement (those created in writing and not by deed or implied) must appear as a notice in the charges section of the register in order to bind a third party. A legal easement is capable of binding a successor in title under the provisions at section 27 of the LRA 2002, and implied easements may bind as an overriding interest under paragraph 3 of Schedules 1 and 3 to the LRA 2002 (as discussed later).

It should also be noted that easements can be *granted* in favour of your neighbour, or *reserved* in favour of yourself where you sell or lease part of your land and reserve for yourself an easement over the part of the land conveyed. If express, any reservation must be clearly written into the conveyance. With implied reservation, the courts have been more reluctant to allow such an easement to succeed as in *Re Dodd* (1843) where an implied reservation of a right of way across the conveyed land was unsuccessful as it was for convenience and not *necessity*.

APPLICATION

Emilia owns a freehold property and agrees that her neighbour Tommy can drive across Emilia's land to get to the main road at the other side of the property. Emilia and Tommy write this into a contract. This must be registered as a notice by Tommy if he wishes the easement to be binding on Emilia against future owners of Tommy's property. If nothing is put in writing, then Tommy must rely on the easement being classified as an implied easement, and as such must hope that it will be classified as an overriding interest under LRA 2002, Schedule 3, paragraph 3 *if* Tommy wishes to protect future successors in title.

IMPLIED EASEMENTS

As explained above, an easement might not be created by deed or in writing. In fact, it is often the case that the parties may not even realise that an easement has been inadvertently created. As such an easement can be implied in a number of ways: necessity; common intention; the rule in *Wheeldon* v. *Burrows* 1879; and LPA 1925, section 62. Easements can also be implied by *prescription* though this is rarely used in practice.

Necessity

This is best described as where, without the benefit of the easement, the land would be useless or impossible to use. Although it is technically possible to exclude 'easement by necessity' through express words in a conveyance, the courts will analyse such a conveyance and will allow such an easement if the facts dictate that the easement really is 'necessary' as in *Hillman* v. *Rogers* [1998]. As above, the case of *Re Dodd* suggests that it is easier to claim the grant of an easement of necessity rather than a reservation. However, as Lord Oliver stated in *Manjang* v. *Drammeh* (1991), it is possible to 'imply the reservation of an easement of necessity' but this must be true 'necessity' and where there is another access route, even access by water rather than on land, the claim will fail as in *Manjang*. In the case of *Adealon International* v. *Merton Borough Council* [2007] Carnwath LJ stated that where there is a 'realistic possibility of alternative access . . . the case for an easement of necessity is much less clear'. In the case of *Wong* v. *Beaumont* [1965] (see Figure 8.3) an implied grant of an easement of necessity was argued in relation to ventilation through a shaft as the land conveyed to Wong specifically for the purpose of a restaurant would have been rendered useless without the easement of the ventilation shaft over the seller's retained land. This case also successfully argued an implied easement of common intention.

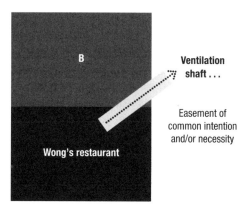

Figure 8.3 *Wong* v. *Beaumont* [1965]

Common intention

The classic exposition of an easement implied by common intention can be taken from the case of *Pwllbach Colliery* v. *Woodman* [1915] where the court stated that the law will 'readily imply' the grant or reservation of an easement of common intention where the facts suggest that it was the intention of both parties that an easement should exist. In *Stafford* v. *Lee* (1992) Nourse LJ explained that common intention will be established where there is evidence that the parties are aware that the land is being used for a particular purpose and the easement would be necessary to give effect to that intention. In *Wong* the common intention was the stronger of the two arguments (the other being necessity) as Wong convinced the court that Beaumont must have intended that there be an easement of ventilation as without it there would be a breach of health and safety law by Beaumont and also they would be 'derogating from grant' – a landlord and tenant doctrine that suggests that what the landlord gives with one hand by way of the lease, he cannot remove with the other.

The rule in *Wheeldon* v. *Burrows*

At first glance, the rule in *Wheeldon* is rather complex. However, once the constituent parts are dissected the rule becomes a little easier to digest and then apply. Referring to the law first:

CORNERSTONE

The rule in *Wheeldon*

According to Thesiger LJ, there are a number of rules that must be applied in order to establish an implied *grant* of an easement in this way. (There are no implied reservations using *Wheeldon*.) First, there must have been *one single owner and occupier* at the outset who then sells or leases part of his land, retaining the rest. Thesiger then explains that 'all those continuous and apparent easements (by which, of course, I mean quasi-easements)', or, in other words, all those easements which are necessary to the reasonable enjoyment of the property granted, and which have been at the time of the grant used by the owners of the entirety for the benefit of the part granted.' In other words, any rights that would be capable of being easements (quasi-easements as an owner cannot have a full easement over his own land) and were continuous and apparent and reasonably necessary for the reasonable enjoyment of the land sold or leased, *and* at the time of the grant were being used by the original owner for the benefit of the part of the land sold or leased, will be implied as an easement for the benefit of the new owner/tenant.

It seems from cases such as *Hansford* v. *Jago* [1921] that this rule can be illustrated by such easements as a rough track used by the original owner over the part of the land sold or leased: where the track is 'permanent and obvious' and is necessary for the enjoyment of the land by the new owner, this will be seen as an easement under the rule in *Wheeldon*. In *Ward* v. *Kirkland* [1967] 'continuous and apparent' was defined as 'a feature which would be seen on inspection and which is neither transitory nor intermittent'. It should also be noted that the rule in *Wheeldon* can be excluded by express words in the conveyance. It should also be noted that 'necessary' here does *not* mean absolute necessity as it does in easements of necessity.

..........APPLICATION

Emilia owns a freehold property that comprises of a large plot of land at 31 Brown Lane. She splits the land into 31A and 31B and sells 31B to Tommy. At the time of the sale, Emilia was using a path across 31B that ran through the boundary and across 31A to the main road. When Tommy bought the property he was aware of the path and now needs the path to reasonably enjoy his property. This could now be classified as an implied easement under the rule in *Wheeldon* to benefit Tommy and his successors in title.

Law of Property Act 1925, section 62

This key section of the LPA states that: 'A conveyance of land shall be deemed to include . . . all . . . liberties, privileges, *easements*, rights and advantages . . .' (emphasis added). This means that, unless there are words to the contrary, every conveyance of land will include the passing of any easements in existence. Once again, it should be noted that section 62 cannot operate in relation to reservation, only grant. It is also true to note that section 62 will create a 'legal' easement as there must be a conveyance of the land to satisfy the provisions at section 62. This also suggests that contrary to the rule in *Wheeldon*, prior to the conveyance there was common ownership but diversity of occupation as there must be a conveyance of the dominant land. This was established in *Long* v. *Gowlett* [1923] but affirmed in *Sovmots* v. *Secretary of State for the Environment* [1979] where Lord Wilberforce stated that section 62 does not operate until 'a separation [of ownership] occurs', as where the land is 'under one ownership one cannot speak in any intelligible sense of rights, or privileges, or easements'. In other words, there is no 'easement in existence' able to pass with the land until there has been a separation of occupation of the two plots. It appears that even a personal right such as a licence may become an easement through section 62 if the conditions are satisfied, as in *Hair* v. *Gillman* (2000) where the right to park a car operated as an easement under section 62.

However, some confusion has arisen due to the case of *Platt* v. *Crouch* [2003], where the Court of Appeal suggested that there was no need for prior diversity of occupation where the use of the easement was 'continuous and apparent'. Here, the defendant owned a hotel and other properties by a river where the hotel was advertised and boats were moored. There was also access to the hotel through the other properties. The hotel was then sold, and the new owner claimed an easement under section 62 over the retained riverside properties to continue to moor boats, advertise the hotel and use the right of way. The confusion arose due to Peter Gibson LJ stating that 'the rights were continuous and apparent and so it matters not that prior to the sale of the hotel there was no prior diversity of occupation' and as such he allowed the section 62 argument to succeed. Though there is some academic support for this view (in Megarry and Wade, *Law of Real Property* (6th edn) – see below), it seems that Gibson LJ aligned the rule in *Wheeldon* with the rule in section 62, blurring the traditional distinction.

REFLECTION

Prescription

This method of claiming an easement is generally: where there is 'long use' of the right (20 years) and can be claimed as a common law right; by the doctrine of 'lost modern grant' which assumes that 20 years' use was based on an original 'lost' grant of an easement; and under the Prescription Act 1832. The right claimed, though, must be 'of right', meaning without 'secrecy, force or permission' (*nec vi, nec clam, nec precario*), and must also be between freeholders and the use must have been continuous and uninterrupted. For more detail, refer to the Land Registry Practice Guide 52 (see Further Reading below).

PROTECTION AND REFORM

Under section 27 of the LRA 2002, any expressly granted easements are subject to compulsory registration and, until this happens, the easement will remain equitable in nature. As above, all equitable easements are only binding on third parties if entered as a notice on the register. All legal easements created expressly, once registered in their own right, will be binding, and all implied legal easements may be binding as an overriding interest under paragraph 3 of Schedules 1 and 3 to the LRA 2002 (see Chapter 4). This states that a legal (implied) easement will be binding on a third party if: (a) it is in the actual knowledge of the new owner; (b) the easement is reasonably obvious on a careful inspection of the land; or (c) the person claiming the benefit of the easement can demonstrate that they have used the easement within the last year leading up to the sale of the land to the new owner.

If the easement has been created and is binding, it can be enforced against a new owner of the burdened land, with remedies such as injunction or damages if a breach occurs. Easements can also be extinguished through express release where the two parties agree to terminate an easement; by implied release though this needs abandonment – even non-user for 175 years is seemingly not enough following *Benn* v. *Hardinge* (1992). If the land returns to sole ownership or the benefit is lost due to a change of circumstances (*Huckvale* v. *Aegean Hotels* (1989)), then the easement may be terminated but *not* through an application to the Lands Tribunal under section 84 of the LPA 1925 as can be the method for restrictive covenants (see Chapter 9).

> **Take note**
>
> In relation to reform, the Law Commission Report *Making Land Work: Easements, covenants and profits à prendre* (Law Com. No. 327, 2011) (see Further Reading below) suggests that Parliament should legislate in order to simplify and codify the law on easements (and covenants).

KEY POINTS

- An easement is a proprietary right which one person can exercise over the land of another.
- Easements are capable of being legal under section 1(2)(a) of the LPA 1925 provided they are created by deed (LPA 1925, s. 52) and are either 'for ever' or fixed term.
- All other easements, including easements created by deed but not yet registered under section 27 of the LRA 2002 are equitable and can only be protected by a notice on the register.
- Easements must satisfy the 'four characteristics' set down in *Re Ellenborough Park* [1956].
- These characteristics are that there must be a dominant and servient tenement; the easement must benefit the land and not the owner; the plots must be owned or occupied by different owners; and the easement must be capable of being an easement. The sub-rules must also be applied within these four characteristics.
- An easement can be express and as such will need to be registered as a legal easement or an equitable easement (by deed or in writing) or it can be implied.
- An easement can be implied by necessity; by common intention; by the rule in *Wheeldon* v. *Burrows*; by section 62 of the LPA 1925; or by prescription.
- Easements can only be implied as a grant or reservation through necessity and common intention but a reservation of an easement cannot be implied through *Wheeldon* or section 62.
- Implied easements can operate as overriding interests under Schedules 1 and 3 to LRA 2002 and as such may bind third parties.
- There is proposed reform under the Law Commission Report No. 327 (2011).

CORE CASES AND STATUTES

Case	About	Importance
Re Ellenborough Park [1956] Ch 131	The right to use parkland.	This is the key case which establishes the four characteristics of an easement – if a 'right' fails one of the tests, it is not an easement.
Bailey v. *Stephens* (1862) 12 CB NS 91	Land in Northumberland and Kent.	For a right to be an easement, the two plots of land must be geographically proximate.
Hill v. *Tupper* (1863) 2 H & C 121	The right to run boats along a canal.	The key case which sets down that the right must benefit the land and not just confer a personal benefit on the owner.
Moody v. *Steggles* (1879) 12 Ch 261	The hanging of a pub sign on neighbouring land.	As above – the right gave a benefit to the business of the occupant and not just the occupant of the business.

→

Case	About	Importance
Moncrieff v. *Jamieson* [2007] 1 WLR 2620	Car parking spaces can be an easement.	This case illustrates that, first, a car park space can benefit the land rather than the owner; and, secondly, that a pool (*obiter*) is also capable of enhancing the value of the land and may not just be recreational – though could involve positive expenditure and therefore would fail as an easement.
Borman v. *Griffith* [1930] 1 Ch 493	Landlord and tenant.	The two plots can be owned by one person providing they are occupied by two.
Aldred's Case [1610] 9 Co Rep 57b	The right to a view.	Too vague – an easement must be sufficiently definite.
Hunter v. *Canary Wharf* [1997] AC 655	TV signals.	Too vague – though could be an easement if through a defined channel – fibre-optically, for example.
Crow v. *Wood* [1971] 1 QB 77	The maintenance of fences.	Usually – no expenditure on the part of the servient land – this was a Lord Denning exception.
Grigsby v. *Melville* [1973] 1 WLR 1355	Cellar storage.	Where the right leads to almost exclusive possession this will not be an easement – an easement is about use not possession.
London & Blenheim Estates v. *Ladbroke Retail Parks* [1993] 4 All ER 157	Car park spaces.	Again, if non-specific it may be an easement – but not a specified exclusive parking space.
Wong v. *Beaumont* [1965] QB 173	Ventilation shaft in a restaurant.	An easement can be implied through necessity or common intention.
Wheeldon v. *Burrows* [1879] LR 12 Ch D 31	Implied easements after a split in land ownership.	The key case and rule which sets down how an easement will be implied once there has been a sale or lease of part of the property. If the continuous and apparent rights enjoyed by the original owner at the time of the grant are now reasonably necessary for the enjoyment of the land by the new owner then an easement will be implied.
Platt v. *Crouch* [2003] EWCA Civ 1110	Hotel claiming an easement of right of way, advertising and mooring of boats.	LPA 1925, section 62 operates to pass an easement to a new owner unless expressly excluded where there is prior diversity of occupation and a conveyance. This case blurs the line between section 62 and *Wheeldon*.

Statute	About	Importance
LPA 1925, s. 52(1)	The need for a deed when transferring land or rights in land.	This section sets down the formalities for a transfer of land by deed – this includes an easement.
LP(MP)A 1989, s. 2	Sets down that land may be transferred equitably but in writing and with a signatory.	No need for a deed – but all conveyances of land must at least be in writing and signed, *not* verbal assurances. Easements are also included here.
LPA 1925, s. 1(2) and LPA 1925, s. 3	Easements can be legal or equitable.	Easements are capable of being legal if by deed, 'for ever' or fixed. Otherwise they will be only equitable.
LPA 1925, s. 62	An easement can be implied to run with the land.	Where there is a conveyance and land is owned and occupied by different owners at the time of the grant.
LRA 2002, Schs. 1 and 3, para. 3	Sets down that an implied legal easement can be an overriding easement.	Only if the new owner has knowledge of, or on a reasonably careful inspection it is reasonably obvious, or the claimant has used the easement at any time in the last year.

FURTHER READING

Land Registry *Practice Guide 62 – Easements* http://www.landregistry. gov.uk/professional/guides/practice-guide-62
Examines the nature of an easement in relation to its creation and protection against third parties.

Land Registry *Practice Guide 52 – Easements by Prescription* http://www.landregistry.gov.uk/ professional/guides/practice-guide-52
Examines the nature of an easement by prescription giving detail on all methods available.

Law Commission *Making Land Work: Easements, covenants and profits à prendre* (Law Com. No. 327, 2011) http://lawcommission.justice.gov.uk/ docs/lc327_easements_report.pdf
Critical evaluation of the current law on easements (and covenants) with proposals for change.

Megarry & Wade, *The Law of Real Property*, 6th edition, 2000, Sweet & Maxwell

CHAPTER 9
Freehold covenants

BLUEPRINT

Freehold covenants

LEGISLATION

- Law of Property Act 1925
- Land Registration Act 2002

CONTEXT

- 80% of freehold properties are subject to restrictive covenants.
- The connection with easements.
- The need for reform.

CONCEPTS

- Legal and equitable rights
- Positive and negative covenants
- Benefit and burden
- Running with the land
- Building schemes and annexation
- Injunctions

- Is the passing of benefit and burden antiquated and convoluted?
- Should covenants be codified to make the process more understandable?
- Is it right that covenants are capable of binding future successors at all?

- Should a covenant be more than just a simple contract – should it be a proprietary right?
- Should there be a distinction between positive and negative covenants?
- Should the law be simplified in line with the Law Commissions proposals [327]?

CASES

- *Tulk* v. *Moxhay* [1848]
- *Smith & Snipes Hall Farm* v. *River Douglas* [1949]
- *Rhone* v. *Stephens* [1994]
- *Federated Homes* v. *Mill Lodge* [1980]
- *Elliston* v. *Reacher* [1908]
- *Jaggard* v. *Sawyer* [1995]

REFORM

- Should Parliament legislate to simplify the law on covenants [and easements] [the Law Commission Reform Paper 327 (2011)]?

SPECIAL CHARACTERISTICS

- The passing of the benefit at common law
- The passing of the burden at common law
- The passing of the burden in equity
- The passing of the benefit in equity

CRITICAL ISSUES

Setting the scene

Land is an extremely valuable asset and the ability to 'sell off' part of your land to a new buyer allows capital to be raised. It is also clear that entering into an agreement with the new buyer to do or not do something on their newly purchased land may have enormous benefits for the seller who has retained part of his land. It may be an agreement that the purchaser will not build on the acquired land, at least, for example, not within 10 metres of the boundary. It may be that the new purchaser agrees that the land will only be used for residential purposes rather than commercial, the seller benefiting from a lack of industrial activity in or around the property or area. These agreements are said to be 'negative' in nature, as the new owner is restricted in his use of the land rather than having any positive obligation to act.

If the agreement is between the buyer and seller, with no third party involvement, then this would be a contractual matter. What is vital in land law is what happens if and when the original seller taking the benefit (the *covenantee*) sells his retained land to another and the original buyer (the *covenantor*) also sells to a new purchaser. Can the two new owners 'on each side of the fence' enforce the original agreement against each other? Generally, if this was a simple contract (with some exceptions) the answer would be no. However, if the law recognises the agreement as a covenant, and that covenant is protected, the new buyer and new seller may be bound by the original covenant. The Law of Property Act 1925, section 3 sets down that covenants are equitable proprietary rights capable of binding third parties (they are not listed as a right capable of being legal at s. 1(2)), and this chapter will explain exactly how and when these covenants may be binding on parties other than the original covenantee/covenantor.

It is also important to note that this chapter deals only with **freehold** covenants, and not covenants between landlord and tenant (leasehold covenants), which fall outside the scope of this book as leasehold covenants are more generally seen as part of the study of landlord and tenant law.

DEFINITION AND BACKGROUND

CORNERSTONE

An equitable proprietary right

A covenant can be described as a legally binding 'promise' between freehold landowners where, as with easements, the affected plots of land are 'sufficiently close'. The original *covenantor* is the one 'burdened' by the agreement, whereas the *covenantee* is the one seen as taking the benefit. So if Emily sells part of her land to Amanda and agrees with Amanda that Amanda will not build on her newly acquired land, then through case law and statute, this agreement may be seen as a proprietary right rather than just contractual. The effect of this, of course, is that the right may be binding on third party new purchasers if the 'rules' of freehold covenants are satisfied.

It is not possible, however, for a covenant to be a 'legal' proprietary right, as it is not listed at section 1(2) of the LPA 1925, so it will always be classified under section 1(3) of the LPA as an equitable proprietary right. It is also vital to note that such a right is also not listed at Schedule 1 or 3 to the LRA 2002 as an overriding interest in its own right. So, for a covenant to be potentially binding on a new owner and 'run with land' it must be protected by a notice on the property register (in the charges section). It would be difficult, if not impossible, as with easements, to use a covenant to trigger a claim for actual occupation under paragraph 2 of Schedule 1 or 3 as the claimant would not be in actual occupation of the other's land, only their own. Hence, a notice on the register would be needed to protect the interest for and against successors in title.

It is, of course, true to say that in recent years, planning law and regulations (the Town and Country Planning Act 1990, for example) govern and control the use of land, but there is no doubt that the 'equitable' law of freehold covenants and its application has played and still plays a major role in regulating the use of land on a more local level between private landowners. In fact, the Law Commission's Consultation Paper 186 in 2008 suggested that almost 80 per cent of registered free-hold titles are subject to restrictive covenants (see Figure 9.1).

APPLICATION

Emily owns 'Grayson Manor' which comprises of a large house and swimming pool and an adjacent cottage known as 'The Beach House'. She retains the main house but sells 'The Beach House' to Amanda. Emily covenants with Amanda that 'The Beach House' will remain as it is, with no extensions or outbuildings added. Amanda agrees and this agreement forms part of the terms of the conveyance and this covenant is placed on the register as a notice. Amanda did as she agreed and did not extend or build.

The following year, Amanda sold 'The Beach House' to Jack and Emily sold the retained main house of 'Grayson Manor' to Nolan. Jack moved in and started to build more properties on his land.

Generally speaking, due to the fact that the covenant agreed between Emily and Amanda was a 'negative' covenant and was protected as a notice on the register, Nolan would be able to argue that Jack was bound by the covenant and as such may have a remedy (such as an injunction) against Jack to stop the building if the 'rules' of restrictive covenants, as will now be explained, can be applied.

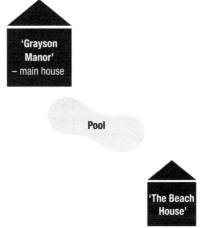

Figure 9.1 Before the sale to Amanda

INTERSECTION

As discussed in Chapter 8, easements and covenants are, *prima facie*, rather similar. They are both proprietary rights, and both are generally applicable where there has been a split of a plot of land, the owner of the retained land agreeing terms with the buyer of the sold land as to the use of the land. However, one key difference is that an easement is generally the right to use your neighbour's land, whereas a covenant is more of a restriction on the use of your own land. However, it is clear as to why the Law Commission Paper No. 327 (2011) argues that the law on easements and covenants is in need of reform.

Positive and negative covenants – benefit and burden explained

The first stage of analysing whether a covenant may be binding on a third party is to try to establish whether the covenant is a 'positive covenant' or a negative or 'restrictive covenant'. The general rule is that if the covenant is 'positive' then it will not 'run with the land' and therefore not be binding on a third party. The reasoning behind this is that the original agreement between the parties is contractual in nature, and the doctrine of *privity* (explained below) will generally not allow third parties to be burdened due to an essentially private contract between the two original parties. As such, if there is expenditure on the part of the covenantor then generally the covenant will be seen as positive and, although binding on the original covenantor (through the contract), it will not bind a successor in title. In the case of *Norwich City College* v. *McQuillin* [2009] a covenant to maintain a fence on the boundary of the two properties was seen as an obligation to perform an act and/or an expenditure of money, and as such was seen as positive and not binding on third parties. However, the key is to interpret the words of the covenant carefully. The key case of *Tulk* v. *Moxhay* (1848) illustrates this point:

CORNERSTONE

The *ratio* in *Tulk* v. *Moxhay*

In the key case of *Tulk* v. *Moxhay* (1848) the original covenantee, Mr Tulk sold land in the centre of Leicester Square, London, to Mr Elms. Elms promised on behalf of himself and successors in title to 'keep and maintain the said parcel of ground and square garden . . . as a square garden and pleasure ground, in an open state, uncovered with any buildings . . .' The land subsequently changed hands and was later owned by a Mr Moxhay who decided to build on the land, even though he knew about the original covenant and paid less for the land because of its existence.

Moxhay's argument was that to 'keep and maintain' involved expenditure and was therefore a positive covenant and not binding. However, the court found that the words 'keep and maintain' referred to the keeping of the land as an open space. This did not involve any expenditure and therefore a negative covenant existed which could bind – especially as Moxhay had 'notice' of the covenant all long. Tulk was able to bring an injunction against Moxhay in relation to the building work. The centre of Leicester Square is still a 'square garden and pleasure ground in an open state' over 160 years later!

Following *Tulk* v. *Moxhay*, if the covenant is negative in nature, then the 'burden' of the covenant may 'run with the land' and be binding on successors in title. The original covenantee, as with Tulk, may then be able to enforce the benefit of the covenant against future owners. If the original covenantee also sells, then it must also be established that the 'benefit' has run with the land, and it is this rather confusing 'formula' that will be explained below. Generally, then, it is necessary to analyse whether the benefit has 'run' from the original covenantee to the new owner (of Plot A), and then to ascertain whether the burden has also run from the original covenantor to the new owner (of Plot B) (see Figure 9.2).

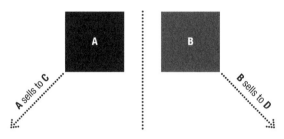

1. **A** agrees with **B** that **B** will 'keep and maintain **B's** land as 'open land'
2. **A** sells to **C**; **B** sells to **D**
3. **C** can enforce the agreement against **D** if the covenant is negative and **if** the benefit has 'run' to **C** and the burden 'runs' to **D**
4. **A's** covenant must also be entered on the register as a notice to bind/benefit successors in title

Figure 9.2 Restrictive covenants

There are, of course, one or two exceptions where the complex rules of freehold covenants do not need to be applied by successors in title, but these exceptions only apply where the successors are at least identifiable at the time of the original covenant. These exceptions are statutory, and are found at section 56 of the LPA 1925 and in the Contracts (Rights of Third Parties) Act 1999.

Privity and section 56 of the LPA 1925 and the Contract (Rights of Third Parties) Act 1999

As stated above, a covenant is essentially a contract between two parties – the covenantee and the covenantor. As such, the general contractual rule of 'privity' applies, and only the two parties may sue or be sued for a breach of the agreement (*Tweddle* v. *Atkinson* (1861)). So, if in our example above, Amanda does build on the plot of land sold to her by Emily, then Emily can sue Amanda for her breach of contract. If there is a sale on both sides, however, the doctrine of privity suggests that any successors in title will not be bound by the original agreement.

However, this common law doctrine was extended by statute – namely section 56 of the LPA and more recently the Contract (Rights of Third Parties) Act 1999. The LPA at section 56 states that: 'a person may take an immediate or other interest in land, or other property, or the benefit of any condition, right of entry, agreement over or respecting land, although he may not be named as a party to the conveyance or other instrument'.

However, this is qualified by only allowing those who are not specifically named to try to enforce the covenant if they are 'existing and identifiable' at the time of the original covenant. This could include 'owners for the time being' of the adjoining land, as was the case in *Re Ecclesiastical Commissioners' Conveyance* [1936]. In *White* v. *Bijou Mansions Ltd* [1938] a covenant which purported to include future landowners fell outside section 56 as they were not identifiable or in existence at the time of the covenant. Unless the covenant purports 'to be a grant to him or a covenant with him', section 56 would not apply (*Amsprop Trading Ltd* v. *Harris Distribution Ltd* [1997]).

However, since 11 May 2000 when the Contract (Rights of Third Parties) Act 1999 came into force, section 56 is no longer the only route available for a third party. Under section 1(3) of the C(RTP)A 1999, a third party may only sue if they are 'named' in the original contract, or are identifiable as a member of a class or description, though they do not need to be 'in existence' at the time of the original agreement. However, the Act is limited in that the remedy is restricted to damages only and only the original covenantor can be sued. As such, and especially where there is a sale of both plots, these exceptions are largely ineffective as future successors are unlikely to be named or identifiable at the time of the original covenant. As such, the 'rules' of the passing of the benefit and burden, both at common law and in equity need to be applied carefully.

DOES THE COVENANT 'RUN WITH THE LAND' AND BIND FUTURE SUCCESSORS IN TITLE?

This is best explained by another look at the scenario between Emily and Amanda:

APPLICATION

Emily owns 'Grayson Manor' which comprises of a large house and swimming pool and an adjacent cottage known as 'The Beach House'. She retains the main house but sells 'The Beach House' to Amanda. Emily covenants with Amanda that 'The Beach House' will remain as it is, with no extensions or outbuildings added. Amanda agrees and this agreement forms part of the terms of the conveyance and this covenant is placed on the register as a notice. Amanda did as she agreed and did not extend or build.

The following year, Amanda sold 'The Beach House' to Jack and Emily sold the retained main house of 'Grayson Manor' to Nolan. Jack moved in and started to build more properties on his land.

If Emily sells 'The Beach House' to Amanda but *does not* then sell the main house to Nolan, then it is clear that Emily, the original covenantee, is still there. There is no need to analyse the 'passing' of any benefit as Emily is still enjoying the benefit of the original covenant. Similarly, if Amanda *does not* sell 'The Beach House' to Jack, then there is no need to analyse the 'passing' of the burden as the burden is still with Amanda. This remains a simple 'contractual' covenant between Emily and Amanda. However, if Amanda sells to Jack, with Emily still in place, then again there is no need to assess the passing of any benefit; only the passing of the burden is relevant. The complexity occurs when Amanda sells to Jack and Emily sells to Nolan. At that point there are two key questions: has the benefit passed to Nolan and has the burden passed to Jack? What follows is a rather convoluted and complex formula that needs to be followed – hence the basis of the Law Commission proposal for reform! The structure of the legal analysis is as follows:

- Does the benefit pass at common law?
- Does the burden pass at common law?
- Does the burden pass in equity?
- Does the benefit pass in equity?

This complex and rather convoluted process has been widely criticised and is the subject of the Law Commission Report No. 327 (2011). It is worth reading the report and deciding whether you agree as to whether the law on covenants is in need of reform. You can find the report at www.justice.gov.uk/lawcommission/areas/easements.htm.

REFLECTION

Benefit passing at common law

Generally speaking, the benefit of a covenant can pass at common law even without expressly assigning it as part of the conveyance. However, there are four conditions that must be satisfied, as stated in *Smith & Snipes Hall Farm Ltd* v. *River Douglas Catchment Board* [1949]. These conditions are as follows:

1. *The covenant must 'touch and concern' the land.* Generally, as with the characteristics of an easement from *Re Ellenborough*, this means that the covenant cannot simply confer a personal benefit but must 'affect the land . . . [or] affect the value of the land' (Tucker LJ in *Smith & Snipes*).
2. *The covenantee must have a legal estate in the land.* This means that the estate must be legal and not equitable.
3. *The assignee of the land must also have a legal estate.* However, the interpretation of section 78(1) of the LPA 1925 was given substantive application by the Court of Appeal, stating that the covenantee and assignee may have different legal estates such as landlord and tenant (as in *Smith*).
4. *The covenant must be intended to run with the land.* This means that it needs to be established that at the time of the covenant there must be an intention that the covenant will benefit successors in title. However, this can be expressed in the conveyance but is implied through section 78(1) of the LPA 1925, which states that a covenant is 'deemed' to run with the land to benefit successors in title.

Burden passing at common law

The general rule is that the burden will *never* pass at common law (for the reasons stated above). Therefore, only the original covenantor will be bound by the covenant at common law. If there is no sale by the original covenantor, then the passing of the benefit at common law to the successor in title of the original covenantee will suffice. However, once the original covenantor sells, then any burden will not pass to the new owner at common law. There are a number of key case law examples which illustrate this point. In *Austerberry* v. *Oldham Corporation* (1885) the burden of keeping a road in good repair did not pass to the successor in title of the original covenantor. Similarly, in *Rhone* v. *Stephens* [1994] the same rule applied and the burden of a positive covenant did not pass at common law. Lord Templeman stated that 'for over 100 years . . . equity will enforce negative covenants . . . but has no power to enforce positive covenants'. He said that this would 'enforce a personal obligation against a person who has not covenanted'. In 1998, the rule was reaffirmed in *Thamesmead Town* v. *Allotey* where Allotey, the successor in title, was not liable to pay for service charges in relation to an earlier covenant.

However, there are a few exceptions to the rule, where the burden of a covenant will run at common law. These include 'enfranchisement' where a long lease is 'enlarged' to a freehold after the tenant has used his right to buy all or part of the freehold. Any leasehold covenants that were pre-existing will then remain binding. Secondly, a 'commonhold scheme' can be created under the Commonhold and Leasehold Reform Act 2002, whereby a number of unit-holders can 'manage' their units under a 'Commonhold Scheme' and contract that covenants will be permanently attached to each unit. Thirdly, the 'mutual burden and benefit' rule can be applied – known as the rule in *Halsall* v. *Brizell* [1957] – where if benefits are enjoyed then burdens must be accepted.

> **Take note**
>
> Generally, the rule is that the burden of a covenant does not pass at common law, so as soon as there is a transfer of land from original covenantor, the passing of the burden in equity must be established. Exceptions such as enfranchisement, Commonhold and the rule in Halsall v. Brizell are possible, but are rare.

Burden passing in equity

This is generally based on the rule in *Tulk* v. *Moxhay* and, as with the benefit passing at common law, strict criteria have been set down by the courts to prevent restrictive covenants being used too broadly:

1. *The covenant must be negative (restrictive) in nature.* The rule has been set out above, as in the case of *Tulk* v. *Moxhay*. Generally, the words of the covenant must be analysed carefully to establish that there is no positive act or expenditure stipulated.

2. *The covenant must be made for the benefit of the land retained by the covenantee.* This means that when the covenant is given, the covenantee must possess land which can take the benefit – there must be a dominant tenement and servient tenement (see Easements – Chapter 8). In *London County Council* v. *Allen* [1914] the LCC did not have 'sufficiently close' land capable of benefiting from the covenant.

> **Take note**
>
> There are a few statutory exceptions to this rule – National Trust and local authority land are two such examples.

3. *The covenant must 'touch and concern' the land of the covenantee.* Once again, this means that benefit cannot be purely personal. In *Re Ballard's Conveyance* [1937] and *Wrotham Park Estate* v. *Parkside Homes* [1974] it was held that it is necessary to establish that the benefit is to the land – but where the land is a large area (such as 4,000 acres in *Wrotham*), a covenant should be taken to mean a benefit for 'each and every part' of the land.

4. *The burden of the covenant must be intended to run with the land.* Once again, this means that it needs to be established that at the time of the covenant there must be an intention that the covenant will burden successors in title. However, this can be expressed in the conveyance but is implied through section 79 of the LPA 1925 which states that the burden of a covenant is 'deemed' to run with the land unless there are express words to the contrary (*Morrells* v. *Oxford United Football Club Ltd* [2001]).

5. *The burden will only pass in equity* ***if*** *it is protected by a notice on the register – it is not an over-riding interest.*

(See Figure 9.3.)

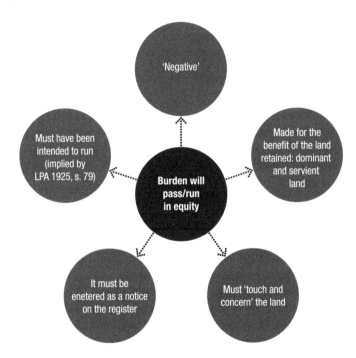

Figure 9.3 The Passing of the Burden

Benefit passing in equity

Once again, for the benefit to pass in equity, the covenant must 'touch and concern the land' as above. However, it must be established that the benefit has been passed in one of three ways:

- annexation
- assignment
- through a building scheme.

Annexation

This means that the covenant is permanently attached to the land, and as such will pass with any subsequent conveyance of that land. There are three main forms of annexation: express; implied; and statutory.

Express annexation

This means that in the conveyance itself clear words are used to make it clear that the benefit is to run. In *Rogers* v. *Hosegood* [1900] the Duke of Bedford covenanted 'with intent that the covenants . . . bind . . . to the benefit of Cubitt & Co, their heirs and assigns'. In *Small* v. *Oliver & Saunders* [2006], following the key ruling of Brightman LJ in *Federated Homes* v. *Mill Lodge Properties* [1980], a covenant is *prima facie* deemed to be annexed to 'each and every part of the land' unless otherwise stated.

Statutory annexation

Especially since the case of *Federated Homes*, it is accepted that the benefit of a covenant can be annexed by way of section 78 of the LPA 1925. As seen earlier, section 78 deems that all covenants are to run with the land unless expressly stated to the contrary. This means that express annexation is largely redundant, as section 78 will operate to annexe a covenant to land automatically. The only exception is where words to the contrary have been used. This can be seen in *Roake* v. *Chadha* [1983] and more recently in *City Inn* v. *Ten Trinity Square* [2008] and *Margerison* v. *Bates* [2008]. Also, as in *Crest Nicholson* v. *McAllister* [2004], the land in question must be identifiable, otherwise section 78 will not succeed.

Implied annexation

Again, due to the operation of section 78, implied annexation is also largely redundant, but annexation may still be implied from the surrounding facts of the case. In *Marten* v. *Flight Refuelling* [1962] it was held that the 'surrounding circumstances' can be used to imply annexation, but this is all rather moot due to the impact of section 78.

Assignment

The successor to the original covenantee's land can argue that there was a chain of assignments of the covenant from the original covenantee to the successor. However, there are many difficulties in establishing the chain, as can be seen in the case of *Newton Abbott Co-Operative* v. *Williamson and Treadgold* [1952].

Building scheme

This is often referred to as a 'scheme of development' or a 'building scheme' and is where there is often a new development where an area of land is being developed. Plots are laid out by the developer with the aim of selling the plots to individual purchasers. The idea here is to create mutually enforceable covenants which will benefit all of the owners. An example may be a covenant only to mow the lawn between 2 pm and 5 pm on a Saturday! The aim would be to bind all owners and their successors in title. In order to achieve this, the case of *Elliston* v. *Reacher* [1908] set down strict criteria:

- All parties must have derived their title from a common vendor.
- Prior to selling the land the vendor must have laid out identifiable plots subject to the restrictive covenants.
- The covenants must apply to all plots with intended benefit for all.
- The purchasers must have bought with full knowledge of the covenants.

In later years, a more relaxed approach was taken. In *Re Dolphin's Conveyance* [1970] it was held that there was no need for a common vendor or identifiable plots. However, it was affirmed that covenants must apply to each plot equally – (*Emile Elias* v. *Pine Grove* [1993]). The modern approach is simply that there must be a scheme of covenants intended to apply to all (*Whitgift Homes* v. *Stocks* [2001]) and that there must be a pre-conceived common intention that the covenants apply equally and to all

(*Small* v. *Oliver & Saunders* [2006]). In *Turner* v. *Pryce* [2008] the claimants successfully claimed an injunction in relation to preventing the defendants developing their gardens as a building scheme provided for the benefit of restrictive covenants to apply to all plots.

REMEDIES AND REFORM

It is, of course, true to say that covenants can be ended through mutual agreement or by the dominant and servient land merging back into the hands of one owner (as with easements). Also as with easements, the Lands Tribunal does have jurisdiction under section 84 of the LPA 1925 to discharge or vary a covenant if it sees fit. In terms of remedies for breach, the contractual remedy of damages is severely limited due to the doctrine of privity. Damages cannot be sought between the original covenantee and successors in title. However, an injunction and/or damages may be sought under the Supreme Court Act 1981, section 50.

As covenants are equitable in nature, the usual remedy is an injunction – *mandatory* to 'pull down' any work that has been done in breach of a covenant or *prohibitory* to stop work going ahead before it starts. It is important to note, though, that the courts may be slow to order demolition of property built in breach of a covenant. In *Wrotham Park* v. *Parkside* [1974] damages were awarded (5 per cent of expected profit). In *Surrey County Council* v. *Bredero Homes* [1993] nominal damages were awarded as there were no tangible losses. In *Jaggard* v. *Sawyer* [1995] damages were awarded as an injunction would have been 'too oppressive'.

As suggested above, the Law Commission has recently published its reform proposals in its report *Making Land Work: Easements, Covenants and Profits à Prendre* (Law Com. No. 327, June 2011). This has already been discussed above – but it is useful to read the report in full to be able to understand the full critique of the current law on covenants. The report can be found at www.justice.gov.uk. lawcommission/areas/easements.htm.

KEY POINTS

- A covenant is an agreement between two freeholders. Essentially this is contractual in nature and is binding only on the original covenantor and covenantee.

- If the 'rules' are satisfied, then a covenant is capable of being a proprietary right which may bind third parties outside the statutory exceptions of section 56 of the LPA 1925 and the Contract (Rights of Third Parties) Act 1999.

- A covenant can only ever be an equitable right, not legal, as it is outside section 1(2) of the LPA 1925 and can never be an overriding interest as it falls outside Schedules 1 and 3 to the LRA 2002. It must be protected as a notice on the register.

- Key cases such as *Tulk* v. *Moxhay* (1848) set down that only a negative covenant will 'run with the land' and if there is a sale of both plots of land already subject to a covenant, then common law and equitable rules must be applied.

- The benefit will run at common law, but *generally the burden will not* – following cases like *Austerberry* v. *Oldham* and *Rhone* v. *Stephens*.

- The burden may run in equity if the covenant is negative; touches and concerns the land; and is intended to run – which, under section 79 of the LPA 1925, it is deemed to do unless contrary intention is expressed. In order to bind a third party the covenant must be protected as a notice on the register.

- The benefit will run in equity through either annexation, assignment or a building scheme. LPA 1925, section 78 states that the benefit of a covenant is deemed to run with the land unless stated otherwise.

- Covenants can be ended through mutual agreement; through merger of the dominant and servient land or by the Lands Tribunal under section 84 of the LPA 1925.

- The most common remedy for a breach of a covenant is an injunction, but damages are available where an injunction is too oppressive (*Jaggard* v. *Sawyer*).

- The recent Law Commission Report (No. 327, 2011) suggests that the law on covenants (and easements) should be reformed and replaced with a system of 'land obligations'.

CORE CASES AND STATUTES

Case	About	Importance
Tulk v. *Moxhay* (1848) 2 Ph 774	Land in the centre of Leicester Square.	This is the first case which established that only a negative covenant is capable of running with the land and binding a third party.
Smith & Snipes Hall Farm v. *River Douglas* [1949] 2 KB 500	Sets down the four main conditions for the benefit running at common law.	This case suggests that the benefit will nearly always run with the land at common law – especially with the statutory provision at section 78 of the LPA 1925.
Austerberry v. *Oldham* (1885) 29 Ch D 750; *Rhone* v. *Stephens* [1994] 2 AC 310; *Thamesemead Town* v. *Allotey* [1998] EWCA Civ 15	These cases suggest the burden will not run at common law.	Along with the later cases of *Rhone* and *Thamesmead* v. *Allotey*, *Austerberry* supports the principle that a burden should not pass at common law due to the doctrine of contractual privity.
Halsall v. *Brizell* [1957] Ch 169	There are some exceptions to the rule that a burden will not run at common law.	The rule here is that of 'mutual burden and benefit' – if you take a benefit at common law, you may need to accept a burden too.
Morrells v. *Oxford United Football Club* [2001] Ch 459	Clear words of a lack of intention that a covenant should run.	Express words to the contrary will defeat the implied intention that a covenant will run at section 78 of the LPA 1925.

Case	About	Importance
Federated Homes v. *Mill Lodge* [1980] 1 WLR 594	A question arose as to the extent of a covenant being annexed to land.	It was held that the substantive effect of section 78 is such that a covenant is deemed to annexe to 'each and every part' of the land.
Roake v. *Chadha* [1984] 1 WLR 40	As *Morrells*, above.	Clear words to the contrary will also defeat the implied intention at section 79 that a burden is deemed to run with the land.
Elliston v. *Reacher* [1908] 2 Ch 374	Discusses the conditions for the running of the benefit in equity through a building scheme.	Sets down the strict conditions under which such a scheme operates – later loosened by *Re Dolphin's Conveyance*.
Jaggard v. *Sawyer* [1995] 1 WLR 269	Remedy for breach of covenant.	Generally the remedy will be an injunction but damages can be awarded where an injunction is too oppressive.

Statute	About	Importance
LPA 1925, ss. 1(2) and 1(3)	Legal and equitable proprietary rights.	These sections demonstrate that a covenant is capable of being an equitable proprietary right only.
LRA 2002, Schs 1 and 3	Set down the list of remaining overriding interests.	A covenant is not an overriding interest and needs protecting by way of a notice on the register.
LPA 1925, s. 56 and the Contract (Rights of Third Parties) Act 1999	The doctrine of privity is extended by these two statutes in relation to covenants.	Third parties may be able to enforce an original covenant – but only if they are named or identifiable at the time of the original covenant.
LPA 1925, ss. 78 and 79	Statutory provisions which set down the rules by which the benefit (s. 78) and the burden (s. 79) of covenants may be deemed to run with the land.	Covenants are deemed to run with the land unless there are contrary words in the conveyance suggesting otherwise.

FURTHER READING

Cooke, E. 'To restate or not to restate? Old wine, new wineskins, old covenants, new ideas' [2009] Conv 448
This article gives a detailed critique of the current law on covenants and looks at the Law Commission's proposals for change.

Federated Homes v. Mill Lodge Properties [1980] 1 WLR 594
A reading of this judgment gives an insight into the simplification of the law through an application of section 78 of the LPA 1925.

Law Commission: *Making Land Work: Easements, covenants and profits à prendre* (Law Com. No. 327, 2011) www.justice.gov.uk. lawcommission/areas/easements. htm
Examines in detail the proposals and need for change in relation to covenants (inter alia).

Tulk v. Moxhay (1848) 2 Ph 774
A reading of this seminal case gives an excellent breakdown of how to make an analysis of whether a covenant is positive or negative.

CHAPTER 10

Mortgages

BLUEPRINT
Mortgages

KEY QUESTIONS

LEGISLATION

- Law of Property Act 1925
- Administration of Justice Act 1970/1973

CONTEXT

- The 'credit crunch' financial crisis.
- 'Sub-prime' lending especially in the US.
- The Human Rights Act 1998 and its impact.

CONCEPTS

- Legal and equitable mortgages
- Possession
- Peaceable re-entry
- redemption
- clogs and fetters
- undue influence

- Is it against Protocol 1 HRA 1998 to take possession by peaceable re-entry?
- Should a lender be able to bankrupt a borrower as in *Alliance* v. *Slayford*?
- Did the *Etridge Guidelines* work?

- Is a mortgage more a simple contract, or is it more a proprietary right?
- Should a lender be able to take possession easily?
- Should unconscionable interest rates defeat a lender's rights?

CASES

- *Four Maids* v. *Dudley Marshal* [1957]
- *Horsham* v. *Clark* [2009]
- *Bishop* v. *Blake* [2006]
- *Samuel* v. *Jarrah Timber* [1904]
- *RBS* v. *Etridge* [2001]

REFORM

- Should Parliament legislate to outlaw foreclosure – the Law Commission Reform Paper 204 (1991)?
- Should the Human Rights Act prevent possession without due process?

SPECIAL CHARACTERISTICS

- The right to take possession from 'before the ink is dry'
- The 'defence' to ask for a reasonable time under AJA 1970, s. 36
- The statutory right to sell
- Common law duties – the lender must try to get the best price possible
- The 'defence' of 'clogs and fetters'
- The 'defence' of undue influence

CRITICAL ISSUES

Setting the scene

For many years, the study of land law included a rather theoretical subject which didn't seem particularly 'living and breathing' to many of those studying. The property market was buoyant, and the warning that 'buying a home may be a great option . . . but only if you're ready for the financial commitment and responsibility of home ownership' (Fannie Mae, 2013 – see Further Reading below) was largely ignored. However, this was before the so-called 'credit crunch' and financial crisis which according to many had 'started in the US housing market where banks had lent money to "sub-prime" borrowers' (such as Fannie Mae) (BBC News, 2013 – see below). This subject is, of course, the law of mortgages.

The law of mortgages from a land law perspective can be split into three main areas of interest. These are the rights and obligations of the lender; the rights of the borrower; and a doctrine 'borrowed' from contract law, the doctrine of undue influence. It is also worth noting that a mortgage, by its very nature, is a contract. As such, some of the general law of contract applies. However, a mortgage is also another form of proprietary right capable of being legal under section 1(2)(c) of the LPA 1925. A lender can and must register this charge (under sections 25 and 27 of the LRA 2002) as a notice in the charges section of the register in order for it to be binding against third parties. A mortgage can also be an equitable mortgage, but this is generally only where the formalities of creation and registration of a legal mortgage have not been satisfied, or where an equitable interest is mortgaged as opposed to a mortgage relating to the entire legal title (see Chapters 1 and 6). However, it is the 'charge by way of legal mortgage' (section 1(2)(c) of the LPA 1925) that will be discussed in detail below.

CREATION OF A MORTGAGE

CORNERSTONE

The LPA 1925

According to section 1(2)(c) of the LPA 1925, a mortgage is one of the key interests that can be created 'at law' by way of a deed. The LPA 1925 at section 23 states that the only way that a legal mortgage of registered land can be created is by way of a 'legal charge'. The lender or *mortgagee* lends the money to the borrower or *mortgagor* and registers the mortgage as a legal charge against the title of the new owner (sections 25 and 27 of the LRA 2002). Until this is completed, the mortgage remains equitable in nature.

A mortgage was defined in the case of *Santley* v. *Wilde* (1899) as the 'creation of an estate or interest in property . . . as a security for the payment of a debt . . . for which it is given'. In simpler terms, it is of course a secured loan given by a lender to a borrower, in return for which the lender takes a charge over the property. The mortgagor takes legal title in return for the 'legal charge' the lender takes over the property (sections 85 and 86 of the LPA 1925). As above, a mortgage of registered land is a 'disposition of a registered estate' and for it to become 'effective at law' it must be registered in line with section 27(2)(f) of the LRA 2002, remaining equitable only up until registration. It should also be understood, however, that a written agreement to create a mortgage (rather than by deed), providing it complies with the formalities set down at section 2 of the LP(MP)A 1989', will also be an equitable mortgage. It is also possible, though rare, to take an equitable mortgage secured against your equitable interest in the property.

RIGHTS OF THE LENDER

The fact that the lender takes a legal charge over the property gives them legal rights to deal with that property in many ways under certain circumstances – usually on default (non-payment of the monthly payments) by the borrower:

INTERSECTION

As discussed in Chapter 6, a co-owner joint tenant with an equitable interest in a property is able to mortgage his equitable interest if a lender is willing to give such a loan, and this will act as an act of severance – creating a tenancy in common interest for the lender.

> There are many different types of mortgage available: the repayment mortgage; the endowment mortgage; the pension mortgage; and a mortgage (usually a 'second mortgage') secured against the property to secure a loan for a business venture. You can, of course, research these different types of mortgage, but in relation to the study of land law, it is not essential to learn the difference between the types of mortgage – this is more to do with finance than law. Land law does not really distinguish – as was said in *Santley* v. *Wilde*, 'once a mortgage always a mortgage' – the type of mortgage is merely incidental.

CONTEXT

The lender can simply *sue the borrower* for the debt as the mortgage is, as stated above, a contract. If the property is sold and 'negative equity' results in money still being owed, then a personal claim can be brought for the debt against the borrower as in *Rudge* v. *Richens* (1873).

The lender can also use *foreclosure* as a remedy, but this method is extremely draconian, extinguishing all rights, both legal and equitable, of the borrower (sections 88 and 89 of the LPA 1925). The court also has the power to grant a sale rather than foreclosure, under section 91 of the LPA 1925 (see Figure 10.1).

Take note

The Law Commission (Report No. 204, 1991) suggested that foreclosure was 'unnecessary and undesirable' as a remedy due to its oppressive nature. The report also gives a very detailed overview of the law relating to mortgages (as it was then) and the need for reform. (See Further Reading below.)

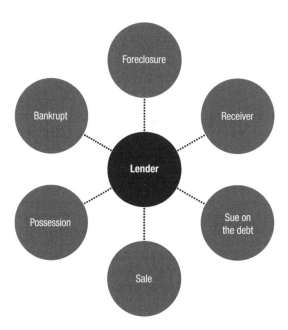

Figure 10.1 Lender's rights

The lender can also appoint a receiver (under sections 101 and 109 of the LPA 1925) but the two key rights of a lender are the right to *possession* and the right to *sell* – these will be discussed in detail as they are the two rights most widely enjoyed by the lender.

Possession

The right to possess the property is, of course, a fundamental right that may be exercised by the lender. It is a common law right rather than statutory and is a right exercisable, as with all other rights of the lender, due to the fact that there is a registered legal charge on the property. As such, unless the mortgage contract contains a specific clause to the contrary, as in *Ashley Guarantee* v. *Zacaria* [1993], a lender may take possession 'even before the ink is dry on the contract' – in other words, from the moment the contract is signed (*Four Maids* v. *Dudley Marshal* [1957]). In practice, of course, a lender would rarely exercise this right unless there was default by the borrower, but it is always a possibility:

....**APPLICATION**

In the case of *Realkredit Danmark* v. *Brookfield House* [2000], a lender took possession without default on mortgage payments (though there were other breaches of the mortgage conditions by the borrower).

The next step is to identify how the lender takes possession, and there are two ways in which this might happen – with or without a court order (see Figure 10.2). Again, due to the fact that there is a registered legal charge over the property, technically and traditionally, the lender can opt for possession without a court order.

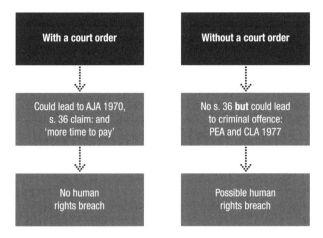

Figure 10.2 Possession methods

Without a court order

This method is known as 'peaceable re-entry' and usually consists of a lender simply informing the borrower by letter that they are to vacate in order to allow the lender to take possession. In *Ropeigealach* v. *Barclays Bank* [1999] the Court of Appeal held that this method could be used, though with a warning that it is both 'dangerous and uncivilised'. The reason for the warning, more recently seen in the case of *Horsham* v. *Beech* [2009], is that 'peaceable re-entry' may soon turn 'un-peaceable' in relation to a residential property, if the lender is aware that the borrower is still in the property at the time of possession, and there is a possibility of intimidation or violence. This would then result in a criminal offence being committed by the lender under section 5 of the Protection from Eviction Act 1977 and section 6 of the Criminal Law Act 1977. In *Horsham* v. *Clark* a human rights issue was also raised, in that it was questioned as to whether taking possession away from a borrower contravened Protocol 1 of the European Convention on Human Rights incorporated within the Human Rights Act 1998:

Protocol 1, Art. 1 of the European Convention on Human Rights provides:

(1) Every natural or legal person is entitled to the peaceful enjoyment of his possessions. No one shall be deprived of his possessions except in the public interest and subject to the conditions provided for by law . . . and by the general principles of . . . law.

(2) The preceding provisions shall not, however, in any way impair the right of a state to enforce such laws as it deems necessary to control the use of property in accordance with the general interest or to secure the payment of taxes or other contributions or penalties.

It was decided that taking possession without a court order *could* contravene the Protocol, but, due to it being heavily qualified in paragraph (2), English common law of possession does not *per se* contravene human rights. However, the Council for Mortgage Lenders, the body which regulates the mortgage lending sector, sent out advice to all its lenders that, following *Horsham*, a court order should be the preferred method.

With a court order

However, there is an advantage for the lender in using the 'peaceable re-entry' method. If this method is used, rather than a court order, the borrower cannot invoke section 36 of the Administration of Justice Act 1970 (as amended by section 8 of the AJA 1973) to ask for a reasonable time to pay any arrears owed. This 'stay of execution' by the court can only be granted if a court order *is* used by the lender – triggering the section 36 'defence' to possession. Prior to the case of *Cheltenham and Gloucester* v. *Norgan* [1996], a 'reasonable time' was rather arbitrarily set by the courts, usually between two and four years. However, *Norgan* clarified that the borrower should have the remaining time left on the mortgage to pay off any arrears provided that the borrower could convince the court that they were not in negative equity; they were able to pay; and that they would not fall into arrears again in the future, providing the court with a budget plan as evidence.

....**APPLICATION**

In *Norgan*, 13 years remained on the mortgage, with over £125,000 in positive equity on the property. The court allowed the arrears to be paid off over the remaining 13 years.

Sale

The power to sell the property after possession is a statutory right set down at section 101 of the LPA 1925, which details when the power to sell *arises*, and section 103 of the LPA 1925, which details when the right to sell becomes *exercisable*. The distribution of proceeds of sale is also set down at section 105 of the LPA 1925. Section 101 sets down that the right to sell only arises in relation to a legal (rather than equitable) mortgage and provided the power of sale is not excluded by the mortgage contract itself. Section 103 sets down when the right to sell becomes exercisable – contingent on default in relation to arrears or any other breach of the contract such as, for example, leasing or altering the property without permission of the lender:

⊕ CORNERSTONE

LPA 1925, section 103

103   Regulation of exercise of power of sale

A mortgagee shall not exercise the power of sale conferred by this Act unless and until –

(i)   Notice requiring payment of the mortgage money has been served on the mortgagor or one of two or more mortgagors, and default has been made in payment of the mortgage money, or of part thereof, for three months after such service; or

(ii)   Some interest under the mortgage is in arrear and unpaid for two months after becoming due; or

(iii) There has been a breach of some provision contained in the mortgage deed or in this Act . . .

In relation to proceeds of sale, section 105 sets down the order of distribution, starting with the payment of sums owing to the lender and their costs, any subsequent secured loans, and ending with money being returned to the borrower if any money remains!

However, the lender also is subject to a number of duties that, although not overly restrictive, do act as a safeguard to try to ensure that a lender acts in accordance with the common law.

Common law duties of the lender on sale

There are a number of key common law duties in relation to a lender selling the property.

There is a common law understanding that although the lender is effectively holding the sale money 'in trust' until the proceeds are distributed (section 105 of the LPA 1925), the lender is *not* a trustee in the legal sense of the word – meaning that there is no actual trust in operation (*Nash* v. *Eads* (1880)).

The lender does, therefore, have an 'unfettered discretion' as to how and when they sell to achieve repayment of the debt, though they are, as with the BSA 1986 above, under a duty to try to obtain the best possible price when they sell. The seminal case on this point is *Cuckmere Brick* v. *Mutual Finance* [1971] but this

> **Take note**
>
> If the lender is a building society rather than a bank, some duties also lie in statute – at paragraph 4 of the Building Societies Act 1986 (BSA 1986) – the duty to take reasonable care to get the best price possible.

was recently affirmed in *Bishop* v. *Blake* [2006] where, although the court held that there was no obligation to aggressively market the property, hiding a very small advertisement for the sale on the back of an obscure trade magazine *The Publican* without any contact number of the seller was, according to Ferris J, 'pathetic' in terms of its marketing and showed no real effort to get the best price possible.

However, the case of *Silven* v. *Royal Bank of Scotland* [2003] illustrates that there is no duty on the lender to delay the sale until the market recovers. There is also technically nothing to prevent a lender from selling the property to a family company even where the lender has a significant interest, though any sale to himself will be void (*Tse Kwong Lam* v. *Wong Chit Sen* [1983]) (see Figure 10.3).

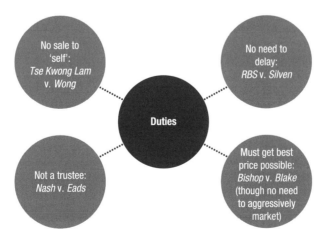

Figure 10.3 Common law duties on sale

It can be argued that the lender does have an almost 'unfettered' power to possess and to sell the property – due to their legal charge over that property from the signing of the mortgage. There are common law and statutory restrictions; however, these restrictions are not too onerous for a lender to overcome. This falls in line with the general policy consideration stated in *Horsham* v. *Clark* – that a lender has a very broad right to realise his asset, especially on default. It should also be noted that the lender can also attempt to 'bankrupt' the borrower if all else fails – as in the case of *Alliance and Leicester* v. *Slayford* [2000] where, although the court referred to the Alliance's choice of method as 'vile', it was ultimately allowed!

RIGHTS OF THE BORROWER

As suggested above, the borrower does have a number of rights that essentially exist to allow the borrower to 'pay off' their mortgage and to redeem their property when the full mortgage debt has been repaid. Other than the statutory provision at section 36 of the Administration of Justice Act 1970 (AJA 1970), the borrower also has a number of equitable rights, known collectively as the 'equity of redemption' (see Figure 10.4).

Take note

Even though the section 36 claim has been discussed above, it should not be overlooked that this is the major right of the borrower and should always take precedence in any illustration you might give on the rights of the borrower.

Take note

The case of *L'Estrange* v. *Graucob* [1934] from the law of contract held that any term in a contract would be binding if that contract is signed – with the exception of operative misrepresentation.

Reasonable time to pay – section 36 of the AJA 1970/section 8 of the AJA 1973

As discussed above, if the lender uses a court order to try to take possession, the borrower is able to counter this with a claim under section 36 as amended by section 8 of the AJA 1970/1973 to ask the court for a reasonable time to pay the arrears. The details of this 'defence' have been discussed above.

Equitable rights of redemption – clogs and fetters

One of the main principles underpinning the law of mortgages is that the borrower should be free to pay off their debt and redeem their property when the debt to the lender is repaid in full. The case of *Samuel* v. *Jarrah Timber* [1904] set down the principle that there should not be any 'clog or fetter on the equity of redemption'. In other words, although the mortgage is a contract, and essentially any term in the mortgage once signed becoming binding, a mortgage is also a proprietary right subject to certain equitable rights and protections that may be capable of voiding certain terms within the contract if they unfairly prevent redemption.

There are two main examples of 'clogs and fetters' – *unfair penalties* and *unconscionable interest rates*.

Unfair penalties and unconscionable interest rates

In relation to unfair penalties, the courts may allow terms in a contract that are merely collateral to the main mortgage contract, but where there is an unfair advantage to the lender that forms part of the mortgage, this may be struck out by the courts as unconscionable. In the case of *Kreglinger* v. *Patagonia Meat* [1914] the advantage (which was a right of first refusal on the sale of sheepskins) was unconnected to the mortgage transaction between the two parties. In the case of *Santley* v. *Wilde* (see above) the unfair advantage to the lender of a share of profits to be paid after redemption of the mortgage was not collateral and was part and parcel of the mortgage agreement. The same conclusion was drawn in the case of *Noakes* v. *Rice* [1902] where a covenant to continue buying 'malt liquors' after the mortgage to the brewery had been paid in full was seen as a 'clog on the equity' to redeem.

The second example of a 'clog and fetter' is where the lender imposes an arbitrary and therefore unconscionable interest rate on the borrower. In *Cityland Holdings* v. *Dabrah* [1968] the national rate was 7 per cent, the initial rate in the mortgage was 17 per cent *but* rising to an unconscionable 57 per cent on first default by the borrower. This was said to 'trouble the conscience of the court' and was struck out as unfair. However, where the borrower is an experienced property developer having taken legal advice, even a 48 per cent rate will not necessarily be seen as unconscionable (*Ketley* v. *Scott* [1981]) or where the 'appalling credit history' of the borrower facilitates a high interest rate (46 per cent) as in *Woodstead Finance* v. *Petrou* [1985].

> It should be noted that the Consumer Credit Act 2006 regulates credit agreements between lenders and borrowers. However, first time legal mortgages of residential land are exempt from the provisions of the Act – so this Act is largely irrelevant in relation to most mortgages.

CONTEXT

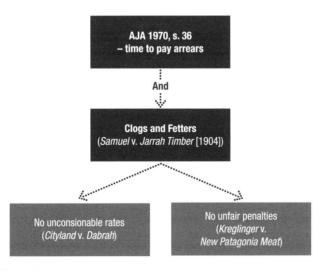

Figure 10.4 Rights of the borrower

UNDUE INFLUENCE

As explained above, the doctrine of undue influence is 'borrowed' from the law of contract. This is essentially where, in any contract, a party can claim 'undue influence' or 'improper pressure' in signing a contract. The effect of this 'pressure' is that a contract can be made void due to the undue influence evidencing a lack of genuine consent – a necessary component of any contract.

> Equity gives relief on the ground of undue influence where an agreement has been obtained by certain kinds of *improper pressure* which were thought not to amount to duress at common law because no element of violence to the person was involved (GH Treitel, *The Law of Contract*).

CONTEXT

Definition – Class 1 and 2A and 2B

Undue influence was described by Lindley LJ in *Allcard* v. *Skinner* (1887) as 'some unfair and improper conduct, some coercion from outside, some overreaching, some form of cheating and generally, though not always, some personal advantage gained'.

'Class 1' undue influence needed the claimant to prove conclusively that improper pressure was exerted. It was traditionally held that there was a need for the injured party to demonstrate some loss or disadvantage when claiming undue influence, but the House of Lords in *CIBC Mortgages* v. *Pitt* [1993] stated that there is '*no further requirement* [of] . . . *manifest disadvantage*', disapproving *BCCI* v. *Aboody* [1989] on this point.

'Class 2 undue influence' was split into class 2A and class 2B – 2A being undue influence exerted in certain accepted common law relationships such as doctor and patient; solicitor and client; and even 'priest and disciple'. In these relationships, the burden of proof would move to the defendant, with the burden on them to demonstrate that improper pressure was not exerted and that the 'injured' party signed the contract voluntarily and in full knowledge of the consequences. The one relationship visibly missing was that of husband and wife – and this relationship was dealt with by the courts under Class 2B – any relationship of 'trust and confidence'. The case of *Barclays Bank* v. *O'Brien* [1993] suggested that the distinction between Class 2A and 2B was artificial as the 'named' relationships within Class 2A were all relationships of 'trust and confidence' as in Class 2B. However, the distinction was not formally 'overruled'.

The *Etridge Guidelines*

In relation to mortgages, the situation was as follows:

....**APPLICATION**

Traditionally, couples (ordinarily husbands and wives) would go and see a lender, asking for a second mortgage to 'prop up' the husband's business. The wife would remain largely silent in the discussion with the lender and then husband and wife would both sign for the second mortgage. Later, of course, the couple would default on their mortgage payments and the bank would come seeking possession. At this stage, the wife would be in a position to argue that the husband had unduly influenced her into signing, without her really understanding that the marital home was at risk. If the bank had played a part in this by allowing her to sign, they would become a party to the undue influence and as such the mortgage would be set aside for undue influence. The debt would remain, but only as a personal debt – the marital home would be safe from the bank's attempts to take possession. Of course, the undue influence may have been genuine, or perhaps the couple were both fully aware of the effect of a claim of undue influence! As such, the courts decided to act, in the main, to protect the lender from any unscrupulous claims of undue influence.

In the key case of *Royal Bank of Scotland* v. *Etridge* [2001] the courts set down what became known as the *Etridge Guidelines* – a set of clear guidelines which stated, almost as statutory provisions, that if a lender was 'on notice' that such a situation might occur – for example, one of the signing parties seemingly lacking in knowledge in relation to the consequences of signing a second mortgage – then the bank was under a duty to send the parties (especially the 'weaker' party) for independent legal advice. The effect of this advice would be to preclude the party from making a claim of undue influence – thereby safeguarding the mortgage.

The full judgment of *Etridge* is valuable in that it clearly sets down the law related to 'mortgage undue influence' – and the speech of Lord Nicholls sets down the guidelines in some detail. It is perhaps interesting to note that since *Etridge* there have been very few cases where undue influence has been claimed in order to set aside a mortgage – hence it would seem that the guidelines are effective. (See Further Reading below.)

REFLECTION

KEY POINTS

- A mortgage is a proprietary right as well as being a contract.
- Mortgages are capable of being legal under section 1(2)(c) of the LPA 1925 provided they are created by deed (section 52 of the LPA 1925).
- Mortgages can also be equitable if not created in line with the formalities or if they are secured against an equitable interest.
- Mortgages in relation to land law can be illustrated by reference to the rights and duties of the lender; the rights of the borrower; and the doctrine of undue influence.

- The rights of the lender are mainly the right to take possession and the right to sell, although the lender has other rights such as suing on the debt and calling in a receiver.
- The right to possess is a common law right and can be exercised from 'even before the ink is dry' on the mortgage contract. It can be exercised with or without a court order.
- A court order can trigger a claim by the borrower for a 'reasonable time to pay' under section 36 of the AJA 1970 but a possession attempt without a court order could lead to a criminal offence being committed by the lender under PEA and CLA 1977.
- The right to sell is set down at sections 101–103 of the LPA 1925.
- The right to sell is countered by common law duties such as the duty to get the best possible price.
- The borrower, as well as rights under section 36, can also argue 'clogs and fetters' on their equity of redemption, such as unconscionable interest rates.
- The borrower could also claim undue influence, and attempt to get a mortgage, especially a second mortgage, set aside. This is unlikely to succeed since the *Etridge Guidelines* were introduced in 2001.

CORE CASES AND STATUTES

Case	About	Importance
Santley v. *Wilde* (1899) 2 Ch 474	The definition of a mortgage.	'Once a mortgage always a mortgage' – it is a proprietary right, not just a contract.
Four Maids v. *Dudley Marshal* [1957] Ch 317	Common law possession.	A lender can take possession 'before the ink is dry on the contract' – no need to wait for default.
Ropeigelach v. *Barclays Bank* [1999] QB 263	The lender can take possession without a court order.	However, this is 'dangerous and uncivilised' and can lead to a criminal offence under the PEA 1977 and CLA 1977.
Horsham v. *Beech* [2009] 1 WLR 1255	As above – though the lender should not use 'peaceable re-entry' after *Horsham*.	This case also gave rise to a human rights argument under Protocol 1 of the HRA 1998 – taking possession may be a breach of human rights.
Cheltenham and Gloucester v. *Norgan* [1996] 1 WLR 343	If a court order is used, the borrower can ask for a reasonable time to pay the arrears under section 36 of the AJA 1970.	What is 'reasonable' is now any time remaining on the mortgage provided the borrower can show evidence that future payments will be made without further default and that there is positive equity in the property.
Bishop v. *Blake* [2006] EWHC 831	'Pathetic' advertising.	The lender must try to get the best possible price but does not need to aggressively market.

Case	About	Importance
Silven v. *RBS* [2003] 1 WLR 997	The lender need not delay the sale.	No burden on the lender to delay – for example, until the market recovers.
Alliance and Leicester v. *Slayford* [2000] EWCA Civ 257	'Vile and disgusting' behaviour.	The court will allow even 'vile' behaviour such as bankrupting the borrower if this is the only way for the lender to realise their asset.
Samuel v. *Jarrah Timber* [1904] AC 323	'Clogs and fetters' on the equity of redemption.	The court may strike out any term in the mortgage contract that is unconscionable and prevents the borrower from redeeming the property after full payment of the debt.
Noakes v. *Rice* [1902] AC 24	Beer contracts.	Where the term is collateral to the mortgage it will be allowed – but where an oppressive term forms part of the mortgage it may be struck out where the effect of the term is to prevent redemption.
Cityland Holdings v. *Dabrah* [1968] Ch 166	Unconscionable interest rates.	Where the interest rate is arbitrary and unconscionable it may be struck out.
RBS v. *Etridge* [2001]	Undue influence.	If a lender follows the *Etridge Guidelines* and sends the 'weaker' party for independent advice they will discharge the burden of any claim for undue influence to set aside the mortgage.

Statute	About	Importance
LPA 1925, s. 1(2) and LPA 1925, s. 3	That mortgages can be legal or equitable.	Mortgages are capable of being legal if by deed; and if registered under section 27 of the LRA 2002. Otherwise they will be only equitable.
AJA 1970, s. 36	A 'reasonable time' to pay the arrears.	This can be triggered by a possession by court order and can allow the borrower time to pay the arrears.
LPA 1925, ss. 101 and 103	The right to sell arises and is exercisable.	These sections set down the rules as to when a bank can sell the property after possession.
LPA 1925, s. 105	Priority of sale proceeds.	This section sets down the priority order of distribution of proceeds of sale – the lender first . . . the borrower last.

FURTHER READING

BBC News: Economy Tracker: House Prices http://www.bbc.co.uk/news/10620450
Examines the background to mortgage lending and explains the nature of the credit crunch and its effect on the housing market.

Fannie Mae.com – Knowing Your Options http://www.fanniemae.com/portal/progress/index.html
This is an overview of the US sub-prime mortgage lender 'credited' by many as being instrumental in the collapse of the mortgage market.

Law Commission Report *Transfer of Land: Land Mortgages* (Law Com. No. 204, 1991) http://www.official-documents.gov.uk/document/hc9192/hc00/0005/0005.pdf
Critical evaluation of the need for reform in relation to mortgages.

The case of *Royal Bank of Scotland* v. *Etridge* [2001] http://www.publications.parliament.uk/pa/ld200102/ldjudgmt/jd011011/etridg-1.htm
The full judgment is a very sound overview of the operation of the doctrine of undue influence on the law of mortgages – with Lord Nicholls setting down the *Etridge Guidelines* for lenders and solicitors.

Glossary

Adverse possession Occupation of land taken to the exclusion of the original owner. The procedure to claim has been made more difficult under the LRA 2002.

Alienability The ability to transfer property from one party to another.

Beneficial interest The rights of a beneficiary in relation to property held under a trust. It is a particular type of equitable interest.

Caveat emptor Buyer beware – especially important when buying a property.

Chattel An item of personal property often referred to as a 'fitting' as opposed to 'real' property (land or rights in or over land).

Commonhold A system of freehold ownership of units created by the Commonhold and Leasehold Reform Act 2002.

Common law Rules of law developed from the decisions of the courts, introduced into English law by William the Conqueror and based on precedent.

Constructive trust A trust imposed by equity to protect the equitable interests of a beneficiary under a trust. In land, the constructive trust is now assessed by 'holistic' contributions (*see Jones* v. *Kernott* [2011]).

Covenant (restrictive – freehold) An agreement between two neighbouring freeholders which may run with the land to bind successors in title.

Deed A special legal document that can be clearly identified as a deed and is signed, witnessed, executed and delivered.

Determinable fee An interest/estate in land which will automatically come to an end on the occurrence of a specific event. After the LPA 1925, it can only exist as an equitable interest.

E-conveyancing The method of electronic conveyancing for which the LRA 2002 paved the way. The aim is that all property will be transferred electronically with completion, stamp duty payment and registration of title all happening simultaneously.

Easement A proprietary right enjoyed by (the owner of) one piece of land (the dominant tenement) to use proximate land (the servient tenement).

Equitable interest A right recognised by equity, as distinct from a legal interest: e.g. a beneficial interest under a trust; a right of estoppel; a covenant.

Equity Part of English law originating from decisions of the Lord Chancellor, and the Courts of Chancery, which developed to provide a remedy where the common law was inadequate. It is now a regulated set of legal principles recognising rights which are not protected under the common law.

Estate The extent and duration of a person's ownership of land. Normally 'freehold' or 'leasehold'.

Estate contract An agreement to create or convey a legal estate: e.g. an option to purchase. This is an equitable proprietary right.

Estoppel (proprietary) A principle which prevents a person unconscionably going back on a promise where there has been reliance and detriment.

Express trusts A trust of land where the details are recorded on a trust instrument or more recently a Land Registry Form JO.

Fee simple absolute in possession A freehold estate in land.

Hereditament *Real* property capable of being passed on/transferred:

- a corporeal hereditament is tangible property such as land or buildings.
- an incorporeal hereditament is intangible property such as an easement.

Joint tenancy Ownership of land by two or more persons where the four unities – possession, interest, time and title – are identical and there are no presumptions to the contrary operating.

Land Defined as being not just the buildings themselves, but fixtures attached to the building and reasonable use of airspace above the property and down into the earth below.

Lease According to Lord Templeman in *Street* v. *Mountford* – an estate in land where there is 'exclusive possession, for a term at a rent'. According to the LPA 1925 – a term of years absolute.

Legal estate Freehold or leasehold ownership of land created by deed.

Legal interest A limited category of interests in land specifically set down by section 1(2) of the Law of Property Act 1925 to be legal interests, e.g. a legal easement, a legal mortgage.

Licence 'Mere' permission to enter or occupy land for an agreed purpose. The right is now said to be purely personal and generally not binding on third parties.

Minor interest Interests in registered land which must be protected by the entering of a 'notice' in the charges section of the register: mortgages, covenants, options to purchase are all such examples.

Mortgage An interest in land created as security for a debt. The lender is the mortgagee; the borrower is the mortgagor.

Overreaching The statutory process by which beneficiaries' interests in land are converted on a sale of land by at least two trustees (legal owners) or a trust corporation into a 'money right' from the proceeds of sale.

Overriding interest (unregistered interests which override) A right or interest (in registered land) which is binding on the registered proprietor and third parties without being entered on the register: e.g. the rights of persons in actual occupation, short legal leases, implied legal easements (Schedules 1 and 3 of the LRA 2002).

Prescription A method of acquiring an easement by long use.

Rectification Correction of errors on the register where there has been fraud, mistake or it is just to 'rectify' but more difficult when the registered proprietor has taken possession.

Redemption (equity of) The right of the mortgagor to redeem the property on repayment of the mortgage. There should not be any 'clogs or fetters' to prevent redemption.

Registered land Land of which the ownership and third party rights affecting it are registered (recorded) at the Land Registry. Proof of ownership is by reference to the Official Copy of the Land Registry entries. Largely governed by the LRA 2002.

Resulting trust A trust created by operation of law, sometimes in order to give effect to the presumed but unexpressed intention of the settlor – based on contributions to purchase price at the time of purchase.

Reversion The interest in land retained by a person who has granted someone else a lesser estate or interest in the land. For example, a freeholder may grant a 99-year lease – at the end of the 99 years the property reverts 'back' to the freeholder.

Tenure The nature of a legal estate – rooted in feudal land-holding.

Term of years absolute A leasehold estate in land.

Title The right of ownership.

Trust of land A trust of land under which the trustees have the power, but no obligation to sell the property (since TOLATA 1996). The property until sold and any subsequent proceeds of sale are held on trust for any beneficiaries. Trustees are also known as the 'legal owners'; the beneficiaries being the 'equitable owners'.

Unregistered land Land of which the ownership is not registered (recorded) at the Land Registry. The 'traditional' form of conveyancing where ownership is proved by reference to title deeds and many other documents such as probate and marriage certificates.

Index

Entries in **bold** type appear in the glossary.